THE INVISIBLE HOUSES

There is an increased interest among architects, urban specialists and design profess-ionals to contribute to solve "the housing problem" in developing countries. *The Invisible Houses* takes us on a journey through the slums and informal settlements of South Africa, India, Colombia, Honduras, El Salvador, Cuba, Haiti and many other countries of the Global South, revealing the challenges of, and opportunities for, improving the fate of millions of poor families. Stressing the limitations of current approaches to housing development, Gonzalo Lizarralde examines the short-, mid- and long-term consequences of housing intervention. The book covers—among others—the issues of planning, design, infrastructure and project management. It explains the different variables that need to be addressed and the causes of common failures and mistakes, while outlining successful strategies based on embracing a sustained engagement with the complexity of processes that are generally invisible.

Gonzalo Lizarralde is a professor at the School of Architecture, Université de Montréal. He has more than 15 years' experience in the field of housing and project management in developing countries. He has authored more than 50 articles on the subjects of housing, post-disaster reconstruction and project management. He is a founding member of i-Rec, an international network for improving post-disaster reconstruction.

THE INVISIBLE HOUSES

Rethinking and Designing Low-Cost Housing in Developing Countries

Gonzalo Lizarralde

Routledge
Taylor & Francis Group

NEW YORK AND LONDON

First published 2015
by Routledge
711 Third Avenue, New York, NY 10017

and by Routledge
2 Park Square, Milton Park, Abingdon, Oxon OX14 4RN

Routledge is an imprint of the Taylor & Francis Group, an informa business

© 2015 Taylor & Francis

Library of Congress Cataloging in Publication Data
Lizarralde, Gonzalo, 1974–
The invisible houses : rethinking and designing low-cost housing in
developing countries / Gonzalo Lizarralde.
        pages cm
    Includes bibliographical references.
    1. Sustainable architecture – Developing countries. 2. Low-income
    housing – Developing countries. 3. Architects and community –
    Developing countries. 4. Urbanization – Developing countries.
    I. Title.
    NA7477.L59 2014
    728´.1091724–dc23   2014017179

ISBN: 978-0-415-84082-8 (hbk)
ISBN: 978-0-415-84083-5 (pbk)
ISBN: 978-1-315-74960-0 (ebk)

Typeset in Bembo
by HWA Text and Data Management, London

Printed and bound in Great Britain by
TJ International Ltd, Padstow, Cornwall

A Sebastián, mi príncipe, e Ili, mi princesa

CONTENTS

FIGURES

THE AUTHOR

A specialist in planning, management and evaluation of international architecture projects, Gonzalo Lizarralde is a professor at the School of Architecture at the Université de Montréal. He has fifteen years of experience in consulting for architecture and construction projects and has published numerous articles in the fields of low-cost housing and project management. Dr Lizarralde has taught at the University of Cape Town (South Africa), McGill University, Université de Montréal, Universidad del Valle and Universidad Javeriana (Colombia), and has given lectures in universities in Europe, the United States and Latin America. He has a post-doctorate from the Department of Construction Economics and Management at the University of Cape Town. Dr Lizarralde has been awarded research grants and/or scholarships from the South African NRF, the Social Sciences and Humanities Research Council of Canada (SSHRC), the Fonds québécois de la recherche sur la société et la culture (FQRSC), the Canadian government and other funding agencies. Dr Lizarralde is director of the IF Research Group (grif) at the Université de Montréal, which studies the processes related to the planning and development of construction projects. He is also the leader of the Disaster Resilience and Sustainable Reconstruction Research Alliance, a scientific research program funded by the Quebec research funds (FQRSC). He is a founding member of i-Rec, an international network for improving post-disaster reconstruction. He is also the co-author of the book *Rebuilding After Disasters: From Emergency to Sustainability* (Routledge, 2009).

ACKNOWLEDGMENTS

Many of the arguments presented in this book are the result of *collective research*. I am particularly grateful to:

- Colin Davidson, who provided important suggestions for the arguments in this book and revised a few chapters.
- Michel-Max Raynaud, Cassidy Johnson and Alexandre Apsan Frediani, who shared pertinent ideas about the importance of the Capability Approach in low-cost housing development.
- Lisa Bornstein, Isabelle Thomas, Kevin Gould, Christopher Bryant, Danielle Labbé, Arturo Valladares, Andrés Olivera, Jennifer Duyne Barenstein and all the members and students affiliated to the *Observatoire universitaire de la vulnérabilité, la résilience et la reconstruction durable (Œuvre durable* or The Disaster Resilience and Sustainable Reconstruction Research Alliance) for their contribution to the arguments related to vulnerability and resilience and for creating the Cuban resilience model case study.
- David Root and Mark Massyn and all the staff of the University of Cape Town for their contribution to the research projects conducted in South Africa.
- Mahmood Fayazi, Georgia Cardossi and Dhouha Bouraoui for creating pertinent case studies in Iran, Nairobi and Tunisia. All the students affiliated to the IF Research Group for their discussions, research results and pertinent ideas.
- The officers of *Compensar* for contributing valuable information about the *Cajas de compensación familiar* in Colombia.
- Venkatachalam Thiruppugazh and Graham Saunders for their inspiring ideas during the i-Rec (Information and Research for Reconstruction) conferences.
- Mario Bourgault and Juan Malo for their contribution to the study on project governance in developed and developing countries.
- The students of the Masters in Architecture—*Orientation mgpa* (Université de Montréal) and the professors and students involved in the workshops, conducted in Haiti in 2012 and 2013, for their inspiring ideas.

- Oswaldo Lopez and Adriana Lopez for their contribution to collecting information in Yumbo, Colombia.
- Alfonso Solano and all the participants of the *Taller Internacional de Vivienda* in Rio de Janeiro for their contribution to the case study of Favela Santa Marta.
- The residents of informal settlements and officers of several public and private organizations that were interviewed during the development of the research projects that led to this book.
- Marjorie Ewing, Robert Lecker and Amy Oliver for revising sections of the book and providing editorial comments.

I acknowledge the contribution of the *institutions* that funded the research initiatives that permitted creating the case studies presented in this publication, notably:

- The Social Sciences and Humanities Research Council—Canada, for funding the research work that permitted building the case studies in Colombia, El Salvador and Honduras.
- *The Fonds de recherche société et culture*—Québec.
- The Canadian Government, the Université de Montréal (*Direction des relations internationales*), the Université d'État d'Haïti, the Fondation Connaissances et Liberté (Fokal) and the architecture firm AEdifica for their contributions to creating the case of housing and reconstruction in Haiti.

CREDITS

Excerpts from *Invisible Cities* by Italo Calvino: Published by Vintage. Copyright © 1972 by Guilio Einaudi Editore, s.p.a. Torino. English translation by William Weaver copyright © 1974 and renewed 1978 by Houghton Mifflin Harcourt Publishing Company. Reprinted by permission of Houghton Mifflin Harcourt Publishing Company. All rights reserved. Reprinted by permission of The Random House Group Limited.

Figure 4.1 Lizarralde, Gonzalo, Colin Davidson, and Cassidy Johnson, eds. *Rebuilding after Disasters: From Emergency to Sustainability*. London: Taylor & Francis, 2009. Figure 1.3. Page 8.

Figure 4.3 Lizarralde, Gonzalo, Colin Davidson, and Cassidy Johnson, eds. *Rebuilding after Disasters: From Emergency to Sustainability*. London: Taylor & Francis, 2009. Figure 1.3. Page 8.

Figure 4.5 Lizarralde, Gonzalo. "Stakeholder Participation and Incremental Housing in Subsidized Housing Projects in Colombia and South Africa." *Habitat International* 35, no. 2 (2010): 175–87. Figure 2. Page 180.

Figure 5.3 Lizarralde, Gonzalo, and David Root. "Ready-Made Shacks: Learning from the Informal Sector to Meet Housing Needs in South Africa." Paper presented at the CIB World Building Congress Construction for Development, Cape Town, South Africa, 2007. Figure 2.

Figure 5.4 Lizarralde, Gonzalo, and David Root. "Ready-Made Shacks: Learning from the Informal Sector to Meet Housing Needs in South Africa." Paper presented at the CIB World Building Congress Construction for Development, Cape Town, South Africa, 2007. Figure 4.

Figure 5.5 Lizarralde, Gonzalo, Colin Davidson, and Cassidy Johnson, eds. *Rebuilding after Disasters: From Emergency to Sustainability*. London: Taylor & Francis, 2009. Figure 1.6. Page 16.

Figure 5.7 Lizarralde, Gonzalo, Colin Davidson, and Cassidy Johnson, eds. *Rebuilding after Disasters: From Emergency to Sustainability*. London: Taylor & Francis, 2009. Figure 2.5. Page 42.

Figure 6.2 Lizarralde, Gonzalo. "Stakeholder Participation and Incremental Housing in Subsidized Housing Projects in Colombia and South Africa." *Habitat International* 35, no. 2 (2010): 175–87. Figure 9. Page 184.

Figure 6.5 Lizarralde, Gonzalo. "Sustainable Low Cost Housing in Developing Countries: The Role of Stakeholders." In *Contemporary Issues of Construction in Developing Countries*, edited by George Ofori, 282–306. London: Taylor & Francis, 2012. Figure 10.4. Page 280.

Figure 10.10 Work by students Stéphanie Boudreau-Chartier and Esther Gélinas.

Figure 10.12 Designed by *ELEMENTAL* (Photo: Tadeuz Jalocha).

Figure 10.13 Designed by *ELEMENTAL* (Photo: Cristobal Palma).

Figure 10.14 Designed by *ELEMENTAL* (Photo: Takuto Sando).

Figure 10.15 Designed by *ELEMENTAL* (Photo: Cristian Martinez).

Figure 10.16 Designed by *ELEMENTAL* (Photo: Cristian Martinez).

Figure 10.17 Designed by *ELEMENTAL* (Photo: Cristian Martinez).

Figure 10.18 Designed by *ELEMENTAL* (Photo: Cristian Martinez).

All other images were produced by Gonzalo Lizarralde.

1

LEARNING FROM THE POOR

Most of What Architects, Urban Specialists, Policy Makers and Design Professionals Need to Know About Housing Can Be Learned from the Informal Sector

> [I]t is pointless trying to decide whether Zenobia is to be classified among happy cities or among the unhappy. It makes no sense to divide cities into these two species, but rather into another two: those that through the years and the changes continue to give their form to desires, and those in which desires either erase the city or are erased by it.
>
> *Invisible Cities*, Italo Calvino (p. 30)

The "housing problem" in developing countries is not actually a problem of missing or inadequate dwellings, and its solution is not merely the provision of shelters. Rather, it involves *creating conditions in which people can live lives they have reason to value*. Much as in Italo Calvino's depiction of the invisible city of Zenobia, the solution to the housing problem lies in enhancing a settlement development process which, through changes over the years, gives shape to needs and desires. This can be viewed as either a self-evident statement, taken as a given by architects, urban planners and decision-makers, or as a complex argument that invites a careful examination of the relationship between these conditions and the role of all the professionals and decision-makers engaged in providing housing. In this chapter, I will argue that the latter is correct.

Sanchez's Journey Toward a Meaningful Retirement

Mr Sanchez wears the hat and thick *ruana* (a garment commonly worn by peasants in cold Latin American regions) typical of rural areas as he pedals a decrepit bicycle loaded with vegetables that seem far too heavy for a man of his age to manage on the hilly roads of central Colombia. When I met him, he introduced himself using his two family names—as was once the custom of rural Colombians. Ruben Sanchez Rodriguez, a soft-spoken older man with dark skin and a few missing teeth, resembles many other immigrants in Bogotá and its neighbouring cities. While his house seems quite conventional, sadly, the story of the man and his house is not.

Mr Sanchez and his wife had never been outside their once paradisiacal northern Colombian home region when, six years ago, paramilitary militias threatened their lives and chased them off their property. Victims of an on-going conflict between leftist guerrillas and extreme-rightist paramilitary forces, Ruben and his wife abandoned their multi-acre property, valuable crops and cattle to follow in the footsteps of their two sons and daughter by migrating to Bogotá, the capital city and economic hub of Colombia. Instead of moving to the capital's urban slums, however, the couple moved to a shantytown in Facatativá, a small city a few kilometres away.

Unlike many other rural migrants in poor countries, the Sanchez family was to stay in the slum for just a short time. Mr Sanchez applied for a housing subsidy and loan through a newly initiated municipal program and the family purchased a 40 m² unit on an 80m² plot in a new Facatativá settlement. The house was only partly finished and was delivered with no floors or ceilings, wall finishes, basic appliances and with doors unpainted. It had neither hot water nor a cistern to mitigate the effects of frequent water supply failures.

The two-story house was good, however, Mr Sanchez recalled. It had running water for most of the week, a sewage system and electricity and telephone service. With two bedrooms and an inside bathroom, the new brick house was somewhat small for the elderly rural couple, who dreamt of reuniting their extended family. It was particularly cold during the rainy season for a couple used to the northern region's tropical weather. An agricultural job near Facatativá allowed Mr Sanchez to save enough money to finish the house and build a backyard extension. Upgrading the house and building the extension was easy—like most men from the country, he had basic construction skills and was able to get some "young men from the region" to help him with the concrete structure, plumbing and electricity. Within a couple of years, the Sanchez family doubled the size of the house.

The extension proved to be very important for Mr and Mrs Sanchez. They built small rooms for their three grandchildren, and an extra bathroom. They are proud to say that their extended family now visits them quite often and their grandchildren stay with them on holidays. They also built a solarium whose translucent corrugated roofing material raises the temperature in the house (see Figure 1.1). "This is the space where my wife and I like to spend our free time," Mr Sanchez says proudly. "It is a small piece of the tropical home that we lost six years ago." Mr and Mrs Sanchez and their family lost the valuable assets gained over a lifetime, and will probably never be able to return to their farm or hometown. They also lost the place where their children were born and raised. They found themselves internally displaced at an age when being forced to start a new life from scratch is demeaning. Despite this, and unlike many millions of families in developing countries, Ruben and his wife were relatively lucky. They escaped, unharmed, a war that has claimed thousands of lives, and avoided the fate of the thousands of rural migrants who find themselves living in urban slums for several generations, where washrooms are public—if they exist at all—and obtaining drinking water means walking long distances. Unlike many other elderly rural peasants who are unable to find a job in Bogotá, they did not end up begging for money in an urban park or on a busy downtown street. After their humiliation and suffering, a housing solution made an important contribution to the resumption of a meaningful life which they value profoundly; one in which they can be useful to their family by helping to raise their grandchildren.

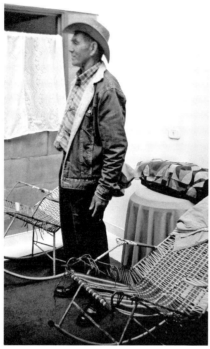

FIGURE 1.1   Mr Sanchez spends most of his free time in this solarium, which reminds him of the home from which he was forcibly evicted. While figures of internally displaced persons (IDP) can vary greatly from one study to another, it is estimated that in 2005 almost two-thirds of the world's IDPs were Colombian.

Slums and Informal Settlements: Part of the Problem or Part of the Solution?

There are various types of slums and informal developments within cities and across regions and countries. It is generally accepted, however, that they are the most tangible representation of qualitative and quantitative housing deficits and evidence of social inequalities and injustices, including segregation, exclusion, marginalization and violation of human rights. The UN-Habitat *Global Report on Human Settlements 2009* estimated that close to 1 billion people—equivalent to 36.5% of the world's urban population—live in slums.[1] This figure rises to 62% in Sub-Saharan Africa and 43% in South Asia, and is expected to increase to 2 billion people by 2030.[2]

Whereas there are ambiguous and controversial definitions of urban slums and other forms of informal settlements, it has been found that they are characterized by increased physical, social and economic vulnerabilities (see Figure 1.2). Chapter 7 will explore the causes of such vulnerabilities, but for the moment let's just state that they represent limited or insufficient access to three types of resources: "hard" resources, such as income, safe shelter, savings and food, and "soft" resources, such as education, insurance, political representation and security, along with services such as sanitation, clean water, roads, electricity, public transportation and health care. Slum dwellers and residents of informal settlements are therefore more susceptible to damage in the wake

FIGURE 1.2   Informal settlements are characterized by increased vulnerabilities. This house in an informal settlement in Cali, Colombia, is at high risk of being destroyed by landslides.

of natural disasters triggered by landslides, floods, earthquakes and fires (see Figure 1.3), to diseases and child mortality (resulting from exposure to toxic and industrial waste, indoor air pollution, polluted water, etc.) and to violence and crime. They typically rely on informal work, and have unclear land tenure and property rights, increasing their vulnerability to social injustices.

It is not surprising, therefore, that slums are often seen as limiting the human potential of their residents[3] and causing significant public health problems. It is estimated that half of the population of Africa, Asia, Latin America and the Caribbean suffer from diseases linked to inadequate water and sanitation.[4] Despite a recent worldwide trend recognizing the merits of urban agriculture, the increased presence of animals in urban slums is also frequently associated with infectious diseases that undermine public health.[5] Slums are also accused of reducing the efficiency of cities and the economic growth of countries. It is estimated, for instance, that every GDP dollar generated in Chile's capital, Santiago, requires 60% more energy than a GDP dollar generated in Helsinki, Finland.[6] More surprisingly, some authors have argued that, contrary to common belief, living in slums is also a financial burden to their inhabitants. In a study conducted in the mid-1980s, housing specialists found that "on average, dwelling units in the squatter sector of Manila would rent for 11 per cent more or sell for 23 per cent more, had they been in the formal sector" (p. 197).[7]

Slums have provoked various responses from governments and decision-makers, including demolition, forced eviction, relocation, rebuilding and upgrading. While the

FIGURE 1.3 Informal settlements are in constant transformation. This one, in Port-au-Prince, Haiti, was destroyed and rebuilt after an earthquake in 2010 that killed more than 200,000 people.

"bulldozer approach" is now largely repudiated by human rights' defenders, scholars and experts, it was a widely applied government policy before the 1980s, and is still practiced in cities in China, Zimbabwe and some other countries.[8] Mike Davis, a writer and activist, refers to this phenomenon as a "contemporary Haussmannian approach" and estimates that more than 750,000 people were evicted in Harare (Zimbabwe) in 2005, and about 500,000 in Jakarta (Indonesia) between 2001 and 2003. The Centre on Housing Rights and Evictions estimates that 5 million people in the world are still forcibly evicted every year.[9] This book will instead argue that slums and informal settlements are themselves both part of the problem and part of the solution to the housing problem. But let's consider first some common myths often associated with urban informality.

Slums and Informal Settlements in Developing Countries are Decaying Environments

The term "slum" carries pejorative connotations in both developed and developing countries. In 19th-century Europe, the term was used to describe decaying environments of squalid and wretched character.[10] This is, however, an inadequate description of the reality of most informal settlements and slums in developing countries today. Most of them are actually vibrant and dynamic neighbourhoods on a path of constant improvement, consolidation and regularization. In the book *The Myth of Marginality*,

Janice Perlman, an anthropologist with extensive experience in the favelas of Rio de Janeiro, describes Brazilian informal settlements this way:

> Beneath the apparent squalor is a community characterized by careful planning in the use of limited housing space and innovative construction techniques on hillsides considered too steep for building by urban developers. Dotting the area are permanent brick structures that represent the accumulated savings of families who have been building them little by little, brick by brick.
>
> (p. 1)[11]

All the Urban Poor Live in Informal Settlements

Again, this myth is only partially true. In reality, not all slum dwellers are poor; instead, the residents are a heterogeneous group that includes professionals, merchants, employees, entrepreneurs, gangsters, pensioners and university students. Besides, in many cities, there are more poor people living outside slum areas than within them.[12] This is extremely important in analysing urban challenges and urban resilience, since it means that cities are more capable of absorbing the poor than is usually believed.

Nothing is Worse than Living in a Slum

Contrary to common belief, slums are not the sites of the worst living conditions in developing countries, and they do not always accommodate the poorest of the poor. In most developing nations, the majority of the poorest citizens still live in rural areas[13] and remote locations, where they have limited or non-existent access to health services, schools, infrastructure and jobs. According to World Bank specialist Martin Ravallion, "urban areas account for less than half—about 30% on average—of the poor" (p. 435).[14] It is true that the poor urbanize faster than the population as a whole in many developing countries. However, if transition countries in Eastern Europe are an indication of what may eventually happen in poor countries, the status of the rural poor will not improve quickly. If trends witnessed since 1998 continue in transition countries such as Belarus, Georgia, Hungary, Lithuania, Moldova and others, researchers predict that "the share of rural poverty in total poverty will further increase in the future" (p. 2174).[15] This tendency is confirmed by poverty specialist Ann Tickamyer, who argues that "rural poverty remains the dominant form of deprivation for the world's poor and, despite rapid urbanization, is projected to continue for many years to come" (p. 416).[16]

According to a UN-Habitat report, almost half of the rural population in developing countries lives below the poverty line, while this is true of less than a third of the urban population.[17] Poor rural residents in Sri Lanka, the Congo region, Colombia, Angola and many other countries are often affected by war and violence, and suffer from additional vulnerabilities, including decreased life expectancy and higher rates of child mortality[18] and illiteracy, among others.

The rather romantic view that slum dwellers are suffering the inconveniencies of informality, while missing an enviable quality of life in the country within pastoral landscapes abounding with productive animals and flourishing crops, does not stand up to serious debate. In fact, conditions for the rural poor remain very harsh when compared to the urban poor.

Slums and Informal Settlements are Places of Misery and Despair

In most of the informal settlements in which my colleagues, my students and I have worked, we have found residents busy with activities such as working, buying and selling goods, taking care of children, cooking, preparing for celebrations or attending church. In Port-au-Prince, Mumbai and Cape Town, we were particularly impressed by the schoolchildren's impeccably clean uniforms, and in Rio de Janeiro's favelas we found happy children flying kites, and devoted mothers and fathers playing with their children. In Colombian slums, we found groups of men meeting to watch a soccer game, and families preparing celebrations. These are not the places of misery and despair that many expect to find (see Figure 1.4). Perlman reveals the strength of character she found among favela residents she interviewed: "No matter how many obstacles they face," she argues, residents were "full of hope for the future." Then she adds, "Their optimism is contagious– while few think that life in Brazil or Rio will become better in the next five years, a majority think that their communities will be better and almost everyone thinks that their own lives will be better" (p. 22).[19]

Residents are Waiting for the First Opportunity to "Escape" From Slums and Other Informal Settlements

While there is little doubt that the majority of people living in informal settlements would like their living conditions to improve, the belief that slum dwellers dislike living in slums and that they would like to "escape" from them has led to poor housing solutions and policies. There are, in fact, several reasons why slum dwellers like living in their settlements. Probably the most significant is the strong network of friends,

FIGURE 1.4 Slums are not places of misery and despair. Here, enthusiastic children pose for a photo in Gugulethu, an informal settlement in the Western Cape, South Africa.

relatives, service providers and clients they find there who play a fundamental role in their lives and reduce some of their economic and social vulnerabilities. When living in close proximity, friends and relatives take care of children while parents are at work; young friends and relatives care for the elderly; the store manager provides credit to a family going through financial difficulties; people in the neighbourhood provide security for children and teenagers; friends and acquaintances help a car owner repair his broken vehicle; godparents living nearby can attend family celebrations and exchange presents; and, generally, most residents feel comfortable living with those who share similar backgrounds, cultural references, life experiences and status. Fragmenting or disturbing these social networks is dangerous in any society, but it is particularly catastrophic for vulnerable communities in impoverished areas.

The "Formal" and "Informal" Sectors and Other Semantic Problems

Settlements, industries, economic sectors and jobs are typically categorized as "formal" or "informal." Informality is often a residual notion whose meaning is derived in relation to something else, and often by specifying what it is not.[20] The term "informal" is used indiscriminately to describe an attribute (given to a company, a sector of the economy, an industry), a way of doing things (an informal process, for instance) or a way of functioning in a particular context.

The informal sector thus comprises a heterogeneous group of unregistered enterprises and employees making a living through informal transactions and income-generating activities.[21] These are typically conducted in the absence of formal contracts, rights and regulations.[22]

It is estimated that fully 43% of the Gross Domestic Product (GDP) of African and Latin American countries is produced in the informal sector.[23] "About 85 per cent of all new employment opportunities around the world occur in the informal economy," according to a UN-Habitat report.[24] This means that the informal sector harbours the most dynamic and significant group of industries in the world. Besides, different types of informal activities regularly collide. The majority of slum dwellers in developing countries earn their living from informal sector activities, and the informal construction sector makes a significant contribution to building most informal and squatters' settlements (see Figures 1.5 and 1.6). It has been found that the informal sector produces about half of the world's housing stock.[25] In the following chapter, we shall see that informality is, above all else, a strategy for adapting to a hostile environment. However, it is important to stress here that classifying human settlements, the building industry and the economy in two categories (formal and informal) is an arbitrary and simplistic approach. Most specialists now recognize at least four problems with this binary classification.

1   *Blurred boundaries:* The boundaries between formality and informality are often blurred in the construction industry, the economy and urban morphology. For instance, formally planned roads and plots are sometimes occupied by informally built structures and, over time, informally built settlements acquire some characteristics of formality, such as addresses, public investment and legal infrastructure. Legally established construction companies subcontract informal workers, while some

FIGURE 1.5   Formality and informality sometimes merge. This is the case in this transition zone between the well established Rio de Janeiro neighbourhood of Botafogo and the Favela Santa Marta.

construction companies only partially comply with administrative, fiscal and legal requirements. Legal retail stores sell illegally imported products, while informal vendors on the street sometimes sell "clean" goods. Additionally, the geographical boundaries between the formal and informal economies are also indistinct (see Figure 1.5). Entrepreneurs located in the slums trade products and services in formal city sectors, while formally established companies distribute goods to retail stores in informal settlements. Finally, a significant proportion of formal workers live in informal settlements and informal workers often operate in established neighbourhoods.[26]

2   *Subjective criteria:* The criteria used to classify settlements, companies, workers and procedures as formal or informal are often arbitrary. For instance, housing units are typically considered informal when occupants do not have a legal title; however, security of tenure is not always necessarily linked to legal titles. Structures built without permits are often considered informal; yet, the vast majority of renovations in formal construction projects are conducted without these permits. Besides this, stores and companies that are generally considered informal sometimes pay certain taxes. A common example of subjectivity, which has a strong influence on architectural discourse, captures this phenomenon: vernacular architecture is typically built informally, but it is seldom subject to the same prejudices of illegality

FIGURE 1.6 Informal settlements and informal labour are often found on the same site. Owners of this workshop in an informal settlement in Mumbai, India, live in the unit's second story.

that are applied to urban squatter settlements. Two standards of assessment seem to apply, one to the rural vernacular and one to the urban informal.

3   *Prejudices*: Characterization as "formal" or "informal" usually implies a biased scale of values.[27] Informality is often associated with chaos, disorder, illegality, insecurity and inefficiency. Yet, as we will see in the coming chapters, the informal construction sector is largely organized and efficient, informal settlements are not necessarily chaotic, and informality and illegality do not necessarily go hand in hand. Pejorative representations of informal settlements, companies, workers and construction have largely been used to justify and legitimize evictions, segregation, persecution and other forms of social injustice.

4   *Context specificity*: Different cultures, sectors and groups have varying levels of tolerance and differing perceptions of informality, making the classification even more arbitrary, biased and impractical for decision-making. Consider labour conditions: hiring employees without formal contracts is not typically considered a crime and is commonly accepted in agricultural activities and within rural communities. The contribution of children to family businesses has traditionally been tolerated (and even promoted) by parents and communities. These conventions do not find the same acceptance in some urban contexts, where they may even be illegal. Finally, community-based organizations sometimes operate without all of the registrations and credentials required in the formal sector.

You might therefore be surprised that, despite these significant limitations, this book uses the terms "formality" and "informality" along with some other terms that have been controversial among scholars and specialists. These terms include "beneficiaries" and "users," which—some experts believe—imply an unequal balance of power between those who "provide" and those who "use" (receive) aid. Because this is not a book on semantics, but rather one determined to highlight the value, skills, importance and qualities of informal workers, slum dwellers, vulnerable communities and community-based organizations, I hope that readers will permit the use of these terms, trusting that I use them without prejudice. There are four additional good reasons for using these terms. First, there are no scales that effectively describe the many gradients (shades of grey, so to speak) between formality and informality in urban morphology, city structures, housing construction, industrial and commercial activities, labour practices, etc. Second, informality is used here as a general term to describe a way of functioning and the strategies used by the poor to secure income, shelter, security and services. As such, it describes a heterogeneous group of mechanisms of resilience and forms of operation commonly used by poor communities and/or individuals. It also conveniently communicates common patterns that are applicable in a variety of contexts. Third, by opposing formal companies, construction and interventions, "informality" (as a term applied to housing, settlements, companies, etc.) is useful in explaining intertwined mechanisms of response and adaptive measures to the environment that rarely occur independently. Finally, I prefer to use the terms "informal" and "informality" as shorthand for what is, in reality, a loose collection of concepts, rather than other commonly used terms such as "marginal," "spontaneous," "irregular" and "subnormal" (e.g. subnormal agglomerations). As we will see, there is very little in informal settlements and the informal sector that is marginal, spontaneous, subnormal or irregular.

Why Some Ideas for Solving the "Housing Problem" Have Failed

Access to adequate housing is an international human right. This is more than a rhetorical argument. In 1966, the United Nations General Assembly adopted the International Covenant on Economic, Social and Cultural Rights, which recognized the "right of everyone to an adequate standard of living for himself and his family, including adequate food, clothing and housing, and to continuous improvement of living conditions."[28] Recognition of housing as a human right has not, however, necessarily translated into sufficient projects or sound policy. While the proportion of urbanities living in slums has been reduced in most developing countries, their actual numbers have increased. In 2007, there were about 29.9 million people living in slums in Bangladesh, 45.3 million in Nigeria and 45.7 million in Brazil. This corresponds to roughly 70%, 65% and 30% of the total urban population in these countries, respectively.[29]

Given that housing is such an important factor in personal well-being and in that of society as a whole, why is there an insufficient supply of adequate housing for all the inhabitants of developing countries? This section and Chapter 3 address this fundamental question by pointing out the difficulties of providing a large quantity of quality houses. During housing crises (particularly those due to the mass destruction of human settlements during disasters), it is common to find well-intentioned architects, urban planners and design professionals who have "a good idea" for solving the housing problem. Newspapers and conferences abound with ideas such as "the government should build houses for the poor," "the government should provide them with land so they can build their own houses," "the poor should receive financial help for housing construction," "a new village must be built to house poor people," and so on. However, easier said than done, these ideas fail to acknowledge their inherent limitations. The following review of housing strategies shows that many good ideas for providing housing have failed utterly, and that devising solutions to the housing problem has been, for most developing countries, a major challenge that has proven difficult to overcome.

Providing Public Housing Through Turnkey Projects

It is often argued that governments interested in improving the well-being of their citizens and respecting human rights should provide affordable housing for the poor. In fact, even before Member States of the United Nations declared housing to be a human right, several governments in developing countries, including India, Mexico, Kenya and Tunisia, among others, had started ambitious public programs to achieve widespread access to housing. In fact, this strategy became national policy in many developing countries, and it is now accepted that public provision of turnkey housing projects is a first-generation policy for solving the housing problem.

This generation of housing policy began immediately following World War II and continued until the 1970s, when the World Bank entered the housing arena.[30] Governments opted for demolishing squatter settlements and making a financial commitment to replacing them with "decent" solutions, principally through the mass construction of units, which were then rented or sold at subsidized prices. Numerous slums were cleared during this period. A well-known case was the favela of Catacumba in Rio de Janeiro in 1970, which was replaced by mid- and high-income residential projects that today form part of a popular tourist destination. Public housing projects in many countries (including Algeria, Colombia, Mexico and many communist countries) often took the form of "new developments" of mass-produced mid- and high-rise buildings located on empty land on the outskirts of urban centres. In many countries, including Cuba, the quest for mass production and economies of scale favoured prefabrication techniques, which typically used precast concrete components in the construction of four- to eight-story buildings.

The policy proved to be inadequate, however. At least seven factors contributed to its failure in countries such as India, Colombia, Mexico, Jamaica, Nigeria, Vietnam, Algeria, Tunisia, among others, when:

1   Government agencies and institutions proved to be inefficient builders; in the end, the core "business" of governments is governing, not building and administering buildings.
2   Resources were not readily available in political environments where health, safety and other social issues were in direct competition with housing provision.

FIGURE 1.7 Direct provision of public housing has proven to be largely disappointing and the policy is now eschewed in most developing countries, with the exception of some communist countries, such as Cuba, where this public housing project was recently built for the inhabitants of Sagua.

3   Public housing programs opened the door to corrupt practices; in some cases, public housing was provided only to civil servants or the military. It was also used to further political agendas and for electoral purposes, often benefitting middle class rather than poor residents.

4   Projects were too often developed on inexpensive land, usually in remote locations where jobs, services and infrastructure were not readily available, thus perpetuating insufficient living standards for the poor. Describing public housing developments in Hong Kong, Mike Davis stated: "The incompatibility of peripheral, high-rise housing with the social structures and informal economies of poor communities is, of course, ancient history: it's an original sin repeated over decades by urban reformers and city czars everywhere" (p. 64).[31]

5   Limited resources did not allow governments to offer subsidies to all who needed them, leaving them unavailable to the poorest families.

6   Even with significant subsidies, affordability still eluded the majority of the poor.[32]

7   Governments found it easier to clear slums than to provide housing. If we believe United Nations estimates, governments were annually destroying more low-cost housing units than they were developing.[33]

Today, the policy of direct provision of turnkey projects is rarely adopted in developing countries. Some exceptions include China and Cuba, which, as socialist states, still consider housing to be an integral component of its welfare system (see Figure 1.7).

Let the Poor Build for Themselves

Frustration with the limited success of public housing led to second-generation housing policy. This time, there was increasing enthusiasm for interventions based on self-help construction. An interest largely generated by John Turner's[34] view of human settlements, which held that since the great majority of households in developing countries were already producing housing solutions for themselves, they could contribute to the construction of their own houses within organized self-help housing programs. Turner, a British scholar trained in architecture, considered housing "as a verb," thus conveying the idea that housing was not simply a *product* but also a *process* in which end-users could play an important role. The self-help approach presupposed that, by involving the users in production, construction costs could be reduced to the point that its beneficiaries could become homeowners.

The World Bank, in particular, espoused this cost-reduction prospect and adopted (or rather "hijacked," according to some observers) the self-help principles to institute, in 1972, a policy that encouraged governments to deliver sites-and-services. The approach was also adopted by the Inter-American Development Bank in Latin America and is now considered to be the "second generation" of international housing policy. According to the bank, governments would develop land and offer plots with access to basic public services to beneficiaries who would then build their own units, thus considerably reducing costs.

Some analysts have seen this approach as a withdrawal of the State from its responsibility to improve housing conditions for the poor, rather than as a tribute to their skills and potential. Some consider it to have been based on a view of the users' involvement portrayed in the original self-help works that was romanticized. Regrettably, this is partly true. Today we know that a great share of self-help construction is not really done by the users themselves, but rather by informal workers and other paid help.[35]

Housing specialist Charles Choguill reports that the results of this strategy, applied as national policy in many countries, were largely disappointing. Let's consider some of the reasons. First, even with a reduced government investment, sites-and-services were still too expensive for at least 20% of most urban populations.[36] Second, developing this type of large-scale project was difficult, particularly due to administrative and legal barriers to land development (see Chapter 3 for a detailed analysis of the problems associated with land markets). Third, this approach implied that governments should agree to support lower housing standards. This caused politically expensive ethical debates in many countries. In fact, some sites-and-services were considered little more than government-supported slums. Fourth, during this period, cities were not really perceived as efficient centres of production (as they are now), but rather as drains on investment and subsidies that attracted rural migrants. This narrow view of urban problems did not help sustain support for this type of policy and was, in fact, one of the most significant contributing causes to the failure of World Bank urban policies in the 1970s. Fifth, projects faced major challenges in providing adequate sanitation. Although underground sewage and water supply systems are very expensive, they are barely visible to the electorate once the projects are completed. This reduces the value these projects hold for politicians and their electoral agendas. Sixth, in many cases, beneficiaries did not like the new locations,

FIGURE 1.8 Sites-and-services has been largely abandoned as a strategy for housing development; however, its basic principle, providing services to unoccupied plots, was recently applied in this "serviced" township of Mfuleni in Cape Town, South Africa.

so they sold the plots and returned to the slums. Finally, in sites-and-services projects, housing provision was dissociated from employment creation, which affected the strategy's popularity among politicians.[37]

Due to major difficulties with the approach, the World Bank eventually abandoned the self-help (sites-and-services) policy in the mid-1980s. Around the same time, the Inter-American Development Bank also recognized that sites-and-services projects were not working as expected in Latin America.[38] It is estimated that from 1972 to 1981, the total output of project-based programs was only 10% of what was required in developing countries.[39] Despite these conclusions, a form of sites-and-services strategy was recently implemented in the Cape Town townships (South Africa). Residents were provided with land titles, roads, electrical and sanitary services (one prefab toilet per family), and users were expected to build their own shacks on these lots. The approach has had mixed results (see Figure 1.8). Whereas it has permitted shelter to thousands of families, it has raised significant criticism regarding the quality of the settlements that are produced in this process.

Improving Conditions in Urban Slums

The remarkable failure of public housing and the unambiguous evidence of the unsatisfactory effects of slum clearance and relocation motivated housing specialists and policy-makers to opt for in-situ upgrading of slum areas. This approach commonly involves improving existing infrastructure and addressing the complex issues of land tenure. It recognizes that upgrades to infrastructure—notably sanitation—profoundly improve the living standards of slum dwellers. Infrastructure investment usually includes improvements to water supply, sewage systems, electrical service and roads. In some cases, it also includes improvements to public transportation, open spaces and community services and facilities.

Securing land tenure not only reduces legal vulnerabilities that facilitate eviction and displacement, but also motivates slum dwellers to accelerate house completion and upgrades. As we shall see in Chapter 3, land tenure is a critical component of the housing equation. However, we will also discover that slum upgrading does not necessarily have to target individual legal ownership. Collective tenure and mechanisms to improve conditions for renters can (and must) also be envisaged. Take the case of slum upgrading conducted under World Bank programs in 1985 in Dharavi[40] (Mumbai's most populous slum and home to more than 800,000 inhabitants[41]). These initiatives were not based on legalizing tenure at the individual level, but rather were achieved through organizing and consolidating cooperatives (see Figure 1.9). In any case, the benefits of slum upgrading often include: reduced disturbances to the social and economic life of communities; enhancement of economic development in informal settlements (see Figures 1.9 and 1.10); and preservation of slum dwellers' invested capital. It also guarantees that the *intended* beneficiaries remain the *actual* beneficiaries of interventions and investment.[42]

FIGURE 1.9 Slum upgrading accelerates housing completion and facilitates the creation of home-based income-generating activities like this barbershop in Dharavi, probably Mumbai's best-known slum.

In the following chapters we will revisit the advantages and controversies around slum upgrading strategies. However, it is important to highlight here that the cost of these operations is usually tremendous. Housing specialists Bruce Ferguson and Jesus Navarrete estimate that the cost of laying infrastructure in slum-upgrading programs is two to three times the cost of providing infrastructure to new formal developments.[43] Resolving land tenure issues and administrative barriers is also very expensive. It is estimated that it would cost US$18 billion annually for 16 years to improve the lives of 100 million slum dwellers and to provide adequate solutions for the roughly 600 million people who may otherwise become slum dwellers by the year 2020.[44] As a consequence of the increased cost of slum upgrading, governments have only been able to afford this approach on a reduced scale. It is now commonly believed that "the best way to deal with urban slums is to decrease or stop their formation and thereby avoid fixing them retrospectively at high cost" (p. 204).[45]

Nostalgia for Productive Small Towns and Villages

Housing deficits and slums have often been associated with rapid and uncontrolled migration to urban centres. There has been a widespread belief that developing countries can (and should) reduce the pressure for low-cost housing in major cities by stopping migration from rural areas to urban centres by creating migration buffer zones, notably small towns and villages. This argument is reinforced by the conviction that slums

FIGURE 1.10 Slum upgrading typically includes public investment in infrastructure and land regularization. Originally a slum built through land invasion, this settlement in Bogotá is now recognized as a "formal" city neighbourhood (*barrio*).

FIGURE 1.11 Traditional lifestyle in villages and small towns, such as this village in Kutch, India, have for decades inspired professionals, decision-makers and politicians. However, the results of attempts to mimic villages in new developments have been disappointing.

and informal settlements suffer from vice and crime (prostitution, promiscuity, drug addiction, drug trafficking, organized theft, etc.), which are supposedly rarely found—or are at least less evident—in traditional villages and rural areas. The argument suggests that rural residents become "contaminated" on arriving in urban centres, particularly in slums (a perception that has been challenged by many experts, including favela-specialist Janice Perlman in her books *The Myth of Marginality*[46] and *Favela*).[47]

According to this logic, the problem of inadequate housing in urban centres can be reduced by creating productive centres in small settlements, and thus attracting and retaining rural residents. These settlements can be provided with schools, agricultural support and healthcare centres, so as to recreate traditional (and highly autonomous) communities. This approach has gained popularity in Southern India, the Caribbean and Africa, where it is seen as a practical way of returning to the "roots" of African, Caribbean and Indian values and "ways of life" (see Figure 1.11). In a recent conference on post-earthquake reconstruction in Haiti, the Haitian president's advisor on urban affairs claimed that by creating productive villages (one of them with a university), not only would the housing pressure on Port-au-Prince be reduced, but residents would also have the privileged opportunity of returning to traditional occupations and values. The same argument has been widely promoted by Ivory Coast expatriates in Canada hoping to develop investments to improve the quality of life of young Ivoirians. Journalist and India specialist Edward Luce reminds us that Mahatma Gandhi espoused this approach for the Asian subcontinent, having found core Indian values in its villages. However, Luce himself is hardly optimistic about the approach:

> India is slowly urbanizing and it is hard to imagine what could stop the continuing expansion of its cities. But *Gandhians* continue to believe the village should occupy a holy place at the centre of Indian nationhood. Their influence continues to undermine attempts to provide better planning for the cities.
>
> (p. 10)[48]

In fact, current urban specialists and economists are convincingly challenging the romantic idea that villages are non-violent, homogeneous communities where members of a cohesive society share edifying values. Discussing gender inequalities, particularly the increased infanticide and "foeticide" of girls in India, Luce argues that: "Naturally, the problem is worse in villages [where] arranged marriages and functional illiteracy are still the norm." According to estimates presented by the same author, "fifteen per cent of girls in India's poorest five states get married at or below the age of ten. Clearly, almost all of this takes place in the villages." He adds: "Children born in the village are also almost twice as likely to die below the age of five as those born in the city" (p. 315).[49]

Unlike other strategies presented in this section, this particular one was not commonly promoted as national housing policy by international financial institutions (World Bank, Inter-American Development Bank, International Monetary Fund, etc.). However, the experience of enthusiasm for village development followed by disappointment has occurred in most African and Latin American countries. During the 1970s, in an attempt to reduce rural migration to Cairo to alleviate pressure for urban housing, the Egyptian government adopted a plan to develop New Towns (towns that would have industries to provide employment for the new residents) and New Communities (village-type settlements near large urban centres). However, new towns such as Tenth of Ramadan became a colossal liability. A study by Gil Feiler found that "in 1983 a network of roads suitable for a town with a population of 150,000 inhabitants was completed while the total number of new settlers was less than 10,000. Educational, housing and health facilities were also under-utilized" (p. 130).[50] Other town and village projects also failed in the Egyptian new town experiment: the 15th of May City lacked basic infrastructure; in Sadat City only "19 out of a total of 158 newly planned industries were initiated. From a total of 12,200 planned units, only 1,000 housing units were constructed" (p. 131). The town of El-Obour suffered a similar fate.

As we will see in Chapter 7, following natural disasters, attempts to relocate vulnerable communities to villages and "new towns" in Tunisia, Indonesia, India, Sri Lanka and Honduras have turned into disasters themselves, in some ways more terrifying than the original events that precipitated the relocation.

Despite recurring nostalgia for rural life, specialists now agree that urbanization is "an inevitable outcome of the development process" (p. 5).[51] In most developing countries, urbanization is a major factor underlying prosperity. UN-Habitat makes this clear in unmistakable terms: "Empirical evidence clearly demonstrates that as a country becomes more urban, its per capita income also tends to rise." It continues:

The level of urbanization (or the proportion of people living in urban areas) is associated in some places with numerous positive societal outcomes, such as technological innovation, various forms of creativity, economic progress, higher standards of living, enhanced democratic accountability and women's empowerment.

(p. 7)[52]

Recent evidence also suggests, however, that there is a limit to urban efficiency in developing countries, at least in Latin America's large metropolitan areas. Medium-sized cities seem to be more productive than large urban centres. According to a recent study published in *The Economist*, medium-size cities (such as Curitiba in Brazil, Toluca and Merida in Mexico, or Medellín in Colombia) perform better economically than large cities and capitals (Rio de Janeiro, Mexico City, Bogotá, etc.). The report argues that "unusually early in their development, Latin America's biggest cities may have ceased to reap economies of scale because their institutional, social and environmental support structures have not kept up with their expanding populations".[53] If the UN-Habitat argument and *The Economist*'s report can provide a guide to policy-making—at least in Latin America—it can be argued that significant positive effects can be obtained from increased urbanization, while avoiding unplanned "megalopolization."

Whereas several scientists still deny that there is a causal relationship between urbanization and reduced poverty, the 2010–11 UN-Habitat report suggests the opposite: "Urban growth is, therefore, both positive and necessary for rural poverty reduction" (p. 25). In any case, investment in urban housing is sound policy. This does not mean, however, that investment in villages and small towns is not also needed. Several UN-Habitat publications advocate for intelligent investment in what it terms "small urban centres." Nonetheless, it has become clear that the reasons for investing must be carefully considered. One of these reports concludes that government investment in small urban centres, as a measure to control the growth of large cities, has had a very poor success record.[54]

Enabling Markets and Providing Subsidies

Discouragement with publicly controlled housing solutions lead to a hopeful turning to (private) market-driven solutions in many developing countries. This represented a shift from project-based solutions, such as public housing, slum upgrading and village development, to solutions based on structural reforms. In the late 1980s and early 1990s, specialists recognized that housing and land markets in developing countries suffered from numerous bottlenecks and over-regulation, largely due to bureaucratic, administrative and legal frameworks.[55] Both international financial institutions and United Nations agencies claimed that the housing agenda should not be based in public projects, but rather in the creation of an appropriate administrative, economic, legal and institutional environment to enable the private housing sector to work efficiently (Chapter 3 will comment on this approach).

By 1993, this strategy was adopted as policy, and the World Bank and the United States Agency for International Development (USAID) were explicitly encouraging the privatization of housing production. In so doing, this approach became the "third generation" of international policy on low-income housing. Not only were governments expected to limit their participation in housing production, but they were also expected to reduce unnecessary involvement in its regulation. By this time, it was largely recognized that housing development provided an important contribution to overall development. With less government involvement, employment and other macro-economic indicators would improve. Generally, the policy recommended:

- developing property rights;
- developing mortgage and financing, including lending and borrowing at affordable interest rates;
- opening up urban land for residential development through provision of infrastructure;
- reforming building and planning regulations concerning land and housing development;
- expanding market activity;
- revitalizing the construction sector by eliminating regulatory barriers;
- developing an institutional framework to enable markets.[56]

Additionally, the approach often included providing subsidies to poor families to enable them to purchase housing units developed by the private sector. Direct subsidies were a marked improvement compared to the approaches implemented during the 1970s and 1980s. However, despite widespread enthusiasm for limiting State intervention and increasing private sector participation in housing provision, the approach of enabling the markets and providing housing subsidies has also proven to be disappointing in both quantitative and qualitative terms. It is now argued that "enabling the markets to work" has not equalled "giving the poor access to better housing."[57]

In fact, the number of squatter settlement residents worldwide increased from 715 million in 1991 to 998 million in 2005, and this number is expected to increase to 1.4 billion by 2020. The challenges remain enormous. An investment of US$3 trillion would be required to overcome the housing and public infrastructure needs of Latin America alone.[58] It is estimated that Bogotá—the city that attracted the Sanchez family in the story at the beginning of this chapter—will need to double its present housing stock by 2025.[59]

Chapter 3 discusses the reasons for the limited success of this strategy. Here, I will touch on just a few. First, structural reforms were not implemented at the pace or on the scale that the World Bank and the International Monetary Fund (IMF) policies anticipated.[60] Secondly, the strategy failed to sufficiently stimulate action and participation from community-based organizations. Third, by concentrating poor residents in specific neighbourhoods built by private developers, most projects undertaken in this approach have exacerbated social segregation. Fourth, the solutions have rarely reached the poorest sectors of society. Finally, and more worryingly, most housing projects have failed to adapt to the needs and aspirations of low-income residents (see Figure 1.12).

Chapters 3 and 7 will argue that the neoliberal policies promoted by the World Bank and the IMF pushed governments to reduce their involvement in housing, thus effectively transferring responsibility for housing planning, financing and procurement to municipalities. This policy was widely implemented in Latin America and in other parts

FIGURE 1.12 "We are making your dreams come true" is the motto of this housing developer, who sells units to subsidized families benefitting from a Colombian government "enabling" program. However, many dreams of the poorest Colombians have failed to come true under this policy.

of the world in the 1980s. Rusen Keles asserts that in the reorganization of the Turkish government conducted in 1984, "rights, powers, duties and functions of the Ministry of Public Works and Settlements in respect to squatter settlements have been transferred to the municipalities" (p. 164).[61] However, small- and medium-size municipalities were given neither the financial mechanisms to intervene nor the administrative and legal structure to effectively respond to this challenge.[62] Most municipalities found themselves incapable of initiating and managing housing programs, and powerless to respond to housing crises and disasters.[63] As we shall discover in Chapter 7, in many cities of the developing world the result has been catastrophic. It is now accepted that "the main single cause of increases in poverty and inequality during the 1980s and 1990s was the retreat of the state" (p. 43).[64] The UN–Habitat Global Report of Human Settlements 2003 asserted that "the redirection of income through progressive taxation and social safety nets came to be severely threatened by the ascendancy of neo-liberal economic doctrines that explicitly "demanded" an increase in inequality" (p. 43).[65]

The NGO Revolution: Providing Housing Through International Development

Few housing projects have attracted as many young architects, urban specialists and design professionals as those falling under non-governmental organization (NGO) based international development. In fact, in an effort to compensate for the inability of both the public and private sectors to solve the housing problem, over the past few decades, the not-for-profit sector has assumed a significant role in housing provision in developing countries. Aid (also known as "Official Development Assistance") has

FIGURE 1.13 Badly hit by Hurricane Mitch in November 1998, a few months later the town of Choluteca, Honduras, became the site of an "NGO storm." At least 16 international NGOs (many of them religiously oriented) worked in the region for three years building this new development, a few kilometres away from the original town.

become an enormous industry. It is estimated that between 2001 and 2005, developing countries received US$368 billion in aid, 129 billion of which went to African countries alone.[66]

However, aid to developing countries has rarely been completely "free." Donor nations use international aid as a foreign policy instrument to promote strategic agendas and to implement international policy. For instance, about two-thirds of the UK's aid has gone to countries belonging to the Commonwealth, with whom it wishes to maintain close relationships. International aid specialists argue that "there was an increase in condition-based lending in the 1980s, based primarily on institutional reform and economic policies with strong neoliberal principles of market-led development in developing countries" (p. 86).[67] These economic conditions (typically known as "the Washington Consensus") required developing countries to embrace Structural Adjustment Programs (SAPs) designed by international agencies. Since then, multilateral aid through agencies such as the World Bank, United Nations and the European Union has assumed an important role in the formulation and implementation of development policy.

Two types of aid exist,[68] development aid and humanitarian aid, both of which have had a strong influence on housing provision (see Figure 1.13). In both cases, aid has largely been administered by bilateral and multilateral funding agencies acting through NGOs, principally those that consider housing to be a fundamental component of development (not all do). Sometimes, government agencies in developed countries also act through international NGOs operating in partnership with local NGOs.

Paradoxically, the aid industry has recently tried to mitigate the negative effects of structural adjustments (such as liberalization, privatization and reduction of welfare) that were widely promoted during the 1980s. According to a recent paper published in the *International Encyclopaedia of Human Geography*, NGO involvement "in implementing World Bank-financed projects grew rapidly during the 1980s and 1990s as many governments' service-delivery capacities were shrinking."[69] The paper adds that "70% of World Bank-financed projects in 2006 had NGO involvement" (p. 85).[70] Today, it is estimated that about 30% of development aid is managed by multilateral donors such as the World Bank,[71] which, for a long time, required that governments involve NGOs and advocacy groups in the preparation of Poverty Reduction Strategy Papers.

Despite good intentions, NGO involvement in providing housing in developing countries has had largely disappointing results. They are not, of course, a homogeneous group. NGOs act in different ways and produce different results.[72] Yet, generally, the majority resort to the same "package" of objectives, including good governance, community empowerment, sustainable development, equity and the strengthening of civil society. Their methods are also often the same, including community participation, partnerships with local institutions and communities, objective-based management and strong community leadership. The following chapters will show, however, that in most cases the descriptions of objectives and the means of achieving them are merely rhetoric. Overall objectives have not been effectively implemented, and noble intentions have remained just that. Community participation typically means that users provide cheap sweat equity; community-level interventions sometimes exacerbate urban fragmentation and segregation; equity often means an equal distribution of goods (irrespective of obvious differences between beneficiaries); and objective-based management becomes a linear task prescription that adapts poorly to dynamic contexts. Other common problems with aid-based interventions are that:

1   NGOs act according to their own agendas and priorities, thereby effectively bypassing the State and creating a parallel system of individual, isolated interventions, rather than acting in support of holistic, long-term strategic plans.
2   External NGOs, which often intervene for short periods of time, regularly abandon beneficiaries and communities once the project funding is exhausted. This short-term intervention strategy rarely results in sustainable long-term solutions.
3   NGOs have adopted many enabling/subsidizing strategy methods, notably the tendency to locate new developments in remote areas, avoid the informal sector and hire large formally-based contractors.
4   The work of NGOs is often fragmented. Although in some cases various organizations will offer a variety of services and products to a group of beneficiaries, in other cases their products and services overlap. The first scenario often creates piecemeal and fragmented solutions, while the second results in redundancy and competition (NGOs often compete for beneficiaries). Both problems have a negative impact on the well-being of beneficiaries and the quality of human settlements.
5   International NGOs and consultants have, all too often, become the real beneficiaries of development aid.[73] Not only are NGOs now staffed by large numbers of well-paid "experts," but they also issue generous contracts to numerous consultants who travel, analyse foreign contexts, propose guidelines and produce reports (which often serve little purpose beyond filling NGO directors' bookshelves).

6   The work of NGOs depends on external donor funding. Despite good intentions, however, the donors' priorities and agendas do not necessarily reflect the needs and desires of the poor.[74]

7   Typically, NGOs justify and legitimize their interventions by emphasizing the inaction, inexperience or negligence of other project stakeholders (particularly public agencies). It is hardly surprising, therefore, that they sometimes have very poor relationships with governments, local authorities and other project participants.[75] These difficult relationships often limit project performance. It has been noted, for instance, that in Mexico "the rivalry between the Mexican government and NGOs limits the possibility of NGOs to address livelihood issues of the Mexican poor" (p. 367).[76]

8   NGOs rarely hire experienced architects, urban planners and design professionals.[77] Instead, designs are often produced by junior professionals whose housing knowledge and experience of the local context is limited. The lack of skills typically undermines project quality and intervention performance.

9   Although they possess neither experience nor knowledge of complex housing and urban issues, hundreds of NGOs, whose experience lies in social development or emergency aid, will initiate permanent housing projects. This lack of knowledge of the social, aesthetic, functional, technical and managerial aspects of housing projects greatly reduces the quality of initiatives, and undermines the sustainability of new settlements.

Implications for Rethinking and Designing Low-Cost Housing in Developing Countries

As we have seen, previous approaches have failed to substantially alleviate qualitative and quantitative housing deficits or improve the living conditions of the poor. Meanwhile, the population of slum dwellers worldwide continues to grow by about 10% yearly.[78] The following chapters will elaborate additional limitations of the approaches previously mentioned. Examples given will illustrate the weaknesses of these strategies as implemented by the public, private and non-profit sectors. We will consider how recently-popularized approaches—the enabling strategy, NGO interventions and current policies—seek to reinforce particular supply-side components, namely formal (private) sector products, services and markets.[79]

The book will construct an argument and a framework for thinking about low-cost housing that focuses on its role in social justice. I will argue, for instance, that although it has successfully created housing solutions for about half of the world's population, adapted to hostile environments and provided innovative and affordable solutions to the poorest of the poor, the informal sector has been largely ignored and excluded. The title of this book derives from this fundamental premise. Worldwide, the informal sector produces millions of innovative, highly adaptable and culturally sensitive housing solutions. These are insufficiently understood by architects, urban planners, design professionals, politicians and other decision-makers, and I have therefore chosen to refer to them as "invisible houses." Informal settlements (the informal sector's most notable outputs) constitute sophisticated social, economic, technological and political systems, yet they go unseen by most professionals, who view them instead as demeaning

FIGURE 1.14 The processes of housing development have become invisible to the majority of non-poor. Busy pedestrians in Mumbai seem to fail to notice the survival strategies happening in the background.

and chaotic (see Figure 1.14). This book will show that, contrary to common belief, slums are not demeaning and chaotic environments where anarchy and disorder prevail and from which residents long to escape. We will highlight the structures and reasons that help determine the economic and social relevance, morphology and functioning of urban slums and other forms of informal settlements.

The book's title also alludes to the fact that the informal sector is so ignored and neglected that it has become an invisible component of both the urban economy and the urbanization process. Its products, achievements, problems and solutions remain unseen by most design professionals and decision-makers. By focusing on the actions that architects, urban planners and design professionals can take when planning and designing housing projects, the book will underline how the informal sector presents opportunities and challenges for both the housing problem and social development.

We shall also see that it is not just the informal sector that is invisible to design professionals and decision-makers. The importance of the housing development process is so commonly underestimated that it is often missing altogether. And yet, as will be shown, the quality of this process is crucial for the development of successful architectural and urban projects. The understanding gained through a careful study of invisible actors, products, processes and settlements is critical to developing sustainable housing solutions that can help redress social injustices.

The book is based on the belief that architects and urban specialists have a crucial role to play in housing and social justice. The challenges and opportunities ahead for improvement are gigantic: a recent World Bank study estimates that the built-up urban areas of developing countries may triple by 2030, which would mean that these countries alone will see the development of "the same amount of built-up urban area in the next 24 years as the entire existing urban world has done up to this point in history" (CD-ROM).[80] This is an opportunity that cannot and should not be missed.

Complexity and a Systems Approach

Responding to this challenge requires that one assume a particular view of the housing problem. More specifically, it involves accepting and grappling with the innate complexity of redressing social injustices; various levels of intervention, variables and temporal frames must be considered simultaneously.

Multiple levels of intervention: Professionals and policy and decision-makers often act within confined mandates: politicians and bureaucrats make policies, urban planners create plans and architects design projects, which are typically organized and coordinated by project managers. This is understandable, given the need for specialization and focused expertise. However, the consequence is that policy-makers and planners rarely understand the constraints of housing projects, and design professionals often have a limited understanding of policy-making and housing policy ramifications. As we shall see in the following chapters, policies and plans repeatedly fail because they have not been tailored to specific project characteristics, and project performance is affected by poor policy and idealistic planning. In reality, finding solutions to housing deficits involves understanding housing development as a complex system in which different levels of intervention, including projects, programs and policies, have a strong influence.

Dynamic variables and trade-offs: Chapter 7 will discuss the phenomenon whereby architects, engineers and designers appear in the wake of major disasters that have attracted public attention, claiming to have a brand new "housing solution." These innovations are too often little more than technical solutions—perhaps a new gadget for building houses. They are rarely comprehensive solutions to the complex variables at play in housing development. While building houses is relatively easy, developing meaningful, liveable settlements that redress social injustices is a complex endeavour.

In fact, the construction of the units is rarely the difficult stage of addressing the housing problem. In most developing countries, houses are relatively easy to build with local resources and know-how. Let me repeat: the difficulty of housing provision is not the construction of structures, roofs and envelopes or the speed of construction or the even the efficiency of the construction site. The real challenge is properly coordinating multiple variables. These variables include land acquisition and transfer, project management, organizational design, project governance, stakeholder participation and management, development of financial mechanisms, solving legal challenges and procedures, considering heritage conservation, infrastructure development, community service establishment and economic activity development. All these variables affect one another: governance mechanisms determine stakeholder satisfaction, infrastructure construction is a prerequisite for economic development, land management is indispensable to the success of housing plans, community services greatly influence settlement sustainability, and so on. Avoiding the (housing) system's complexity by focusing on any particular element, such as construction methods, materials or resources,

FIGURE 1.15 Complexity must be embraced in order to deal with the multiple variables, time scales and levels of intervention that must be considered in housing development—some of them portrayed in this view of Ahmedabad, India, where the challenges are enormous: transportation, heritage conservation, infrastructure, income-generation, pollution, etc.

is hardly a sound solution. Rather, architects, urban specialists and design professionals need to deal with the problem's complexity by integrating all these variables into the solutions they devise and managing the way they interact (see Figure 1.15).

Temporal frames and scales: Most housing solutions proposed by "experts" (including those proposed by public agencies and NGOs—which often work with short-term mandates) typically focus on the delivery of housing units; that is, the short-term processes occurring immediately before they are occupied. However, developing sustainable settlements is a process that can take several years, or even decades. This book will demonstrate that successful housing solutions are those that incorporate short-term actions, mid-term results and long-term impacts, and include planning and following-up post-occupancy phases.

Most professionals know that housing design requires the consideration of interventions on various scales—from the unit to the overall urban level—that determine the relationship between settlements and neighbourhoods (some even argue that the regional scale must be carefully considered). The relationships between the outputs at these different levels are, nonetheless, seldom understood or analysed when planning housing interventions. As we shall see in the following chapters, the relationships between the housing unit and the plot are habitually neglected, and this causes severe limitations to incremental construction. The relationship between plot size and family income are usually ignored in housing projects, which often propose identical plot sizes. The relationships between neighbourhood development and urban integration are sometimes underestimated by NGOs concentrating on responding to the needs of a particular community. In sum, the relationships between units, plots, clusters, neighbourhoods, settlements and cities need to be carefully considered to provide comprehensive solutions to the housing problem.

Gathering and Using Information

Making decisions about housing often involves accepting significant trade-offs. Consider density: there is no doubt that community involvement in decision-making increases end-user satisfaction (in Chapter 9 we will review the evidence for this). Users and communities usually demand or expect lower-density settlements. There is usually a preference for detached units, large open spaces and parks, lower buildings rather than tall ones and generous front yards. Urban planners know very well, however, that lower density has a negative effect on public infrastructure sustainability, transportation and economic activities. Both variables (user satisfaction and long-term sustainability) are certainly desirable, but achieving both simultaneously is not always easy. Consequently, experts in project collaboration have found that users often need information and training sessions to understand how their desires and expectations affect the project. Only this way can they significantly contribute to the decision-making process without feeling frustrated when they fail to see their hopes and expectations reflected in designs and plans. As we shall see in the following chapters, failure to provide these training and information opportunities leads to an imbalance of variables that ultimately reduces user satisfaction and long-term sustainability.

In some aspects, housing interventions are more difficult than other architectural projects. In housing projects and programs, it is especially difficult for decision-makers to collect sufficient information about users to respond to their individual needs and expectations. Not only would a large amount of data about each individual family need to be collected (every user is different), but this data is dynamic, meaning that it is constantly changing as living conditions evolve. Factoring in all the information needed for each stage of the project (land acquisition and transfer, project management, organizational design, project governance, stakeholder information, financial mechanisms, legal challenges and procedures, infrastructure needs, expectations about community services, factors influencing economic activities, etc.) is virtually impossible. As we have seen, even if all the information were available in real time (promptly updated as it changes), using it in decision-making would remain difficult because some variables negatively affect others. So, how can housing projects be properly designed when all the information required to respond to users' individual needs and expectations is not available?

This book argues that common housing strategies concentrate decision-making power and thus exacerbate the information problem described above. As such, it is particularly necessary to decentralize decision-making power in housing projects and initiatives. This decentralization enables both individual and collective agency to be considered. The following chapter describes how informal solutions capture a vast amount of dynamic information required to develop convenient housing solutions. Architects, urban planners and design professionals need to learn *about* and *from* this sector. When it comes to low-cost housing we all need to learn from the poor.

Subsequent Chapters

Throughout this book, a series of case studies in Colombia, Honduras, El Salvador, Cuba, India, Haiti, Iran, Tunisia, South Africa and other countries illustrate the book's central argument. I conducted most of these case studies with colleagues and the help of students affiliated with the IF Research Group (under my direction). Chapter 2 explains how informal settlements and the informal sector function. It clarifies the identity of the urban poor and informal workers by addressing the question of whether they are criminals, wrongdoers, victims or heroes. It also defines the boundaries of informality and attempts to categorize informal activities. Finally, it describes the limitations of informality. Chapter 3 explains how the housing market functions, describing its distortions and the so-called "gap" in the housing ladder. It also analyses the major financial mechanisms operating in the residential market. Chapter 4 deals with the problem of land, concentrating on the issues of land tenure, density, land management, corruption and land-use vulnerabilities. Chapter 5 focuses on the argument presented in the first chapter, exploring the concept and operational mechanisms of the informal sector's most common housing development strategy—incremental construction. Chapter 6 claims that housing is not really about houses, but rather about infrastructure, community services and economic activities. In explaining this, it focuses on public services (water, sewage, electricity, telephone, Internet, etc.), collective services and transportation. The issues of vulnerability, resilience and reconstruction will be explained in Chapter 7, which argues that disasters are not actually "natural" and that, when not properly handled, reconstruction projects themselves are often another disaster.

Chapters 8 through 10 introduce a theoretical framework for addressing low-cost housing in developing countries, focusing on social justice. Drawing from human rights theories, Chapter 8 explains the role and strength of individual agency and the freedom to make decisions, while also discussing the limitations of a freedom-based approach to housing. In response to these limitations, Chapter 9 explores stakeholder theory to build a case for sound governance mechanisms in housing interventions. Chapter 9 presents an innovative framework that creates strong links between individual and collective agency, which helps establish housing as a matter of social justice. Chapter 10 examines the strength and viability of this approach in situations of extreme inequality, and the advantages of a sustained commitment to core values. We look at a demanding approach to planning, design and research and policy-making that calls for the sustained engagement of multiple stakeholders. This chapter returns to the argument of complexity and clarifies the scope for architects, urban planners and other professionals and decision-makers. It also discusses the design challenge we face and which, to paraphrase Italo Calvino's description of Zenobia, must ultimately create the conditions in which people can live lives they have reason to value. But which people? Let's first consider who the invisible millions are.

Notes

1 UN-Habitat. *Planning Sustainable Cities: Global Report on Human Settlements 2009*. London: Earthscan, 2009.
2 Mehta, B. and A. Dastur, eds. *Approaches to Urban Slums: A Multimedia Sourcebook on Adaptive and Proactive Approaches*. Washington: The World Bank, 2008.
3 Ferguson, B. and J. Navarrete. "A Financial Framework for Reducing Slums." In *Contemporary Readings in Globalization*, edited by S. Sernau, 183–96. London: Sage, 2008.
4 UN-Habitat. *Planning Sustainable Cities.*
5 *The Economist.* "Hot Spots: Plagues and Livestock." *The Economist*, February 10, 2011.
6 *The Economist.* "City Limits." *The Economist*, August 13, 2011.
7 Friedman, J., E. Jimenez, and S.K. Mayo. "The Demand for Tenure Security in Developing Countries." *Journal of Development Economics* 29, no. 2 (1988): 185–98.
8 *The Economist.* "Let Them Shoot Hoops." *The Economist*, July 30, 2011.
9 Mehta and Dastur, eds. *Approaches to Urban Slums.*
10 UN-Habitat. *The Challenge of Slums: Global Report on Human Settlements 2003*. London: Earthscan, 2003.
11 Perlman, J. *The Myth of Marginality: Urban Poverty and Politics in Rio De Janeiro*. Los Angeles: University of California Press, 1980.
12 UN-Habitat. *The Challenge of Slums.*
13 Ravallion, Martin. "On the Urbanization of Poverty." *Journal of Development Economics* 68, no. 2 (2002): 435–42; Rodriguez, A.G. and S.M. Smith. "A Comparison of Determinants of Urban, Rural and Farm Poverty in Costa Rica." *World Development* 22, no. 3 (1994): 381–97.
14 Ravallion, "On the Urbanization of Poverty."
15 Macours, K. and J.F.M. Swinnen. "Rural-Urban Poverty Differences in Transition Countries." *World Development* 36, no. 11 (2008): 2170–87.
16 Tickamyer, A.R. "Poverty, Rural." In *International Encyclopedia of Human Geography*, edited by R. Kitchin and N.Thrift, 416–20. Oxford: Elsevier, 2009.
17 UN-Habitat. *State of the World's Cities 2010/2011*. London: Earthscan, 2008.
18 UN-Habitat. *State of the World's Cities 2010/2011.*
19 Perlman, J. *Favela: Four Decades of Living on the Edge of Rio De Janeiro*. Oxford: Oxford University Press, 2010.
20 Hansen, K.T. "Informal Sector." In *International Encyclopedia of the Social and Behavioral Sciences*, edited by N.J. Smelser and P.B. Baltes, 7450–53. Oxford: Pergamon, 2001.
21 UN-Habitat. *The Challenge of Slums.*
22 Davis, Mike. *Planet of Slums*. London: Verso, 2006.
23 UN-Habitat. "Measuring the Size of the Informal Economy." *Habitat Debate* 13, no. 2 (2007): 19.
24 UN-Habitat. *State of the World's Cities 2010/2011.*
25 Bhatt, V. and W. Rybczynski. "How the Other Half Builds." In *Time-Saver Standards for Urban Design*, edited by D. Watson, A. Plattus and R. Shibley, 1.3.1–1.3.11. New York: McGraw-Hill, 2003.
26 Werna, E. "Shelter, Employment and the Informal City in the Context of the Present Economic Scene: Implications for Participatory Governance." *Habitat International* 25, no. 2 (2001): 209–27.
27 Doherty, G. and M.L. Silva. "Formally Informal: Daily Life and the Shock of Order in a Brazilian Favela." *Built Environment* 37, no. 1 (2011): 30–41.
28 Office of the United Nations High Commissioner for Human Rights. "International Covenant on Economic, Social and Cultural Rights." Office of the United Nations High Commissioner for Human Rights, www.ohchr.org/EN/ProfessionalInterest/Pages/CESCR.aspx.
29 *The Economist.* "Slumdog Millions." *The Economist*, March 24, 2010.
30 Choguill, C.L. "The Search for Policies to Support Sustainable Housing." *Habitat International* 31, no. 1 (2007): 143–49.
31 Davis, *Planet of Slums.*
32 Choguill, "The Search for Policies to Support Sustainable Housing."
33 Zanetta, C. "The Evolution of the World Bank's Urban Lending in Latin America: From Sites-and-Services to Municipal Reform and Beyond." *Habitat International* 25, no. 4 (2001): 513–33.

34 Turner, J.F.C. *Housing by People: Towards Autonomy in Building Environments.* New York: Pantheon Books, 1977.

35 Datta, K. and G.A. Jones, eds. *Housing and Finance in Developing Countries.* London: Taylor & Francis, 1998.

36 Choguill, "The Search for Policies to Support Sustainable Housing."

37 Davis, *Planet of Slums.*

38 Gilbert, A. "Helping the Poor through Housing Subsidies: Lessons from Chile, Colombia and South Africa." *Habitat International* 28, no. 1 (2004): 13–40.

39 Keivani, R. and E. Werna. "Refocusing the Housing Debate in Developing Countries from a Pluralist Perspective." *Habitat International* 25, no. 2 (2001): 191–208.

40 Mukhija, V. "An Analytical Framework for Urban Upgrading: Property Rights, Property Values and Physical Attributes." *Habitat International* 26, no. 4 (2002): 553–70.

41 Davis, *Planet of Slums.*

42 Mehta and Dastur, eds. *Approaches to Urban Slums.*

43 Ferguson, B, and J. Navarrete. "A Financial Framework for Reducing Slums: Lessons from Experience in Latin America." *Environment and Urbanization* 15, no. 2 (2003): 201.

44 Mehta and Dastur, eds. *Approaches to Urban Slums.*

45 Ferguson and Navarrete, "A Financial Framework for Reducing Slums."

46 Perlman, *The Myth of Marginality.*

47 Perlman, *Favela.*

48 Luce, E. *In Spite of the Gods: The Strange Rise of Modern India.* London: Abacus, 2006.

49 Ibid.

50 Feiler, G. "The New Towns in Egypt." In *Housing Policy in Developing Countries*, edited by Gil Shidlo, 121–39. London: Routledge, 1990.

51 UN-Habitat. *State of the World's Cities 2010/2011.*

52 Ibid.

53 *The Economist.* "City Limits."

54 UN-Habitat. *Meeting Development Goals in Small Urban Centers: Water and Sanitation in the World's Cities.* London: Earthscan, 2006.

55 Choguill, "The Search for Policies to Support Sustainable Housing."

56 Keivani and Werna, "Refocusing the Housing Debate"

57 Ibid.

58 The Economist. "City Limits."

59 Ibid.

60 Keivani and Werna. "Refocusing the Housing Debate."

61 Rusen, K. "Housing Policy in Turkey." In *Housing Policy in Developing Countries*, edited by Gil Shidlo, 140–72. London: Routledge, 1990.

62 Lizarralde, G. "The Challenge of Low-Cost Housing for Disaster Prevention in Small Municipalities." In *4th International i-Rec Conference 2008. Building Resilience: Achieving Effective Post-Disaster Reconstruction*, edited by i-Rec, Electronic publication. Christchurch, New Zealand: i-Rec, 2008.

63 Wisner, B. "Risk and the Neoliberal State: Why Post-Mitch Lessons Didn't Reduce El Salvador's Earthquake Losses." *Disasters* 25, no. 3 (2001): 251–68.

64 UN-Habitat. *The Challenge of Slums.*

65 Ibid.

66 Desai, V., R. Kitchin, and N. Thrift. "Aid." In *International Encyclopedia of Human Geography*, edited by R. Kitchin and N. Thrift, 84–90. Oxford: Elsevier, 2009.

67 Ibid.

68 Ibid.

69 Ibid.

70 Ibid.

71 Ibid.

72 Vakil, A. "Confronting the Classification Problem: Toward a Taxonomy of NGOs." *World Development* 25, no. 12 (1997): 2057–70.

73 Davis, *Planet of Slums.*

74 Rahman, M.M. "Problems of the NGOs in Housing the Urban Poor in Bangladesh." *Habitat International* 26, no. 3 (2002): 433–51.

75 Rahman, "Problems of the NGOs in Housing the Urban Poor in Bangladesh"; Sanyal, B. and V. Mukhija. "Institutional Pluralism and Housing Delivery: A Case of Unforeseen Conflicts in Mumbai, India." *World Development* 29, no. 12 (2001): 2043–57; Faranak, M. "Flirting with the Enemy: Challenges Faced by NGOs in Development and Empowerment." *Habitat International* 21, no. 4 (1997): 361–75.

76 Faranak, "Flirting with the Enemy."

77 Rahman, "Problems of the NGOs in Housing the Urban Poor in Bangladesh."

78 UN-Habitat. *State of the World's Cities 2010/2011.*

79 Keivani and Werna, "Refocusing the Housing Debate."

80 Mehta and Dastur, *Approaches to Urban Slums.*

2

INVISIBLE MILLIONS

The Multiple (and Contradictory) Faces of Poverty and Informality

> They also believe, these inhabitants, that another Beersheba exists underground, the receptacle of everything base and unworthy that happens to them, and it is their constant care to erase from the visible Beersheba every tie or resemblance to the lower twin.
>
> *Invisible Cities*, Italo Calvino (p. 100)

The Perfect Columns

Hernando Murielo was, in many aspects, an informal construction worker like any other. He was often hired on a daily basis to contribute to construction fieldwork in different places of El Valle, a region in western Colombia. Unlike many other temporary workers, however, he saved enough money to buy basic construction tools. This allowed him to conduct work directly, without the need to be hired by a general contractor. With time and discipline, his equipment improved and he started to build as a general (informal) contractor in places like Santa Helena, near the city of Cali, where he ultimately set up a workshop and established his business. He later developed a piece of equipment that was to change his fate and the future of his family. He found that casting columns with the timber and metal supports used in traditional concrete forms was both expensive and time consuming. By recycling large PVC pipes, he conceived a concrete form that needed not be lost in every use, allowing him to build as many as ten columns (see Figure 2.1.). Not only were the columns cast faster and more efficiently (without losing the form in every use), but also they had fewer defects and errors in dimensions.

Reputation about Hernando's technique and good quality of work granted him enough informal contracts to afford sending his son to study in a university in Cali, where he ultimately graduated in architecture. When I visited Hernando in 2012, he had partnered with his son, who now had obtained the right to practice architecture. Their business was then a "formal," duly registered enterprise that paid income tax, collected and paid sales tax and complied with most employment regulations. The

FIGURE 2.1 Mr Murielo's equipment to cast round columns allowed him to obtain profitable contracts. By recycling PVC pipes, his concrete forms can be easily handled and used as many as ten times (top picture). The result is perfectly cast columns that reduce costs and time in construction (bottom picture).

company now has a Facebook page that promotes their activities and features pictures of their best projects.

It took twenty years in the path from informality to formality to transform the Murielos' business. Is this a successful, uplifting story that represents the entrepreneurship of millions of informal residents and workers or, instead, one that masks (and distracts us from) a very different reality? This is a charged question, but one that must be answered in order to develop appropriate interventions in low-cost housing in developing countries.

Multiple Representations and Perceptions

A cornerstone of any change in housing conditions for the poor is to know *who we are working with*. Note that by "we," I refer to, among others, architects, design professionals and decision-makers, and that I prefer the expression "working with" rather than "designing for" or "planning for" when I refer to both users and builders. I will further describe the implications of this particular phrasing in Chapters 8 and 9. Nevertheless, as we shall see in this chapter, defining *who we are working with* is not an easy task, particularly because divergent views of the poor often compete—and coexist—in both literature and policy.

This tension is especially relevant considering that varied representations and perceptions of the poor have contributed to justify and legitimize urban housing interventions. Housing specialists Graham Tipple and Suzanne Speak have shown, for instance, that homeless people are wrongly portrayed and perceived as "villains," "beggars," "mentally ill," "immoral," "transients," "loners" and "helpless." Tipple and Speak argue that these largely false perceptions of homeless people, and the representations that people and institutions create of them (usually accompanied by judgmental and pejorative language), have contributed to institutionalize their stigmatization and segregation.[1] Rightly disturbed by the size of the homeless population in developing countries, they refer to the homeless as "the hidden millions" in an excellent book with the same title.

Consider also the case of planning and design of rental space for the poor. Rental solutions are some of the most ignored aspects of housing development in the Global South. Many reasons explain this flaw in policy, including misconceptions about landlords, who are often portrayed as ruthless exploiters of poor tenants. Alan Gilbert, a professor at University College London, has shown, however, that landlords in many Latin American cities are instead owner-occupiers that have one or two properties. "In certain Colombian cities," he finds, "absentee landlords rarely own more than two or three properties." He continues:

> Not infrequently, the principal form of accommodation is provided in consolidating self-help settlements where resident owners rent out individual rooms. Petty landlordism seems to be the rule and is part of the process by which more established owners try to increase their incomes.
>
> (p. 133)[2]

He also found this pattern in Guadalajara and Puebla (Mexico), where he revealed that the majority of landlords were rather poor and built their houses through self-help.[3]

Given these misconceptions, who actually are the residents of informal settlements, the urban poor and the informal workers? Before we explore the world of informal entrepreneurs such as Mr Murielo, let's consider the multiple representations that are generally created of slum dwellers and the urban poor.

Slum Dwellers and the Urban Poor: Criminals, Wrongdoers, Victims or Heroes

Criminals

The perception that slums are home to dangerous criminals has provoked and justified the most hideous reactions towards informal settlements. Millions of Brazilians have been forcibly evicted and are still persecuted in favelas in Rio de Janeiro and other cities accused of collaborating with guerrillas and drug dealers.[4] Linking slum dwellers with subversion also justified brutal persecution in Egypt, Chile, Argentina and Algeria during the 1970s.[5] Similarly, recent slum demolitions and evictions in Zambia, Malaysia, Bangladesh, China and Zimbabwe have been justified with arguments that link slum dwellers to criminal activities.[6] Probably the most famous segregation, persecution and repression of the urban poor occurred in South Africa during the Apartheid regime, with dramatic consequences that still remain two decades after the end of the regime (see Figure 2.2). Housing expert Marie Huchzermeyer argues, nonetheless, that policy-makers in South Africa still define the problem of informality "with a focus on the illegality of the settlement process, of the land use and the building type" (p. 334).[7]

Alas, various indicators suggest relationships between informal settlements and both urban crime and violence. According to a UN-Habitat report, the number of homicides in certain slums can be more than five times higher than in other districts.[8] Another

FIGURE 2.2 The criminalization of informal settlements has led to increased segregation, exclusion and persecution. In few places these are as noticeable as in urban South Africa.

report by UN-Habitat highlights, for instance, that much of the crime in Nairobi, Kenya, originates from informal settlements, where 60% of the population lives in just 5% of the city's land.[9] Some physical characteristics of slums seem to contribute to higher rates of crime, including poor lighting, limited transit of people in some areas, lack of surveillance, increased densities, etc. Other studies claim, however, that these characteristics have less influence than cultural and social ones. "Cultural and social expectations of violence, coupled with young male "hyper masculinity" values," argues the UN-Habitat report, "pervade many Brazilian favelas, Colombian barrios, Jamaican slums and North American ghettos—where marginalized young men are expected to revenge insults with injury or death" (p. 67).[10] The concurrence of informal settlements and gangs seems also to explain several crimes in South Africa. It is estimated that there are as many as 100,000 gang members in the Cape Flats in South Africa, who are considered responsible for 70% of crime in the region.

Wrongdoers

Slum dwellers are usually accused of negatively affecting other citizens, cities and the environment. Gangsters and other inhabitants of informal settlements commit crimes that affect non-slum-dwellers. Besides, it is often believed that slums and other informal constructions deteriorate the image of cities. This perception has justified major interventions aimed at "beautifying" key urban areas. In too many cases, though, this approach has taken the form of forced and market evictions that reinforce social injustices. Unlike forced removals, market evictions are caused by more subtle developmental pressures such as urban gentrification, rental increases, land-titling programs, land development and land grabbing. These evictions are often triggered by infrastructure projects (in the last five decades, 50 million people have been evicted in India for the construction of dams), by international mega events (it is estimated that 1.7 million people were evicted in Beijing ahead of the 2008 Olympic games)[11] and by other "urban beautification" initiatives.

In Chapter 7, we shall see that the informal construction sector has been unfairly accused of causing major natural disasters, exacerbating the perception of informality as a dangerous phenomenon. An additional common complaint is that slums and other forms of informal settlements cause important environmental damage, including contamination of water sources, air pollution and deforestation. Pollution of water sources is caused, among others, by open sewers, their use as public toilets or places to wash clothes and by the accumulation of waste. In fact, pollution of water channels is considered today one of the most important environmental challenges in Port-au-Prince, Haiti (see Figures 2.3 and 2.4). For some (even local) observers, this is the inevitable result of the inherent laziness and dirtiness of informal residents.

Air pollution is often caused by the burning of waste, the use of charcoal and wood for cooking and energy generation, and the lack of maintenance in equipment. Deforestation is often linked to illegal occupation of green, agricultural or environmentally protected areas. Beach-flanked mountains (a scenic attribute of Rio de Janeiro, Brazil) are, for instance, considered increasingly threatened by the expansion of favelas, prompting authorities to erect concrete walls to restrain the "spill" of informal construction (see Figure 2.5).

FIGURE 2.3 This open-air market in Port-au-Prince, Haiti, is, in reality, a highly polluted water spring and an urban gully where residential and commercial uses collide.

FIGURE 2.4 Polluted water sources are a threat to both the environment and public health in Cité Lajoie in Port-au-Prince.

FIGURE 2.5 In an attempt to control the expansion of Favela Santa Marta (Rio de Janeiro, Brazil, top picture) and protect green areas, authorities recently built a protective wall (bottom picture), a public measure that has been rightly accused of being exaggerated, inefficient and humiliating.

Victims

Informality in economy and construction has a price too; part of the tag is paid by slum dwellers themselves. The poor are often victims of unreliable public service providers, violence, inadequate transport infrastructure, natural hazards, pollution, marginalization, forced evictions and other social ills. Studies have shown that rates of urban violent crime across neighbourhoods "vary considerably, with higher rates correlated with lower incomes" (p. 12).[12] Child abuse, for instance, is frequently associated with perceived "high densities" in some South African settlements.[13] Even though crime is one of the most important worries of the urban poor, they also fall victim to other subtle abuses linked to informality. Perlman's research results on Brazilian favelas show that *favelados* (residents of Brazilian favelas) often pay proportionally more for public services than people with sufficient means. She explains that they live in a "controlled monopolistic territory," and are typically obliged to purchase from a sole source at a premium rate (p. 184).[14] These findings echo the observations of Edward Luce, a journalist and specialist in Indian affairs. Luce finds that, in order to obtain water, the Indian poor often have to pay private truckers, who belong to a "water mafia" (p. 213).[15] Finally, informal dwellers also suffer from poor political representation and public voice, which together limit their possibilities to act as agents in their own development. Given these social injustices, several experts now agree that informality is more a manifestation of the informal dwellers' infringement of rights than of their contravention of law.

Heroes

The urban poor are sometimes portrayed as heroic survivors of a ruthless economic and political system. This approach has justly led to creating a more positive view of informal dwellers and low-income urbanities. A recent report published by the World Bank illustrates this view: "Residents in [slums and informal] communities contribute substantially to the broader economy, through the provision of services, industrial production and construction. They are usually hard working, entrepreneurial, resourceful and self-reliant" (DVD).[16]

Following this line of thought, recent studies have shown that the urban poor develop significant resilience strategies to adapt to the environment (I will return to this argument in Chapter 7). These strategies eventually allow *favelados* in Rio de Janeiro, for instance, to exit slums and move to formal residential areas within one generation.[17] A more positive view of the poor has prompted the emergence of studies of their own social capital, their mechanisms of adaptation and their capabilities (concepts that we will explore in Chapter 8). Let's consider now other perceptions of informality in economic production.

Informal Businesses and Workers: From Supporting Them to Keeping Them at Bay

There are a significant number of business owners among the urban poor. This has led many experts to believe that—despite the paradox—there is an enormous economic potential *in poverty*. Perceptions about the informal sector and economy are, nonetheless, typically based on anecdotic evidence or econometric data that do not distinguish between different forms of informality. Thus optimistic and suspicious views of informal businesses and workers often compete for prominence in academic publications and policy. Almost every expert or decision-maker can point to examples of workers that were mistreated or exploited in hostile labour conditions, or successful single mothers who built up a thriving company from almost nothing. Are informal entrepreneurs and workers resourceful drivers of change, illegal opportunists, or victims? What characterizes the people that offer barbequed *cabrit* (Haitian goat) in the streets of Port-au-Prince, delicious *pupusas* (Salvadoran tortillas) in the plazas of San Salvador, hot *phở* (Vietnamese soup) in the crammed alleys of Hanoi, cell phones, plastic combs, Chinese toys, acetaminophen pills, massages, tarot reading, photocopies, haircuts, beer and other products and services in almost every city of the developing world?

These are crucial questions for architects, design professionals and decision-makers interested in improving low-cost housing conditions in developing countries. Let's consider why. First, several informal economic activities occur in informal settlements. Second, income-generation activities conducted in the informal sector are sometimes linked to domestic activities. Production and domestic uses merge in the same space or are in great proximity, influencing and feeding each other. Finally, informal productive activities sometimes occur in public space and collective areas, greatly defining the configuration, functioning and character of human settlements. Given this importance, we should now consider different emphases in the representations that are often made of informal businesses and workers.

Resourceful Productive Agents

Many specialists see a significant source of employment and production in informal businesses in developing countries. For them, these businesses provide an opportunity for unskilled labour to participate in production and service provision. Informal enterprises fulfil an important social role, particularly because they allow women to work without fixed working hours and to produce income from home-based activities, which allow them to take care of children or elderly family members. A study conducted in the 1980s by W. Paul Strassmann, an expert in low-cost housing and home-based enterprises, seems to support this view. Strassmann found that the majority of workers believed that a home-based enterprise was better than working in a factory or other large organizations. For them, switching to a formal sector job would be justified only by a significantly higher income.[18]

These experts believe that business operators embrace informality as a result of overregulation and legislation (in taxes, labour conditions, business registration, etc.) that hinder their capacity to enter the regulated markets and sectors of the economy.[19] Running micro-businesses is, in this view, a natural response to the inefficacy of public sector service provision. This line of thought, often called the *legalist approach*, emphasizes a rather heroic view of informal entrepreneurs. For instance, Peruvian economist Hernando de Soto, a poverty expert, believes that "micro entrepreneurs will continue to produce informally so long as procedures are cumbersome and costly" (p. 4).[20] These specialists typically imply that informal businesses appear as a rational choice made by the poor when confronted with a hostile economic and legal environment (see Figure 2.6).

FIGURE 2.6 The informal sector largely comprises women who run their own micro-business, like this one, who offers hot meals in the streets of Port-au-Prince. Is she a convinced or reluctant entrepreneur?

The resourcefulness of informal entrepreneurs and workers provide, according to this approach, a relevant contribution to development—which can be enhanced by leaving the State out of the free market and eliminating bureaucratic procedures and fees that hinder legalizing business operations.

Motivation-related theorists also agree on a heroic perception of informal workers, but they emphasize different causes for the emergence of informal businesses. They argue that informal entrepreneurship emerges when an individual or group recognizes and exploits an opportunity.[21] Informal entrepreneurs, according to this approach, exploit opportunities that others have discarded, such as collecting and transforming trash or recycling materials.

Opportunistic Competitors

Sceptics note that legalists tend to "romanticize" informal entrepreneurs as "struggling against great odds to provide needed goods and services" (p. 505).[22] Assuming a different perspective, they observe that informal businesses and workers also exploit opportunities that regulations do not allow the formal sector to exploit easily (for example, exploiting natural resources such as wood or water). Like the legalist approach, this view recognizes that the poor make a rational choice in the face of need. However, here observers emphasize the opportunistic approach of remaining in the informal sector. They argue that informal businesses and workers take advantage, in different ways, of the fact that the State and formal institutions often turn a blind eye to certain sectors of the economy and relinquish law enforcement. They notice, for instance, that informal traders escape penalties by selling only small quantities of goods that they can easily carry away and hide;[23] several businesses try to remain small and home-based in order to evade law enforcement; informal businesses skirt pollution regulations allowing them to operate outside institutional boundaries; and several informal activities do not respect labour condition standards in order to reduce production costs. Business specialist Justin Webb and his colleagues contend that informal entrepreneurs may find it more efficient to operate informally because the benefits provided by formality are lower than the costs required to obtain formal status.[24]

Perceiving an opportunistic attitude among informal vendors and artisans in Port-au-Prince, for instance, has contributed to a long history of forceful measures to evict them from public sidewalks and open areas. However, this strategy has repeatedly failed, and Haitians have grown used to seeing street merchants being violently chased only to see them reappear (in increasing numbers) a few weeks later in the same street or in a different part of the city.

Victims of the Economic System and Institutions

Other specialists emphasize that informal workers and businesses are victims of an economic system and an inefficient labour environment that forces the poor to accept lower standards of production and income-generation. What economists call "the dualist school of thought" subscribes to the notion that the informal sector comprises marginal activities "distinct from and not related to the formal sector" caused by the fact that "not enough modern job opportunities have been created" (p. 4).[25]

According to this perspective, informality is associated with the "uneven nature of capitalist development" that degrades labour conditions for the poor.[26] Defenders of this approach find that casual labour (simultaneously seen as a cause and a consequence of informality) impoverishes the most vulnerable sectors of society.[27] "Instead of upward mobility," writes Mike Davis, an opinion writer and activist, there is only a "down staircase by which redundant normal-sector workers and sacked public employees descend into the black economy" (p. 179).[28] Thus, informality is seen as a form of exploitation in which certain firms and decision-makers turn a blind eye to (or even subcontract and encourage) informal activities and labour to lower production costs. Left-wing defenders of this viewpoint argue that "informalization" is a mechanism to weaken the rights of workers and unions, disenfranchizing the working class with the acquiescence of the State.[29]

Informality in this sense comprises simultaneously of substandard labour (undeclared, exploitative), conditions of work (often hazardous and unprotected) and forms of management (unreliable, dishonest) that significantly affect the urban poor. Informal workers are thus considered "downgraded labour" resulting from poor or selective regulation and opportunistic behaviour by those who control the means of production. Observers point to a number of examples that illustrate this form of exploitation. They find that women working in domestic cleaning, men distributing calling cards provided by telecom giants, and people distributing newspapers on the streets work under dangerous and unfair conditions that are not accepted in the formal economy.

Victims of Informality Itself

It is also argued that being neglected from formal economic, legal and political systems, the urban informal workers and entrepreneurs resort to informal services and institutions that exacerbate their vulnerabilities. One of these services is credit, where unreliable moneylenders and opportunistic traders are most often the financing institutions involved. Analysts point to common examples. If you live in a developed country, you probably pay between 15–18% annual interest rate on your credit card. This is roughly a 0.05% daily interest rate. Just imagine for a moment that you had to pay a 4.7% interest rate per day! As it turns out, this is the daily interest rate that informal fruit sellers pay in Chennai, India, to wholesalers, according to a study presented by poverty specialists Abhijit Banerjee and Esther Duflo in the book *Poor Economics*.[30] Banerjee and Duflo, as well as many other economists, explain that the poor pay high (sometimes absurd) costs for borrowing money. But this is not the only financial problem these informal entrepreneurs must face. Being neglected by the financial system—which rarely allows them to open a bank account—means that they also cannot protect their savings in financial products. Both problems significantly hinder their chances of growing their businesses to a profitable level.

There are many other services that informal business people have to pay at (proportionally) very high costs: these include security, water provision and transportation. In a recent study that my students and I conducted in the street markets of Port-au-Prince, we found that food sellers who display a small cart on the pavement pay almost the same amount of monthly "rent" (in this case to a mafia of informal street managers) that food sellers pay to the municipally run formal market. Informal businesses also spend considerable resources in order to avoid crime and abuse (see Figure 2.7). Furthermore, informal home-based enterprises, according to some experts, negatively affect family members. According to this view, informal family businesses overexploit employees, notably because family members work too hard for too little, and often work in unsafe conditions.[31]

Reluctant Entrepreneurs

The idea that the poor are natural entrepreneurs who enthusiastically embrace business ownership has been recently challenged by Banerjee and Duflo. The majority of the poor, they contend, resort to entrepreneurship out of lack of choices, notably, due to their inability to find a good job. The studies conducted in India by these renowned economists show that the small informal businesses of the poor are most often unprofitable. They find that the poor rarely have the capital, talent and skills to transform their small informal activities into successful businesses. These authors even challenge the idea that the poor have the enthusiasm and commitment required by a real entrepreneur. Citing the case of a female micro-entrepreneur who runs a shop but soon realizes that her business is not effectively profitable, they argue: "Given that her

FIGURE 2.7 Protection against crime is one of the most common priorities of informal entrepreneurs. This home-based workshop of clothing alterations in Yumbo, Colombia, is protected by steel grids against increasing drug-related violence and crime.

business is destined to remain small and never make much money, she may decide to devote her attention and her resources to other things" (p. 224).[32] These economists conclude that micro-credit, and other mechanisms to help informal businesses, play a role in the reduction of poverty, but they are hardly the magic solution that most micro-credit defenders typically claim.

Making Sense of These Different Viewpoints

In order to make sense of these different perspectives, it is necessary to distinguish between different forms of productive units, different types of employment, different forms of occupation of space and between informality and illegality. This is a rather technical discussion, but we shall see that it is important for providing clarity to the links between informal activities and housing.

Let's consider first the two types of informal productive units that exist: informal sector enterprises and productive households. The International Labour Office (ILO) considers that informal sector enterprises are private *unincorporated* enterprises owned by individuals or families and that produce goods or services for sale or barter. They are generally *unregistered,* small or micro-productive units. Households are not typically permanent enterprises, but they can become productive units when they produce goods for their own final use (for example for building the house) or when they employ paid domestic workers.

Let's examine now different forms of employment. The ILO does not embrace a strict dualistic approach. Instead, it recognizes that formal sector enterprises sometimes generate informal employment and that informal sector enterprises sometimes employ formal employees. Thus it considers informal employment as the total of informal jobs, whether carried out in formal sector enterprises, informal sector enterprises or households. It also recognizes that there are five different statuses in formal and informal employment: own-account workers, employers, employees, members of producers' cooperatives, and family workers that contribute in productive units (the latter is almost exclusively an informal job that does not include explicit, formal contracts).

By matching the different combinations that might occur between production units and statuses of employment, we find that there are nine categories of informal employment (note that not all combinations between types of production units and statuses in employment are possible):

1   employees holding informal jobs in formal sector enterprises
2   employees holding informal jobs in informal sector enterprises
3   employees holding informal jobs in households
4   family workers informally employed in formal sector enterprises
5   family workers informally employed in informal sector enterprises
6   own-account workers employed in their own informal sector enterprises
7   own-account workers engaged in the production of goods exclusively for own final use by their household
8   employers employed in their own informal sector enterprises
9   members of informal producers' cooperatives.

This analysis illustrates the blurred boundaries between the formal and the informal sectors. Even though, micro- and small-sized enterprises are more likely to engage in the informal sector,[33] numerous medium- and large-scale enterprises carry out a significant part of their activities informally (1 and 4 are types of informal employment that occur outside the informal sector).

Let's move now to the different needs and relations with space that may exist in informal productive units. Households and informal enterprises can be classified according to the type of outcome they generate, the type of production they carry out and their location. Table 2.1 presents a matrix of some of the combinations that may result from this analysis (impossible combinations are highlighted in grey). This taxonomy shows that both households and informal enterprises can generate products and services. However, the very nature of households (which aim at production for household own consumption) means that offering space for rent or sale can only apply to informal enterprises.

Informal enterprises can engage in product distribution (retail shops, for instance), while both informal enterprises and households can include transformation of products (for instance, recycling and transforming waste), production (construction, for instance) and services (cleaning, transportation, repairs, etc.). The type of production can be artisanal or industrial. The former often corresponds to low-tech and less sophisticated means of production almost completely based on crafting and manual skills, whereas

TABLE 2.1 Matrix combining two frequent informal production units and three forms of classifying informal income-generation activities. Impossible combinations are shaded in grey.

Category	Group	Subgroup	Households (Production for household own consumption)	Informal enterprises (Production for economic exchange)
Type of outcome	Products	Distribution	(grey)	
		Transformation		
		Production		
	Services		(grey)	
	Space	Rent	(grey)	
		Sale	(grey)	
Type of production	Artisanal			
	Industrial			
Location	Home-based			
	Private space		(grey)	
	Public space	Sedentary		
		Semi-sedentary	(grey)	
		Mobile	(grey)	
		Itinerant	(grey)	

the latter typically implies some machinery, lines of production and more sophisticated means of manufacturing.

Informal enterprises can also differ according to their location: within homes (a form that often combines domestic and production activities in indoor and/or outdoor spaces), in private spaces outside of the residential property (in buildings, rooms or open spaces not linked to the house and which imply transportation for the operators) or in public spaces. There are different types of activities that are conducted in public spaces such as streets, parks and plazas. Some of them are decidedly sedentary, notably when permanent fixed structures, such as booths, roofs, deposits or shacks are installed. Others become semi-sedentary, when temporary structures are installed in public spaces but they are not removed or transported on a daily basis (see Figure 2.8 for an example). Mobile activities are those conducted by merchants or service providers that have transportable carts, booths, tarps, equipment or furniture, and that change their location every day or that return the merchandise or equipment to their homes or storage spaces every day. Itinerant activities are conducted by merchants or service providers who are constantly moving and thus who carry the products, tools or equipment used for their activities with them all the time.

Of course additional combinations can be found when combining different categories and units of production. A semi-sedentary activity, for instance, can have artisanal production; a home-based activity can have industrial transformation, and so on.

FIGURE 2.8 Whereas some informal businesses are mobile, others become sedentary or semi-sedentary by using permanent or temporary structures installed in public spaces, like this semi-sedentary barber shop located in a sidewalk in Hanoi.

Finally, let's consider the difference between informality and illegality. Hussmanns and the ILO distinguish *illegal* from *underground* production. The former corresponds to a contravention of the *criminal* code and thus, to production activities, which are forbidden by law or which become illegal when carried out by unauthorized producers (for instance, selling illegal drugs). The latter often corresponds to a contravention of the *civil* code, notably in activities that are legal when performed in compliance with regulations, but which are deliberately concealed from public authorities (for instance, selling imported toys or hot meals in the street without tax declaration).[34] Given the previous taxonomies, let's consider now the implications of the different viewpoints presented earlier in this chapter.

Informal Activities and Value

The somehow sweeping arguments explained above are often affected by the tendency to confuse different types of informal income-generation activities. A careful look shows that several distinctions are necessary to avoid futile generalizations. Owning an unregistered taxi to deliver transportation services, owning a shop or renting space in a house in an urban slum are all examples of informal income-generation activities. Yet, all produce different value for the poor, and thus performance measures for each of these activities are probably different, and the expectations of their owners may significantly differ.

Banerjee and Duflo seriously doubt the idea that:

> … the average small business owner is a natural "entrepreneur," in the way we generally understand the term, meaning someone whose business has the potential to grow and who is able to take risks, work hard and keep trying to make it happen even in the face of multiple hardships.
>
> (p. 225)[35]

It is probably true that poor entrepreneurs disappoint the expectations of many economists concerning the performance of informal enterprises. But the argument of underperformance cannot be easily applied to all informal activities. Take, for instance, business growth, a performance criteria that—when applied to informal businesses—largely disappoints Banerjee and Duflo. One could argue that business growth is not equally important for all types of informal activities. In fact, a woman who works in cleaning activities (an own-account unit of production) and who occasionally hires one or two cousins to help with her activities is not necessarily interested in business growth; at least, not in the same manner that formal enterprises are.

Another common mistake is to believe that the only purpose of all informal businesses is to create profit (Banerjee and Duflo get particularly disappointed by the low overall return of the entrepreneurial activities of the poor). In fact, Webb and colleagues remind us "individuals pursue entrepreneurial activities to create value for themselves in other ways as well" (p. 606).[36] There is, for instance, a significant value that emerges from merging domestic and income-generation activities in household production units (home-based enterprises). Analysing about 2,000 cases of home-based enterprises in Lima (Peru), Kalutara and Colombo (Sri Lanka), W. Paul Strassmann found that a large percentage of operators argue that if they did not have the business in their dwelling (or site), the business would not exist, and without the home business, they could not afford to live in their settlement.[37] This means that home-based informal businesses offer "extended fungibility" (economist jargon for the capacity to exchange, combine and convert resources swiftly, conveniently and without loss). Thus, resources devoted to income-generation and to domestic activities can be shifted at a very low cost. Housing specialists Peter Kellett and Graham Tipple argue that many women and children are not "available for full-time employment, but can divide their time between household chores, education and home-based enterprises" (p. 205).[38] These experts have demonstrated that one of the principal resources that benefits from extended fungibility is space. There is nothing surprising in this finding. In fact, sharing, superposing and/or connecting domestic and income-generation activities is often simultaneously a traditional form of housing design and a strategy of adaptation in the informal sector (see Figure 2.9).

Enterprise life expectancy, another common indicator of performance that interests economists, can also be seen in different ways in different productive units. Banerjee and Duflo lament, for instance, that "in Indonesia, only two thirds of the businesses of the poor survived five years" (p. 213).[39] However, this lack of continuity doing the same activity is not seen in a negative light by all experts. Instead, some of them recognize that one of the main benefits of the informal sector is precisely its low entry and exit barriers,[40] which allow enterprises to adapt to fluctuating environments

FIGURE 2.9 Very often, the combination and proximity of domestic and income-generation activities constitute simultaneously a traditional form of housing in city centres in developing countries (like in this central district of Hanoi) and a strategy of adaptation of the informal sector.

and allow business owners to adapt to insufficiently available and dynamic information.

Architects, planners, design professionals and decision-makers are responsible for recognizing the monetary and non-monetary value of informal activities. By recognizing the intangible, individual and collective value of these activities, projects can better respond to households' needs and aspirations.

Informal Activities and Needs

Informal productive units usually combine different strategies of income-generation. It is not surprising to find a retail shop that offers clothing repair services, sells lottery tickets and provides a laundry service. However, different relationships with the space also mean different needs for business development and residential use. For instance, people who work away from their residences require specific facilities or spaces at home to store equipment and tools used in income-generation activities (see Figure 2.10). Edmundo Werna notes, for instance, that rickshaw pullers in India suffer from the lack of such facilities or spaces. He explains that a significant number of pullers "sleep in their rickshaws in order to prevent them from being stolen, because they do not have a safe place to leave the vehicles at night" (p. 222).[41] Architects, planners, design

FIGURE 2.10 Different informal activities have different needs inside and outside the house. Mobile vendors like the one photographed in first plan here (in Ahmedabad, India) typically need space to safely store equipment, tools and merchandise.

professionals and decision-makers must be able to recognize when families operate as production units; they need to identify the families' needs and those of informal enterprises, and to recognize the close relationships that might exist between domestic and income-generation activities.

When Informality is Not Necessarily Pretty

The boundaries between informality, transgression and crime are sometimes blurry. For instance, building a house on the green mountains of Rio (destroying an important environmental capital for the society) contravenes several laws and regulations. However, building concrete walls to prevent this sort of development is probably both inefficient and humiliating for *favelados*. More sensible solutions to these and other transgressions are required; notably through approaches that recognize that informality is, in itself, the consequence of rights infringements.

It is crucial to recognize the situations and the conditions in which informality becomes an adaptation strategy that allows the poor to produce value for themselves. Nevertheless, it is also necessary to be able to identify the situations and the conditions in which certain forms of informality hinder their own development. Water mafias, unreliable monopolies of public service provision, underground "security" services that resort to violence and intimidation, opportunistic dons who rent and control open space, and other forms of coercion and exploitation often reduce the capacity of individuals, families and groups to achieve their own objectives and aspirations. Professionals and decision-makers need to distinguish between these different forms of informality in order to enhance the ones that genuinely create benefits and avoid—and seek to replace—the ones that produce or reproduce social injustices. This cannot be easily done through deterministic generalizations based on prejudices. It requires a comprehensive understanding of the singular situations and conditions in which informality occurs at the different scales of families, households, businesses, communities and neighbourhoods. In other words, it implies making the characteristics, the motivations and the processes of the millions of urbanities that resort to informality *visible*.

Implications for Rethinking and Designing Low-Cost Housing in Developing Countries

Informal settlements and slums are home to devoted parents, hard-working adults, respectful elders, enthusiastic children and talented youngsters. Sometimes, they are also home to prostitutes, drug dealers, opportunistic traders, drug addicts and careless gangsters. It might seem obvious, but this variety of people only demonstrates that homeless citizens, residents of informal settlements and informal workers are, above anything, human beings. As such, the majority are virtuous people who have noble objectives and dreams for themselves and their families; some have less honourable interests and values; all have a combination of qualities and flaws. Architects, planners, design professionals and decision-makers interested in low-cost housing development can benefit from avoiding generalizations and from engaging instead in a careful understanding of the singularities of poor families and communities. Neither policy-making nor planning need to be based on the characteristics of the majority or the result of a statistical mean if they are instead intended to allow individuals, families and groups to identify their own needs, priorities and expectations, and to actively participate in developing appropriate responses to them. It is our role as professionals and decision-makers to develop structures, institutions, policies and plans that allow individuals and social groups to identify their own particularities and characteristics, and to work on systemic solutions that carefully respond to each situation.

It is still difficult to radically determine whether entrepreneurs enter informality out of necessity (as Banerjee and Duflo suggest) or to pursue an opportunity (as the motivational theorists seem to imply). However, what is certain is that architects, design professionals and decision-makers must often decide whether they are to be encouraged and supported, or restricted and kept at bay. Generalizations and prejudice usually lead to bad policy and poor design. Given the reactions commonly provoked by informal entrepreneurs (ranging from praise to distrust and reject), engaging informal activities and businesses is unavoidable in a serious approach to low-cost housing in developing countries.

Notes

1 Tipple, G. and S. Speak. *Hidden Millions: Homelessness in Developing Countries*. New York: Taylor & Francis, 2009.
2 Gilbert, A. and A. Varley. *Landlord and Tenant: Housing the Poor in Urban Mexico*. New York: Taylor & Francis, 1991.
3 Ibid.
4 Perlman, J. *Favela: Four Decades of Living on the Edge of Rio De Janeiro*. Oxford: Oxford University Press, 2010.
5 Davis, M. *Planet of Slums*. London: Verso, 2006.
6 Ibid.
7 Huchzermeyer, M. "From 'Contravention of Laws' to 'Lack of Rights': Redefining the Problem of Informal Settlements in South Africa." *Habitat International* 28, no. 3 (2004): 333–47.
8 UN-Habitat. *State of the World's Cities 2010/2011*. London: Earthscan, 2008.
9 UN-Habitat. *Enhancing Urban Safety and Security: Global Report on Human Settlements 2007*. London: Earthscan, 2007.
10 Ibid.
11 Ibid.
12 Ibid.
13 Huchzermeyer, "From 'Contravention of Laws' to 'Lack of Rights.'"
14 Perlman, *Favela*.
15 Luce, E. *In Spite of the Gods: The Strange Rise of Modern India*. London: Abacus, 2006.
16 Mehta, B. and A. Dastur, eds. *Approaches to Urban Slums: A Multimedia Sourcebook on Adaptive and Proactive Approaches*. Washington: The World Bank, 2008.
17 Perlman, *Favela*.
18 Strassmann, P. "Home-Based Enterprises in Cities of Developing Countries." *Economic Development and Cultural Change* 36, no. 1 (1987): 121–44.
19 Aguilar, A.G. and E.P. Campuzano. "Informal Sector." In *International Encyclopedia of Human Geography*, edited by Rob Kitchin and Nigel Thrift, 446–53. Oxford: Elsevier, 2009.
20 Alter Chen, M. *Rethinking the Informal Economy: Linkages with the Formal Economy and the Formal Regulatory Environment, Research Paper No. 2005/10*. Helsinki: UNU-WIDER, United Nations University (UNU), 2005.
21 Webb, J.W., G.D. Bruton, L. Tihanyi and R.D. Ireland. "Research on Entrepreneurship in the Informal Economy: Framing a Research Agenda." *Journal of Business Venturing* 28, no. 5: 598–614.
22 Rakowski, C.A. "Convergence and Divergence in the Informal Sector Debate: A Focus on Latin America, 1984–92." *World Development* 22, no. 4 (1994): 501–16.
23 Webb, Bruton, Tihanyi and Ireland, "Research on Entrepreneurship in the Informal Economy."
24 Ibid.
25 Alter Chen, *Rethinking the Informal Economy*.
26 Rakowski, "Convergence and Divergence in the Informal Sector Debate."
27 Werna, E. "Shelter, Employment and the Informal City in the Context of the Present Economic Scene: Implications for Participatory Governance." *Habitat International* 25, no. 2 (2001): 209–27.
28 Davis, *Planet of Slums*.
29 Rakowski, "Convergence and Divergence in the Informal Sector Debate: A Focus on Latin America, 1984–92."
30 Banerjee, A.V. and E. Duflo. *Poor Economics: A Radical Rethinking of the Way to Fight Global Poverty*. New York: PublicAffairs, 2011.
31 Strassmann, "Home-Based Enterprises in Cities of Developing Countries."
32 Banerjee and Duflo, *Poor Economics*.
33 Aguilar and Campuzano, "Informal Sector."
34 Hussmanns, R. "Measuring the Informal Economy: From Employment in the Informal Sector to Informal Employment." *Integration Working Paper*, no. 53 (2004).
35 Banerjee and Duflo, *Poor Economics*.

36 Webb, Bruton, Tihanyi and Ireland, "Research on Entrepreneurship in the Informal Economy."
37 Strassmann, "Home-Based Enterprises in Cities of Developing Countries."
38 Kellett, P. and G. Tipple. "The Home as Workplace: A Study of Income-Generating Activities within the Domestic Setting." *Environment and Urbanization* 12, no. 1 (2000): 203–14.
39 Banerjee and Duflo, *Poor Economics*.
40 Khavul, S., G.D. Bruton and E. Wood. "Informal Family Business in Africa." *Entrepreneurship Theory and Practice* 33, no. 6 (2009): 1219–38.
41 Werna, "Shelter, Employment and the Informal City in the Context of the Present Economic Scene."

3

INVISIBLE MARKETS

On Why to Buy a $60,000 House in a Slum, and Other Distortions in Housing Markets

> On the day when Eutropia's inhabitants feel the grip of weariness and no one can bear any longer his job, his relatives, his house and his life, debts, the people he must greet or who greet him, then the whole citizenry decides to move to the next city, which is there waiting for them, empty and good as new.
>
> *Invisible Cities*, Italo Calvino (p. 56)

House for Sale

Haiti is the poorest country in the Americas. Its capital, Port-au-Prince, has some of the most impoverished areas in the Hispaniola Island. One of them is Cité Lajoie, a seashore slum built on land reclaimed from the sea, partly through the deposit of rubbish and debris resulting from the earthquake that destroyed the city in 2010. Cité Lajoie gets flooded very often. Houses sink due to poor foundations and the instability of the soil, open sewages serve as garbage deposits, water gets contaminated, violence has escalated and electricity must be stolen from rare networks in the area. It is hard to imagine that someone would like to buy a house in this slum. Yet, there are many houses for sale in Cité Lajoie. One, located just beside an open sewage, costs US$6,500. This house (pictured in Figure 3.1) has four rooms and one latrine toilet (locally known as *confort moderne*). Another house located in a slightly better area (closer to the main road and less prone to flooding) costs US$11,200. Nevertheless, neither the presence of small signs advertising houses for sale in slums nor the prices of the units are actually surprising. For example, an 80m^2 house in a slum in Yumbo, Colombia costs an average of US$60,000, and one in Favela Santa Marta in Rio de Janeiro costs US$30,000 (see Figure 3.2). None of them has official deeds; yet, they have entered the residential market.

Given that houses (even informal houses) can be produced and exchanged in residential markets in most developing countries, one might assume that selling and buying them follows the rules and principles of efficient markets wherein demand is balanced by supply. Why then are there not sufficient houses for the poor?

FIGURE 3.1 A house for sale in Cité Lajoie, Port-au-Prince.

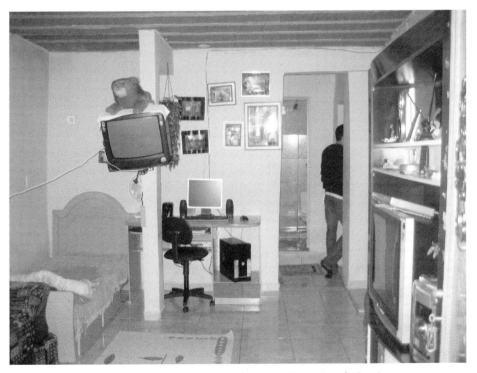

FIGURE 3.2 Interior of a house for sale in Favela Santa Marta, Rio de Janeiro.

When Supply Does Not Meet Demand

The concept of efficient markets in economic theory anticipates that free markets usually balance supply and demand (with more or less success depending on the product and the environment). The concept assumes that when a product is in high demand, its price will rise, allowing for higher profits for producers and providers, thereby motivating them to increase supply in order to keep up with the increased demand. Even though there are several variables that affect prices, neoclassical economic theory sustains that, generally, profit incentives attract new market entrants, thus increasing competition, which in return reduces the bargaining power of suppliers and balances the price of the service or commodity.

Housing units, however, do not behave like other products and services that are exchanged in free markets. When low-cost housing units are in high demand—the case of most developing countries—the supply sector is not able to balance this need with additional production. Consequently, prices keep rising, failing to reflect the natural tension between consumers and suppliers, thus making it more difficult for poor people to purchase a unit. This ultimately translates into qualitative and quantitative deficits of housing units. Economists consider this situation an "inefficiency" in the market, and recognize that it prevents supply and demand from organically responding to each other.[1] There are at least six intertwined factors that are typically associated with the inefficiency of the housing market. Housing specialists Ramkin Keivani and Edmundo Werna contend that, together, they cause "a perpetual state of disequilibrium between demand and supply" (p. 98).[2] Let's explore the influence of these factors.

Capital market failures: Acquiring a house normally requires financial assistance. Purchasing a housing product, therefore, depends on the availability of an external product, credit, which typically takes the form of loans, micro-financing or mortgages. However, we shall see in this chapter that capital markets in developing countries often fail to offer sufficient financial services that are accessible to poor families, thus limiting their capacity to enter the housing market.

Imperfect information: The adjustments between supply and demand require that both suppliers and consumers have access to sufficient information about products, market conditions, regulations, standards, financial options, fiscal incentives, procedures for purchasing, etc. However, the construction industry and the real estate market are highly fragmented and, therefore, information—which is highly dynamic, as we saw in Chapter 1—is often inaccessible and expensive to obtain.

Land and "inelasticity" of supply: Economists refer to "inelasticity" of supply when an increase in the price of the product does not result in an increase in its supply.[3] There are many factors linked to the inelasticity of supply. First, housing units are site-dependent (they are obviously attached to soil) and therefore—unlike other products—they cannot be easily transferred from one site to another in order to meet high demands. This means that houses can be available in one place but unavailable in other places where demand is higher (for example, in areas where jobs and services are available). Second, land is increasingly scarce, and thus expensive, in inner cities. The price of housing units is therefore highly dependent on the price of land, which typically reflects its most profitable use. Alas, it is rarely low-cost housing. Third, land speculation affects the possibility of obtaining plots that can be used for housing development. Keivani and Werna explain: "The problem of excessive land speculation by landowners, including building firms and developers, in unregulated land markets poses a serious challenge to the efficiency of the private market mechanism" (p. 112).[4] Finally, builders and developers in the low-cost housing sector must accept slim profits per unit to maximize affordability. Thus, the activity is only profitable if it can be delivered in large numbers to obtain economies of scale (a South African contractor once told me that building less than 300 units is just "suicidal"). However, due to the lack of large pieces of land in desirable locations, it is difficult to develop projects that are sufficiently profitable.[5] In response, developers and builders often prefer housing development in remote areas and the urban periphery, where plots are larger and cheaper. This preference exacerbates the inelasticity of low-cost housing in central urban areas.

Uniqueness of products: Every site is, of course, different. It has a different climate, topography, zoning, neighbours, etc. The price of a house is, therefore, largely affected by externalities in the context in which it is located. This means that the market price does not necessarily reflect the tension between costs of production and demand.

Housing markets are not truly free markets: Clients and suppliers do not act freely within the housing market. Instead, the housing sector is largely influenced and controlled by institutions and agencies that regulate supply, standards and transactions. These institutions include urban planning agencies, deeds registration agencies, banks and financial institutions, property companies and landowners. Public policies and regulations sometimes act as a barrier to free transactions. Given these characteristics, the World Bank concludes that "policies that restrict the housing market or the building industry decrease housing supply elasticity" (p. 238).[6]

Political inference: The close relationship that exists in some countries between politicians, builders and land developers favours political interference in housing supply. Consequently, projects do not necessarily get developed when and where demand is high (notably where the poor can have access to jobs and services). The interests of politicians, landlords and decision-makers sometimes interfere with the development of projects and plans that can potentially benefit the poor. Keivani and Werna explain:

> The deep rooted involvement of politicians, political parties and local officials in the illegal activities of informal settlements in developing countries such as sanctioning land invasions and protecting informal subdivisions indicates that the implementation of policies and application of regulations in the field of land and housing are intrinsically tied to, and a result of, interplay between different political and economic interest groups which is often manifested in the form of clientelism and political mediation.
>
> (p. 112)[7]

Given the previous factors, the supply and demand of new formal housing do not balance each other in the low-cost housing market (as it is often expected in regular free markets), preventing poor people from obtaining affordable units. In Colombia, for instance, there are on average 245,000 new households every year, but there is a formal supply of only 140,000 units.[8] Like in many other developing countries, this deficit in supply is largely fulfilled by the informal sector, which ends up providing solutions for the lowest levels of the housing ladder (imagine this ladder as a series of steps that allow access to better quality units).

However, if the houses of the informal sector do enter the residential market, why don't the poor "just" climb the housing ladder? Ultimately, the capacity to buy and sell informal units should facilitate that poor families (at least those having the capacity to save a little money or make a loan) sell substandard units in order to buy a better one. Eventually, they could keep adding capital and selling and buying units until they acquire a good quality unit. This process would certainly allow them to slowly improve their living conditions.

Difficulties in Climbing the Housing Ladder

The effective mobility of the poor is a contentious issue among economists and social scientists. Some researchers, such as Janice Perlman, have found that households remain in slums only for a period of time (in Perlman's case in *favelas*).[9] Many of these specialists thus see slums as a transitory phenomenon characteristic of the Global South on its path to development. Challenging this argument, other analysts, such as Benjamin Marx, Thomas Stoker and Tavneet Suri, three economists at MIT, have found evidence that slums and shantytowns are, in reality, poverty traps that reduce household social mobility.[10] The evidence to support these two stances, however, is still inconclusive. It suggests, nonetheless, that many poor families in developing countries do follow the pattern explained above and do climb the housing ladder. But as they do it (sometimes very slowly and with major difficulties) other poor families enter the bottom of the pyramid. Some remain for many years or decades in the lower levels of the ladder, incapable of exchanging the capital invested in their houses for money they could use to improve their living conditions or to face particularly harsh moments.[11] Why can't more families climb the housing ladder faster?

In order to answer this question, Professors Mark Massyn, David Root and I conducted a research project at the University of Cape Town, South Africa in 2006 and 2007.[12] We first developed a theoretical model to identify the different elements of the market. Given that the urban housing market in developing countries reflects the participation of two delivery systems—the informal and the formal sectors—David, Mark and I imagined the housing stock (and the ladder) as a pyramid, where low-cost products are at the bottom and highly priced units are at the top (see Figure 3.3). We subdivided the pyramid into two sections with the boundary between the informal and formal outputs corresponding to the affordability level. Of course, we knew that formality and informality often merge, and that there are many "grey" zones between the two sectors; however, we anticipated that this level represents the minimum housing product available in the formal market. Dots in the model represent housing units at different scales or sub-markets of the pyramid. Arrows represent the mobility of units in the market.

Housing policies in many developing countries (including South Africa, where we conducted the study) often result in the creation of what could be represented as a separate zone in the housing pyramid. Even though this zone belongs to the formal sector, it does not follow the rules that govern the "relatively free" market of medium and upper class housing. Instead, it is more significantly affected by the intervention of government and public agencies. We called this zone the "induced" formal sector. In many countries, the final products of this sector are houses built by profit-driven or non-profit developers within the framework and financing of public subsidies allocated

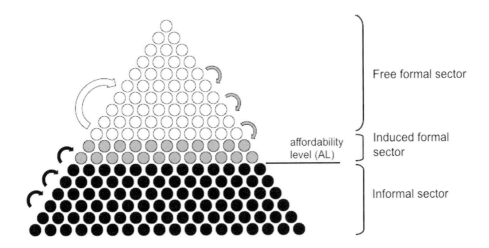

Legend:

$\curvearrowleft$ Residential upgrading

$\supset$ Filtering

$\subset$ Gentrification

FIGURE 3.3 The urban housing market in developing countries (the arrows show different forms of mobility).

to individual beneficiaries. It is not surprising that the housing products of the induced formal sector also correspond to the affordability level; thus, the subsidized units are the minimum-cost product available in the formal sector.

Mobility of the Residential Stock in the Housing Pyramid

The previous model anticipates that the different levels of the housing pyramid (the sub-markets) are not impermeable or static. It recognizes three processes that generate mobility of units in the sub-markets, and that eventually have an influence on the mobility of households themselves.

The first process is residential upgrading. This happens when units move upwards in the housing pyramid, including the possibility that they ultimately enlarge the stock of the formal sector. This transition can take two forms (which can happen simultaneously or sequentially). First, individual houses are modified, consolidated and/or extended by their owners to improve their living conditions. Second, urban revitalization or upgrading programs are used in neighbourhoods or slums in order to improve infrastructure and/ or services, legalize properties and integrate the area in the formal structure of the city (see Figure 3.4). The advantages and disadvantages of slum upgrading are explained in Chapters 1 and 6; however, it is crucial to note here that these individual or collective processes facilitate not only the mobility of housing products but also families (provided they keep ownership of their units in the process). Moreover, by legalizing and regularizing

FIGURE 3.4 Urban upgrading typically increases the value of residential properties. Here a house for sale in a slum in Yumbo, Colombia, recently serviced with running water infrastructure and electricity. The signs reads *"se vende esta casa"* (house for sale) and *"Hay cola grande y pequeña"* (Large and small cola drinks sold here).

ownership, this process potentially allows owners to formally sell their units and thus, it makes it easier for them to purchase a better product.

The second process, known as "filtering," corresponds to the situation in which aging of housing stock in the upper levels reduces relative rents and prices as previous higher-income occupants leave for newer buildings and pass the older dwellings to lower-income households. This process (also called "welfare filtering") implies the movement of housing stock from higher-income to lower-income households, allowing the poor to improve their living conditions[13] (see Figure 3.5). It might contribute to improving the living conditions of poor households, but it is also often associated with less desirable effects such as neighbourhood deterioration and the loss of homeowners' equity in their dwellings.

The third process is known as "gentrification" and it can be seen as reversed filtering. Broadly speaking, housing gentrification occurs when housing at the lower levels of the pyramid attracts higher-income households that gentrify the neighbourhood or settlement, displacing lower-income households to other urban or peripheral areas (see Figure 3.6). Much like neighbourhood upgrading, this process often involves improvements in the housing stock and abrupt increases in property values. However, original residents do not keep their properties due to market pressures or to significant increases in the cost of living (higher taxes, more expensive services, costlier retail shops, etc.). Considering that there is usually insufficient supply of good quality units for the poor, this process easily leads to the worsening of their living conditions.

FIGURE 3.5 Deterioration and subdivisions in historic buildings, such as this one in central Bhuj, India, can contribute to the filtering down of properties in the market.

FIGURE 3.6 Urban interventions in numerous historic districts (including Barrio Candelaria in Bogotá, Colombia, pictured) swiftly increase property values favouring gentrification.

Mobility of Households in the Housing Pyramid

The mobility of residential stock in the housing pyramid improves or deteriorates living conditions for the poor. But how important is the mobility of households themselves? Given that they have the possibility to climb the housing ladder through residential upgrading of their own units and their neighbourhood, is it actually important that they have the capacity to sell their houses?

Answers to these questions are a frequent matter of debate. However, my short answer is "yes." Let's consider why. Other than through residential upgrading of their own units, the possibility for poor households to climb the housing ladder in both the formal and informal sectors—or across these two—is linked to the availability of products across a wide range of prices (to sell a property and be able to buy another one slightly better) and the ability of the household to repeat this process various times. In this context, mobility has several advantages. First, it increases the capacity of households to adapt their living conditions to changes in family size, to reduce commuting time and costs when jobs change, to move closer to desired schools, services, family members or friends. Second, it also allows them to sell their units and transform their capital into cash in case of illness, unemployment, family crises and other adversities. Third, an active secondary market facilitates the entry of households into homeownership. Finally, the capacity to buy units favours certain vulnerable groups, notably because buying a house is the only possibility for many households headed by a woman or elderly person (who cannot easily embrace self-help construction) to become homeowners.[14]

Mobility among the poor, nonetheless, is a phenomenon that does not occur very often.[15] The main reason is that low-cost houses—and notably informal housing—do not often get sold, whether formally or informally. The fact is that most of the small signs announcing a house for sale in informal settlements therefore will not be successful.[16] The work we conducted with David Root and Mark Massyn shows that there are at least nine fundamental factors linked to lack of mobility among the poor.

1. Restrictions in the Induced Sector

There are often important restrictions to the selling of units that are produced by the induced formal sector. Beneficiaries of free housing delivery in Colombia, for instance, are not allowed to sell their units (called "*viviendas gratuitas*") for at least ten years after they have received them. Should beneficiaries want to sell their units after these ten years, they are obliged to offer the unit first to the public agency that built it. Similar restrictions apply to subsidized housing in South Africa and many other countries. Furthermore, self-help programs developed within the induced sector typically prohibit selling units in order to prevent housing filtering and foster community participation (naturally, these measures often backfire by leading beneficiaries to illegally sell their units).[17] In a comprehensive study about housing markets in Johannesburg, Rust and the FinMark Trust argue that when there are not buyers to purchase the subsidized house, the end-user "can't realize the real asset value of his house (replacement value plus appreciation) and use this to improve his housing circumstances" (p.5).[18] Economists tend to believe therefore that value in use also has to be correlated to a real possibility of value in exchange.

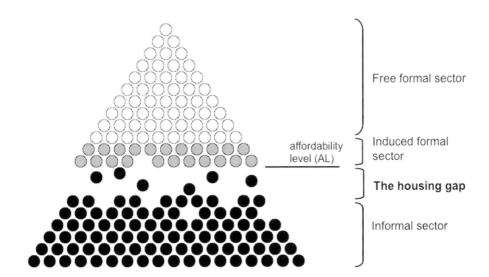

Free formal sector

affordability
level (AL)

Induced formal
sector

The housing gap

Informal sector

FIGURE 3.7   The housing gap in low-cost residential markets.

2. Economic Gap

Insufficient supply of low-cost housing affects different levels of the pyramid. However, another important reason for insufficient mobility is that the limited amounts of units that do get built typically supply only the very bottom of the pyramid (supplied by the informal sector) and at the bottom of the formal sector sub-market (supplied by the induced sector). There is a zone of *almost no supply at all* in the price segment between the affordability level (of the formal sector) and the product of maximum value found in the informal sector. Given the increased lack of new units in this zone, David Root and I called it "the housing gap" in the South African market.[19] Other studies have shown that this gap also exists in other contexts such as Haiti and Colombia (see Figure 3.7).

Building the minimum product offered by the formal sector in South Africa cost, in 2006, approximately R40,000 (US$5,450). This price included the development of the site plus the subsidy for a top structure, but excluded the price of the land and administrative fees. By contrast, the perceived value of units in the informal sector was about R4,000, and the perceived value of a house that had been built with a public subsidy (an output of the induced sector) was about R20,000 (US$2,724). This means that selling a house in the informal sector is not truly useful for purchasing another one in the formal sector. Households thus perceive that the "next" step is too difficult to reach.

What justifies this gap between the prices of the products of both sectors? It is important to remember that the commercial price of a unit is largely the result of construction costs plus profits, plus the cost of land. Profits from projects at the affordability level are slim; thus, profit cannot fully explain the difference in overall price. Land, instead, plays a fundamental role. Housing specialists Bruce Ferguson and Jesus Navarrete[20] argue that the value of land is a key element of the equation for low-cost housing prices in Latin America. It significantly increases the gap between formal and informal prices. Given that informal housing often follows land invasion, the perceived value of informal construction does not fully account for the real cost of land in which it is located. The overall price of formal housing, on the other hand, largely depends on the market price of land.

Other factors also play a part in the gap between sectors. The most obvious one for most observers is that the formal sector provides a product that is largely better than an informal one (it has, for instance, better foundations). There is naturally some truth to this argument. However, the notion of "better" reflects a perspective largely defined by common familiarity with the products of the formal construction sector and little familiarity with the outputs of the informal sector and its competitive advantages. We shall come back to this argument in Chapters 5, 6 and 8.

3. The Technological and Moral Gap

In 2006, Juan Lozano, a Colombian Housing Minister announced that his government "would never subsidize a single housing unit having less than two bedrooms."[21] This was not a surprising announcement for most Colombians, who have grown used to politicians defending the right to "*vivienda digna*" (dignified houses) and assuring that their government will "finally" enforce minimum standards of housing. By contrast, housing specialists know that many informal units often start having a single common space used for several activities. For them, the Minister's comment was yet another piece of evidence that the housing sector is affected by, what can be considered, a moral threshold. That is, the interest of institutions in guaranteeing a minimum standard for the outputs of the induced formal sector.

This moral threshold, which makes some officers think that anything below certain standards is not a "decent" house, is one of the most common obstacles to the development of core-housing projects in developing countries. However, I will consistently argue in this book that unfinished and core-housing units can potentially bridge the gap between the informal and the induced formal sectors, and facilitate mobility for the urban poor (see more in Chapters 6, 8 and 10). However, in order to be adopted more broadly, this strategy requires revising several legal barriers and standards that limit the participation of the informal sector in formal housing development.

4. The Legal Gap and Standards

Legal requirements and regulations limit the capacity of the informal sector to provide housing solutions that could otherwise supply the housing gap. For instance, in order to be able to build low-cost housing and to participate in subsidized housing programs, construction companies in South Africa must meet at least three legal conditions:

1   Register with the National Home Builders Registration Council,[22] which "represents the interests of housing consumers" and provides "protection to housing consumers in respect to the failure of home builders to comply with their obligations."[23] By registering, companies are recognized by their financial, technical, construction and management capacity.[24]
2   Comply with performance specifications and standards defined by the National Department of Housing.[25]

3   Register with the Construction Industry Development Board[26] which categorizes contractors according to their capability to perform construction projects with the public sector.[27]

Other standards and regulations limit the capacity of informal suppliers and manufacturers to participate in housing provision. Consider for instance, the case of the South African People's Housing Process or PHP, a low-cost housing program that aims at involving households in the housing development process. While pretending to integrate end-users, the program encourages the engagement of large companies by asking decision-makers to purchase materials on a large scale, hindering the possibility of small and medium enterprises to enter the subsidized scheme.[28]

5. The Costs of Legalization and Registration

Legalizing property titles and formal registration of sales is cumbersome and expensive in most developing countries. Peruvian economist Hernando de Soto reports that the procedure to formalize informal urban property in the Philippines—for instance—can take up to 168 steps and between 13 to 25 years. He further argues that the procedures to legally occupy a piece of land in Haiti can take 19 years and 111 steps.[29] These costs (in money and time) discourage the effective marketing and purchase of units at the lower levels of the housing ladder.

6. Moving Costs and Informal "Taxes"

Moving from one informal settlement to another implies costs that the poor cannot easily afford. On top of regular moving costs, sometimes residents have to pay informal "taxes" to be accepted in new neighbourhoods or to be able to squat somewhere in a slum. This was the case of some South African households we interviewed in the Cape Town townships, who had paid up to R500 to informal street councils to be accepted in a new informal settlement.

7. The Notion of Family Patrimony

Studying low-cost settlements in Bogotá, Colombia, professor Alan Gilbert of University College London found that about 55% of households in self-help settlements would move if they had more money to do so. The figure rises to 77% in formal low-income settlements.[30] However, this willingness to move should not be taken for granted in all contexts. In fact, besides difficulties in buying and selling units, mobility among the poor is sometimes constrained by their own unwillingness to move. There are two natural reasons for this. First, informal units are often built by long and complex processes of land invasion, financing, protection against threats and harassment, self-help construction, etc. Second, given that the poor have access to limited or no formal financial services at all, building the house is both a savings strategy and an opportunity to secure an inheritance for children or kin. The struggle of family members during these complex processes, combined with the value attached to the family patrimony, creates a sense of attachment that discourages household mobility in many contexts.[31]

8. Community and Ethnic Ties That Bond Communities Together

Having limited access to services and resources, the poor are largely dependent on family and community ties for babysitting, having access to credit, transportation and other daily needs. These close links to kin and community members that require physical proximity sometimes discourage them to move from one neighbourhood to another.

9. Lack of Interest in Formalization

Formalization of informal properties is a prerequisite for formal transactions in the market. However, legalization of properties typically implies paying taxes and public services. These costs discourage some informal dwellers from applying to formalization processes and limit their capacity to sell their units in formal residential markets.

Distorted Mobility

The different variables presented in this chapter become simultaneously a cause and a consequence of the inefficiency of the housing market, and bring negative consequences for both economy and society. They reduce the possibility of transferring housing products and limit the chances of low-income families to climb the housing ladder and improve their socio-economic status. Finally, they contribute to the creation of poor urban environments in which housing is not easily consolidated and remains incomplete for longer periods of time, and in which low income suburbs remain fragmented and disconnected.

The previous arguments do not mean that there is absolutely no mobility of households and housing stock between the sub-markets. However, several studies have found that—even when they exist—these exchanges are often highly distorted. For example, when sold, the value of houses of the South African induced sector depreciate a great deal.[32] In fact, they are most often informally transferred by a value (of R6,000 to R10,000 in 2000) significantly lower than the original replacement cost. Furthermore, many of these units are sold on (illegally) to wealthier clients who buy them at very reduced price. A Housing Minister in the province of the Western Cape in South Africa once complained that bar owners and drug lords are "buying up the government's low-cost housing stock for a fraction of what it costs to build" (p. 23).[33]

Furthermore, when consolidated, informal units also "filter up" instead of filtering down. Given that there is a considerable lack of financial mechanisms for the poor, once consolidated, these units are more accessible to better-off households (who have better access to financing) rather than to those who have a lower income than the seller[34] (incidently, this factor is believed to explain why an informal unit in Yumbo, Colombia, is advertised for a price of US$60,000). Of course, this distortion only exacerbates the lack of supply for the poor.

"Fixing" the Markets

Given the previous inefficiencies and distortions, decision-makers and scholars have consistently searched for ways of "fixing" the housing markets; in Chapter 1 we saw that "enabling the markets to work" has even become an obsession in international policy and among financial institutions.[35] The strategies often concentrate on four main variables: securing property rights, subsidizing housing, facilitating access to financial solutions and preventing idle land. Let's consider now the merits and limits of each of these strategies.

Securing Property Rights

One of the most animated debates in housing studies in developing countries concerns the role of property rights in the alleviation of poverty and subsequent improvements in living conditions for the poor. The debate was significantly fuelled by Hernando de Soto's book *The Mystery of Capital*, in which he claimed to have found a powerful tool for poverty reduction in developing countries.[36] De Soto recognizes that informal houses and land are a social capital for the poor. However, without formal property titles, he contends, they are not a means of wealth production that can be used for other purposes or as collateral for credit. According to de Soto, housing assets therefore become a "death capital" for poor families. He goes on to argue that, by ensuring secure property rights, poor families can potentially obtain loans, enter formal systems and eventually exit poverty. From this standpoint, titles permit converting assets into useable wealth. Politicians and decision-makers should therefore create the conditions for the development of private, tradable, and enforceable property rights and efficient land registration systems. They should also undertake land registration and regularization of insecure tenure.

Imagine, for instance, that through institutional reforms and legalization processes, residents of Cité Lajoie in Haiti could transform the capital invested in their housing units (we know now that it amounts to a lot of money) into wealth… They could escape poverty! The idea is of course persuasive. However, contributions by several researchers, including Geoffrey Payne and Associates,[37] a consultancy, and World Bank aids Robert M. Buckley and Jerry Kalarickal[38] have demystified the functioning of land markets and have challenged this approach. At least six arguments are typically exposed to challenge de Soto's argument.

1   Cost-benefit imbalance. Solving contradictory claims and dealing with cumbersome administrative procedures significantly increase the legal cost of titling processes.
2   Ambiguity regarding tenure. Titling implies providing amnesty to households or landowners that benefitted from land invasion and illegal squatting in the first place. Therefore, it leads to ambiguity regarding the capacity and interest of institutions in respecting and enforcing land tenure rights.
3   Different forms of tenure. De Soto's argument has led many people to confuse tenure informality with tenure insecurity. However, the former does not necessarily imply the latter. Alain Durand-Lasserve, a researcher at the National Center for Scientific Research in France, and Harris Selod, a World Bank economist, demonstrate that countries and cultures have multiple formal and informal systems and levels of tenure that cannot—or should not—be systematically replaced by one Western type of cadastral titling.[39] Instead, they find a continuum of (often vernacular) land tenure rights in many places. Similarly, Nora Aristizabal and Andrés Ortíz find up to fourteen forms on tenure in Colombia,[40] and Emma Porio

and Christine Crisol find eleven urban tenure categories (*de facto* and *de jure*) in Metro Manila, Phillipines.[41] Durand-Lasserve and Harris Selod conclude that the delivery of property rights (usually titles) is only one of the alternatives to formalize tenure. Administrative recognition of occupancy rights is often a secure and more popular form of formalization in developing countries. They even argue that titling processes can, in some cases, reduce tenure security; notably because they can cause conflicts that result in evictions, imply exclusion of some groups that are not entitled or eligible to formalization, favor the displacement of tenants (who often cannot participate in the process) and overlook the existing forms of collective and customary tenure.

4   Difficulties with maintenance. One thing is to provide titles and another one to sustain institutions and practices that can enforce them in the long term. Intentions to regularize cadastral records in Africa and Latin America have demonstrated that the principal difficulty does not lie in collecting the information and creating the databases but in maintaining the institutions and funding the frequently-required data updates.

5   Reduced mobility. Paradoxically, legalization may also contribute to reducing mobility, because the process itself is so lengthy that it forces households to stay in their units for long periods of time, or because they have additional reasons to stay in their units after suffering the long process of regularization.

6   Inexistent or undesired credit. De Soto's argument presupposes that there would be financial products that would use titles as collateral for loans and mortgages, and that the poor desire credit in order to improve their living conditions and overcome other needs. However, both claims have been seriously challenged. Financial services are often absent for the poor, even in countries with relatively developed formal financial systems. Besides, many informal dwellers work in the informal sector. Therefore, it is difficult for them to prove income—which is a common prerequisite to obtain credit—even when titles are used as collateral.[42] Additionally, it cannot be systematically assumed that poor households are desperate for credit. In fact, many poor households are afraid and suspicious of debts. Housing specialist Alan Gilbert explains: "Many poor families are less than enthusiastic about borrowing from formal lending agencies or indeed from anyone else" (p. 168).[43]

   The previous section showed that lack of titles is only one of the reasons that limit mobility and housing supply. Titling is therefore only one of the multiple options for reducing inefficiencies in the housing market and for increasing housing mobility. Even if titles are provided to informal dwellers, there are still a number of variables that need to be tackled to "fix" the housing market: reduce restrictions on selling units produced by the induced sector, facilitate land development to motivate supply, reduce political interference, collect information and provide access to it, etc. More importantly, households would still need to perceive that the tangible and intangible benefits of selling their units to buy another one would offset the monetary and non-monetary costs of the transaction—a perception that cannot always be taken for granted.

Subsidizing Housing

A different premise maintains that "free" private markets inherently create significant disparities, and that their capacity to fulfil demand has been over-estimated. Defenders of this approach include researchers Paul Strassmann,[44] Ramin Keivani and Edmundo Werna. Keivani and Werna argue:

> In the current climate of accepted wisdom of privatisation and market deregulations in all spheres of economy, the issue of exaggeration of formal private sector capacity, excessive market deregulation and over reliance on the formal market for solving low income housing provision in developing countries can seriously undermine efforts for the stated objectives of the enabling housing strategy (i.e. to enhance better quality low income housing provision and to make housing markets more efficient in developing countries).
>
> (p. 105)[45]

Deregulations in the financial market, some specialists argue, have led to abusive interest rates, and deregulation in land markets have led to increased speculation and more benefits for the elites and well-off than for the poor. Defenders of capitalism, they reason, have not fully acknowledged the limits of the "enabling the markets to work" approach. Several developed and developing countries have now recognized that, if markets cannot efficiently offer appropriate solutions for the poor, governments must intervene and help them achieve ownership.

Subsidized housing is, today, one of the most important strategies used in developing countries to alleviate low-cost housing shortages.[46] There are many forms of subsidized housing (including subsidized interest rates on housing loans, subsidized housing-related savings schemes and State-sponsored insurances).[47] However, the most popular one in countries such as Chile, Colombia and South Africa is the provision of upfront subsidies to potential buyers. Upfront subsidies permit targeting specific families that require assistance, thus focusing the scope of the financial aid. The subsidy allows poor households to reduce financial costs, and it permits them to purchase units produced by the private sector. The strategy therefore permits keeping policies that encourage the private sector, while creating a financial alternative for the poor that increases demand for the privately-generated supply. Since the 1990s, governments in Chile, South Africa, Colombia and other countries have seen subsidies as an important tool for discouraging land invasions, generating employment, increasing household self-sufficiency and even responding to disasters.

Subsidies, however, can also produce several effects that exacerbate the problems found in residential markets.[48] First, subsidized housing schemes typically propose restrictions on sales that reduce mobility and prevent families from climbing the housing ladder.[49] Second, they distort the prices of houses in the secondary market. Third, they often require that residents buy units only in new settlements approved by authorities (typically large scale projects built by large construction companies). They therefore rarely permit appropriate levels of participation and significant decision-making power from beneficiaries during the project process. Fourth, in many cases, the beneficiary selection system suffers from manipulation and political interference.

FIGURE 3.8 An upfront subsidy by the South African government permits to purchase a house like this one, located in Freedom Park, Western Cape. However, waiting lists for obtaining a subsidy are long in countries such as South Africa, Colombia and Chile.

Examining subsidized housing programs in Chile, South Africa and Colombia, Alan Gilbert[50] found that the strategy faces a few additional difficulties:

1   The subsidies given to families are insufficient for purchasing a unit offered by private developers. Having to choose between quality and quantity of subsidies offered, decision-makers (particularly in South Africa) have chosen quantity.
2   While the South African program targets the most needy, the Colombian and Chilean programs have had real problems reaching the poorest families (in the case of Colombia, the program targets families that are employed and have savings). In South Africa and Chile, waiting lists are particularly long.
3   Units are very small and they are largely criticized for their lower standards (see Figure 3.8).
4   The programs have not homogeneously reached all regions in their countries.
5   Projects are far from city centres and areas near services, which increases patterns of urban segregation.
6   Projects have deteriorated rapidly, creating new forms of slum neighbourhoods.
7   Beneficiaries cannot easily have access to matching funds and credit from financial institutions.

Let's explore one additional challenge to this approach. Subsidized programs are rarely backed with appropriate project governance mechanisms. In many countries, central governments manage the subsidies while municipalities and regional governments must procure the housing projects.[51] In South Africa, the provincial administration is allocated funds from the national government. Municipalities identify programs and the provincial government allocates the funds to the Municipality, which acts as the project developer or employs an organization to act as a developer on its behalf. However, municipalities do not often have the resources required to administer the projects[52] and require financial assistance and knowhow from external sources, including international support, participation of central governments, private capital, etc. We shall see in Chapter 7 that small municipalities in other places also face significant problems in acquiring safe land, matching public and private resources, encouraging individual savings, selecting, evaluating and approving beneficiaries and choosing minimum standards.

Developing Financial Mechanisms

If lack of financing prevents the poor from purchasing housing units, it is not surprising that defenders of free markets highlight the importance of improving the availability of credit for the poor. Given the relative success of mortgage systems in developed countries (amid the last residential market crisis in the United States), which typically includes public insurance to protect financial institutions from defaults, international institutions such as the World Bank have strongly promoted the development of housing finance mechanisms in developing countries.[53] The premise is that private mortgage financing can reduce the need for public subsidies, and thus their secondary effects.

However, the rather embarrassing fact is that private institutions have seldom reached the poor through financial mechanisms. Several reasons explain this failure. First, formal financial mechanisms are not designed for house improvements, for housing consolidation or for purchasing an unfinished core house. Second, institutions rarely lend to informal workers who cannot prove stable incomes. Third, the small profits that can be obtained from lending to the poor discourage most institutions from developing special mechanisms for them.[54] Fourth, informal units and land cannot be easily used as collateral for credit. Fifth, the typical term of mortgage loans (20 to 30 years) is too long for low-income households to sustain, given their vulnerability to economic changes.[55] Finally, written or *de facto* policies in many countries do not allow for house eviction in case of payment default, so collateral can hardly serve its original purpose.

The consequence is that in countries such as Vietnam, less than 20% of housing finance credit is provided by banks. The main source of housing finance in most developing countries continues to be household savings, informal credit and help from family and friends.[56]

Preventing Idle Land

It is usually argued that making urban land markets more efficient is a prerequisite for enhancing low-cost housing markets. Specialists claim that land development is a key aspect to solving the quantitative and qualitative housing deficits, and a relevant tool to halt slum formation.[57] According to Ferguson and Navarrete,[58] and Datta and Jones,[59] land market failure prevents the conversion of agricultural land into urban land. They argue that governments can play an important role in this process, particularly by reducing standards and streamlining the land development process in order to stimulate private developers and builders. Keivani and Werna add: "The relaxation of land use regulations and increased government provision of basic infrastructural services, for example, are undoubtedly positive actions which increase formal private sector access to suitable residential land and help in reducing the price of urban land in developing countries" (p. 111).[60]

Despite the merits of deregulation, the principle typically competes with other open and hidden interests that make it particularly difficult to implement. In fact, there are many reasons (some people would say "good reasons") for the existence of land-use regulations. Green belts and buffer zones, for instance, protect residential areas from pollution generated by industrial activities and from floods caused by water bodies. They create (almost) natural environments in the city, which sometimes reduce heat, facilitate water flows, beautify urban sectors, motivate open-door recreational activities and increase property values for neighbouring buildings. Limiting urban growth through development boundaries protects agricultural activities and reduces the urban footprint. Restricting building heights helps create urban uniformity, prevents shadows over small buildings and open areas, permits views of relevant landmarks and historic buildings, etc. Finally, restricting uses through enforced zoning protects residential areas and historic districts from polluting activities and demolitions (or rapid transformations), and while doing so, protects property values.

The problem is that these well-intended measures often help reduce residential development for low-income residents. At the same time, they satisfy pressure and advocacy groups and political lobbyists such as environmentalists, heritage preservation advocacy groups, sustainable development militants, and—of course—urban elites that take advantage of property values. These regulations are so common that Datta and Jones conclude that land market development is one of four issues that appear to be largely invisible on current agendas (the other three are: rental housing, savings, and residential mobility) (p. 335).[61]

There are also more hidden (some would say "obscure") interests that compete against deregulation aimed at encouraging low-cost housing development. They include land speculation (which again benefits the well-off and urban elites) and land grabbing and monopolies. But do not believe that these artifices are only a sub-product of savage capitalism. In many countries, the government holds significant land monopolies that hinder residential development. Statistics from the Vietnam Ministry of Construction show, for instance, that in 2009, 3.7 million m^2 of the available 6.3 million m^2 in Ho Chi Minh City were controlled by State-owned groups, and corporations and were not being used.[62]

Understanding the importance of land management in housing development, in the late 1990s Bogotá created Metrovivienda, a city agency devoted to land development and equipped with several legal mechanisms to facilitate land acquisition and transfer. However, after just a few years of operation, land policy and political interests interrupted the agency's role. The consequence is that producing market-driven low-cost housing in Bogotá and many other cities remains difficult. In the face of these difficulties, Datta and Jones conclude: "Research and policy on housing finance has continued to emphasise a "housing" problem rather than one of land market access which is the initial difficulty many low-income households face when attempting to acquire urban shelter" (p. 335).[63]

Implications for Rethinking and Designing Low-Cost Housing in Developing Countries

The approaches to market development presented here have failed to fulfil the expectations of both observers and those most concerned: the poor. There is, it seems, no simple answer or magic solution to widespread insufficient access to housing. In a significant publication on land markets and mobility in developing countries, housing specialist Paul W. Strassmann argued—now, already 20 years ago—that the complex variables that interact in low-cost housing lead experts to simplify the problem of housing deficits. Nonetheless, Strassmann reasoned, simplification tends to become oversimplification, and thus solutions rarely tackle the dynamic attributes of the variables, which become inappropriate or insufficient.[64] Even World Bank policies, typically accused by urban experts of missing the complexity of poverty issues, recognize that several dimensions need to be tackled simultaneously for enhancing the role of markets in developing countries. Measures must, the bank unsurprisingly argues, include the four strategies explained above, but also: regulating land development (see more on Chapter 4), providing infrastructure for residential development (see more on Chapter 5), developing an institutional framework for managing the housing sector (see Chapter 9), and organizing the building industry. This last point includes creating greater competition in the industry by eliminating regulatory barriers to entry, breaking up monopolies, facilitating participation of small firms, removing constraints on the development and use of local building materials and construction methods, and reducing trade barriers that apply to housing inputs.

Understanding the functioning of housing markets is of prime importance for architects, urban planners and other design professionals. In fact, it has also become obvious that innovative approaches are required in dealing with their complexity. However, it should not be assumed that solutions to housing shortages and deficient housing conditions could be fixed through markets alone. Instead, it becomes important to consider alternative forms of housing provision that are not regulated by residential markets, such as cooperative housing. It is also relevant to understand and reinforce informal social arrangements that allow residents to provide collective housing solutions for the poor (such as Salvadorian *mesones* or South American *casonas* or *inquilinatos*). I shall come back to this argument in Chapter 10.

As we shall see also in Chapter 10, real solutions require refusing the neoliberal disengagement of public agencies. They require, instead, innovative mechanisms of project governance in which more stakeholders are increasingly engaged in housing development for the poor. It also implies leaving behind an almost exclusive obsession in a reduction of housing quantitative deficits and embracing also the alleviation of qualitative deficits through punctual interventions in informal and unconsolidated settlements. More importantly—and more controversially—it implies considering different standards of housing that, by having different commercial value, can feed the housing pyramid at different levels, eventually filling the housing gap. The significant challenges to developing credit solutions for the poor invites us to consider savings mechanisms that would allow them to access ownership. Yet, ownership—much like markets—should not be over-estimated. The challenges presented in this chapter remind us of the obsession with homeownership in most housing strategies in developing countries, and this should not always be the case. Innovative programs aimed at promoting rental housing can provide fruitful alternatives to deal with both quantitative and qualitative housing deficits, while at the same time reinforcing and consolidating the housing stock in particular, and human settlements in general.

Welfare strategies must also be reconsidered to mitigate the common shortfalls of subsidized programs. Subsidizing inadequate housing in undesirable locations does not alleviate structural vulnerabilities. Innovative forms of capital, asset and land distribution which are not driven by market forces alone or by the interests of a reduced number of stakeholders are required. Design professionals and decision-makers must certainly contribute to identify them.

Finally, this chapter has revealed that an exaggerated perception of markets has led several actors to consider housing as a commodity that is exchanged through the rules of supply and demand, and that is valued purely for its material and physical attributes. As such, the most important values of housing have been largely ignored, including its natural capacity to create a social narrative, a meaningful life, a dignified livelihood, collective goods, a culturally rich settlement, a built environment harmoniously embedded in a complex natural ecosystem, and an engaged society that does not leave its most vulnerable members behind. In this obsession with markets, land has played a significant role. It has been used simultaneously as a commercially driven commodity, as an abstract source of utility and as a political tool that manipulates supply and demand and feeds selfish interests. Let's consider now why and how it has been so.

Notes

1 Keivani, R. and E. Werna. "Modes of Housing Provision in Developing Countries." *Progress in Planning* 55, no. 2 (2001): 65–118.
2 Ibid.
3 The World Bank. "Housing: Enabling Markets to Work. A World Bank Policy Paper." ed The World Bank. Washington, DC, 1993.
4 Keivani and Werna, "Modes of Housing Provision in Developing Countries."
5 Datta, K. and G.A. Jones. "Housing and Finance in Developing Countries: Invisible Issues on Research and Policy Agendas." *Habitat International* 25, no. 3 (2001): 333–57.
6 Buckley, R.M. and J. Kalarickal. "Housing Policy in Developing Countries: Conjectures and Refutations." *The World Bank Research Observer* 20, no. 2 (2005): 233–57.
7 Keivani and Werna, "Modes of Housing Provision in Developing Countries."
8 Mesa V.I.S. and D. Echeverry Campos. "Reflexión sobre la propuesta del gobierno nacional en el tema de vivienda 2010–2014." In *Presentaciones 2011*, 2011.
9 Perlman, J. *Favela: Four Decades of Living on the Edge of Rio De Janeiro*. Oxford: Oxford University Press, 2010.
10 Marx, B., T. Stoker and T. Suri. "The Economics of Slums in the Developing World." *Journal of Economic Perspectives* 27, no. 4 (2013): 187–210.
11 Gilbert, A. "A Home Is for Ever? Residential Mobility and Homeownership in Self-Help Settlements." *Environment and Planning A* 31 (1999): 1073–92.
12 Lizarralde, G. and D. Root. "The Informal Construction Sector and the Inefficiency of Low Cost Housing Markets." *Construction Management and Economics* 26, no. 2 (2008): 103–13.
13 Canada Mortgage and Housing Corporation. "Filtering in Housing." *Publications and Reports* (2013), http://www.cmhc-schl.gc.ca/odpub/pdf/63795.pdf.
14 Gilbert, "A Home Is for Ever?"
15 Ibid.
16 Datta and Jones, "Housing and Finance in Developing Countries."
17 Ibid.

18 Rust, K. and FinMark Trust. "Analysis of South Africa's Housing Sector Performance." (2006), http://www.hic-net.org.

19 Lizarralde and Root, "The Informal Construction Sector and the Inefficiency of Low Cost Housing Markets."

20 Ferguson, B. and J. Navarrete. "A Financial Framework for Reducing Slums: Lessons from Experience in Latin America." *Environment and Urbanization* 15, no. 2 (2003): 201.

21 Lozano, J. "Juan Lozano, Senador." http://www.juanlozano.com.co/noticias/2006/noviembre/20061126_01.html.

22 NHBRC. "Registration of Home Builders." http://www.nhbrc.org/Registrations/Registrationofhomebuilder.htm.

23 Department of Housing South Africa. *Housing Programs and Subsidies*. Pretoria: Department of Housing, Communication Services, 2006.

24 NHBRC. "Registration of Home Builders."

25 Department of Housing South Africa. "Design and Construction of Houses, Republic of South Africa."

26 Construction Industry Development Board (CIDB). *Annual Report 2004–2005*. Pretoria: CIDB, 2005.

27 Ibid.

28 P.H.P Policy Working Group. *Report on Progress in the P.H.P. Policy Working Group*. Pretoria: CSIR, 2006.

29 De Soto, H. *The Mystery of Capital*. New York: Basic Books, 2000.

30 Gilbert, "A Home Is for Ever?"

31 Datta and Jones, "Housing and Finance in Developing Countries."

32 Boaden, B. and A. Karam. "The Informal Housing Market in Four of Cape Town's Low-Income Settlements." In *Working Papers*. Cape Town: University of Cape Town, 2000.

33 Ibid.

34 Datta and Jones, "Housing and Finance in Developing Countries."

35 The World Bank. "Housing: Enabling Markets to Work. A World Bank Policy Paper." ed The World Bank. Washington, DC, 1993.

36 De Soto, *The Mystery of Capital*.

37 Payne, G. "Land Tenure and Property Rights: An Introduction." *Habitat International* 28, no. 2 (2004): 167–79.

38 Lall, S.V., M. Freire, B. Yuen, R. Rajack and J.-J. Helluin. *Urban Land Markets: Improving Land Management for Successful Urbanization*. Washington: Springer, 2009.

39 Durand-Lasserve, A. and H. Selod. "The Formalization of Urban Land Tenure in Developing Countries." In *Urban Land Markets: Improving Land Management for Successful Urbanization*, edited by S.V. Lall, M. Freire, B. Yuen, R. Rajack and J.-J.Helluin, 101–32. Washington: Springer, 2009.

40 Aristizabal, N.C. and A. Ortíz Gómez. "Improving Security without Titles in Bogotá." *Habitat International* 28, no. 2 (2004): 245–58.

41 Porio, E. and C. Crisol. "Property Rights, Security of Tenure and the Urban Poor in Metro Manila." *Habitat International* 28, no. 2 (2004): 203–19.

42 Buckley and Kalarickal, "Housing Policy in Developing Countries: Conjectures and Refutations."

43 Gilbert, A. "Financing Self-Help Housing: Evidence from Bogotá, Colombia." *International Planning Studies* 5, no. 2 (2000): 165–90.

44 Strassmann, P. "Oversimplification in Housing Analysis, with Reference to Land Markets and Mobility." *Cities* 11, no. 6 (1994): 377–83.

45 Keivani and Werna, "Modes of Housing Provision in Developing Countries."

46 Ferguson, B. and J. Navarrete. "New Approaches to Progressive Housing in Latin America: A Key to Habitat Programs and Policy." *Habitat International* 27, no. 2 (2003): 309–23; Ferguson, B., J. Rubinstein and V. Dominguez Vial. "The Design of Direct Demand Subsidy Programs for Housing in Latin America." *Review of Urban and Regional Development Studies* 8, no. 2 (1996): 202–19.

47 Hoek-Smit, M.C. and D.B. Diamond. "Subsidies for Housing Finance." *Housing Finance International* 17, no. 3 (2003): 3–13.

48 Ibid.

49 Lizarralde, G. "Stakeholder Participation and Incremental Housing in Subsidized Housing Projects in Colombia and South Africa." *Habitat International* 35, no. 2 (2010): 175–87.
50 Gilbert, "A Home Is for Ever?"
51 Department of Housing South Africa. *Housing Programs and Subsidies.*
52 Goebel, A. "Sustainable Urban Development? Low-Cost Housing Challenges in South Africa." *Habitat International* 31, no. 3–4 (2007): 291–302.
53 The World Bank. "Housing: Enabling Markets to Work. A World Bank Policy Paper." ed. The World Bank. Washington, DC, 1993.
54 Gilbert, "A Home Is for Ever?"
55 Tomlinson, M.R. "The Development of a Low-Income Housing Finance Sector in South Africa: Have We Finally Found a Way Forward?" *Habitat International* 31, no. 1 (2007): 77–86.
56 F.M.O Finance for Development. "F.M.O Low Income Housing Roundtable Hanoi, Vietnam." 4: F.M.O, 2012.
57 Ferguson and Navarrete, "A Financial Framework for Reducing Slums."
58 Ferguson and Navarrete, "New Approaches to Progressive Housing in Latin America."
59 Datta and Jones, "Housing and Finance in Developing Countries."
60 Keivani and Werna, "Modes of Housing Provision in Developing Countries."
61 Datta, K. and G.A. Jones, eds. *Housing and Finance in Developing Countries.* London: Taylor & Francis, 1998.
62 Institut des métiers de la ville. "Policies Sough to Manage Housing Industry." (2011), http://www.imv-hanoi.com.
63 Datta and Jones, *Housing and Finance in Developing Countries.*
64 Strassmann, "Oversimplification in Housing Analysis, with Reference to Land Markets and Mobility."

4

INVISIBLE LAND

About Houses Built on Distant, Wasted and Fragmented Land

> Olinda is certainly not the only city that grows in concentric circles, like tree trunks which each year add one more ring. [...] the old walls expand bearing the old quarters with them, enlarged but maintaining their proportions on a broader horizon at the edges of the city.
>
> *Invisible Cities*, Italo Calvino (p. 117)

Distant Housing in Choluteca

Commuting by public transport from Tegucigalpa to Choluteca is a long journey. The overcrowded bus, which has no air conditioning and poor suspension, makes endless stops on the bumpy road that extends from the highlands of central Honduras to the southern valleys. What really makes this journey special is not the considerable heat, the view of the furious rivers that often flood the southern valleys or the colourful shacks standing along the road. It is to realize that Choluteca is an impoverished enclave surrounded by no apparent economic activity. As the bus approached Choluteca, I had the impression that income and production sources had disappeared—or never existed—in the region. Agriculture, manufacturing, tourism and construction are all scarce; their incipient development is simultaneously a cause and a consequence of poverty in the region.

Honduras is one of the poorest countries in Latin America. Before Hurricane Mitch hit Choluteca in 1998, only 40.8% of the potentially economically active population was working. The figure was as low as 33% after the disaster. In the 1990s, almost 60% of the population was still rural, but Choluteca remained a striking example of unequal distribution of land. When torrential winds and rains caused by Mitch washed out the region in 1998, one third of the population was badly affected, in particular poor, informal dwellers.

Floods caused by heavy rain were soon followed by a flood of international NGOs that rushed to Choluteca to build low-cost housing. These organizations included Caritas, UNICEF, Atlas Logistique, Iglesia de Cristo, Médecins Sans Frontières (MSF),

FIGURE 4.1   View of the units built in Nueva Choluteca. All the houses built by the residents using a labour-intensive technology were identical.

the International Organization for Migration and about 18 additional NGOs. The extensive damage in Choluteca, and the lack of affordable safe land in the city, led these organizations to believe that a low-cost housing plan was necessary for relocating residents living in slums and vulnerable zones. Banco Occidental, a local financial institution, proposed the use of one of its properties—a 117ha plot located in a "safe" area 15km from the city centre. Without leadership, each organization assumed the construction of a sector in Nueva Choluteca (as the new town was eventually called). The Spanish neighbourhood was built by the "Cooperación Española," the Samaritana neighbourhood, by an NGO with the same name, and so on.

The land was subdivided in 2,154 individual lots of 10×20m. They were not large enough to allow agricultural activities but neither were they well-arranged enough to contribute, with a higher density, to the sustainability of the settlement. The coarse urban distribution included two principal streets of 12m width—certainly too wide for a residential neighbourhood of one-story units. In Nueva Choluteca the units were set back 3m from the street and separated by 4m. This means that there was only room for expansion in the front and the back of the houses (see Figure 4.1). This spread-out plan of detached units made construction and maintenance of basic infrastructure unviable and the provision of other services (security, post, cleaning, waste collection, etc.) improbable.

Yet, Nueva Choluteca didn't have to adopt this configuration. The suburban plan of the new town contrasted with the elegance, compactness and effectiveness of the old Choluteca city, where vernacular housing, narrow streets and shaded public spaces respected pedestrian scales and created liveable open areas (see Figure 4.2).

Individual lots were sold by Banco Ocidental to affected families for monthly payments of 1,701 lempiras over ten years (roughly US$100 in 2003). However, given

FIGURE 4.2 Vernacular housing typologies and higher densities in old Choluteca create graceful urban spaces—features that are missing in Nueva Choluteca.

that only a small fraction of residents in *Nueva Choluteca* was working in 2001[1] and that 80% of the employed received less than 2,000 lempiras per month, the scheme represented a significant economic burden for most families. Even though numerous organizations were working in place, the only infrastructure built was a small health centre, a water tank to supply a few units, an improvised police station and two schools. In the first few years of development, none of the organizations assumed the responsibility for building roads, parks, sidewalks, water, electricity, sewage or drain systems; not even planting a tree, or building a market.

The Centre for International Studies and Cooperation (CECI)[2]—a Canadian NGO—recognised that what Nueva Choluteca needed was infrastructure.[3] Yet the organization chose to build even more houses with funding provided by the Canadian International Development Agency (CIDA) and the Ministry of Foreign Relations of Quebec. In partnership with the French NGO Atlas Logistique, CECI created a program to produce 52 additional units through labour-intensive self-help construction. This strategy ignored the fact that 40% of the families in Nueva Choluteca were single-parent and female-headed. Even more absurd, CECI also decided that self-help-induced activities had to be conducted by users (mostly mothers) without knowing which house they would be allocated. Officers later explained that this measure was adopted in order to mass-produce standardized units and—ironically—to prevent people from personalizing or putting more care into the construction of their own dwelling!

The result was a neighbourhood of identical units of $6 \times 6m^2$ with neither washroom nor kitchen, and only two small windows on the façade. Because the interior floor level was elevated only 15cm from the ground, the houses were still prone to seasonal floods. Yet, these were expensive houses. Construction materials for one house cost

FIGURE 4.3 An abandoned house in Nueva Choluteca.

approximately US$2,000. Furthermore, later changes and additions made by users proved (three years later when I conducted research in the settlement) that the units initially provided were nothing more than basic structures that residents needed to complete in order to have a space for bathing, a kitchen, a washroom, and, in many cases, an extra room and a space for economic activities. Not only did these additions represent extra costs for residents, but also many of them were made with poor-quality materials and without hazard-resistance standards.

Trying to overcome the limitations in infrastructure outlined above, other outputs provided by CECI in Nueva Choluteca included the construction of 118 kitchens and 172 latrines. A program of leadership and "reinforcement of democratic and participative structures" was also conducted with a meagre budget of US$7,000. But it was too little, too late. By 2001, a socio-economic study conducted by FUNDEMUN-USAID showed the results of this collective failure: 4,704 people lived in Nueva Choluteca, but only 42% of the houses were occupied by the original owners. The rest were rented, transferred to friends and family or simply not used (see Figure 4.3). Ten percent of the houses were already in irregular or bad condition. Out of the population that was economically active (a small fraction), only 27% produced their income in the settlement itself. The poor quality of housing, absent infrastructure, increased segregation, unemployment, high rates of crime and public health problems characterised Nueva Choluteca in 2002.

Why did so many people—presumably intelligent and well intended officers from the municipal and regional governments, the local bank, the international NGOs, the development agencies—make so many mistakes?

The "Is"

Economists Abhijit V. Banerjee and Esther Duflo argue that common mistakes are made in the fight against poverty due to *ideology, ignorance* and *inertia*.[4] In their recent publication *Poor Economics*, they convincingly show that the problem of the "three Is" often negatively affects development efforts and prevents the design of good policy in developing countries. Conversely, one of the most respectable public servants responsible for low-cost housing in Gujarat, India, recently claimed that bad decisions in housing development are often directly or indirectly linked to three types of mistakes: mistakes motivated by *ignorance*, mistakes in *implementation* and mistakes motivated by *intention* (that is, by the intention to serve a particular interest or agenda). I do not know whether the resemblance of the "three Is" of the acclaimed academics and the public officer are a coincidence or the result of shared inspiration. However, I will borrow (and adapt with a little twist) both arguments to contend that, when it comes to low-cost housing in developing countries, politicians, planners, designers and other decision-makers make significant mistakes led by *ideology, ignorance* and (selfish) *interests*. Let's consider some of the common mistakes in the use of land and their effects on low-cost housing development.

Distant Land

The tendency to allocate distant land for housing development is not exclusive to NGOs working abroad. It is also common practice among public institutions, which often try to concentrate decision-making power for the sake of increasing efficiency and, while doing so, favour vacant, large and inexpensive pieces of land for the mass production of units. A recent study developed in our research group, and based on fieldwork research conducted by Douha Bouraoui in Tunisia, confirms this argument. In response to damages and vulnerabilities caused by river floods in Bou Salem, Tunisia, the (pre-Arab Spring) government created two commissions that proposed the relocation of affected families to Erroumani, a piece of land located 6km away from the town centre. The first phase of the project began in 2004 and was completed by 2006. It comprised 211 homes on a plot of 11.5ha. Unlike Choluteca, this new settlement included comprehensive infrastructure: a primary school, a centre for disabled persons, a care unit, a post office, a national guard post, a sanitation station and a pumping unit. Given that the project was constructed relatively quickly and included several services and facilities, did 6km make a difference for local residents?

Bouraoui found that this displacement—albeit short—did make a difference and that residents valued very much their original proximity to services and facilities. Several residents lost their jobs, many of them found that transportation costs were an increased burden to their tight budgets and some worried that their children had to take public transport to go to school.

Developing housing on the outskirts of cities is arguably a rational choice (I noted in previous chapters the reasons linked to it—notably the availability of large and inexpensive land), but it is a decision potentially loaded with significant negative effects for the poor. It is a bad decision that often finds justification in *ideology*—sometimes of the well-intended kind. Consider the Tunisian case, for instance. Relocation was justified as a social initiative aimed at promoting "solidarity, tolerance, democracy and human rights" (p. 155).[5] It was seen (or at least presented to the public) as a way of protecting people from future threats, notably floods; thus, as a mechanism for reducing vulnerability among poor households. However, it reflects decision-makers' *ignorance* about the social consequences of distant displacement. In many cases, the vulnerability of the poor is in fact augmented when they are forced to settle far away from jobs, high densities, services, family and community members. There are many reasons for this, including the fact that transportation costs and commuting time and hassle do not equally affect the well-off, who can rely on more comfortable and rapid forms of individual transportation, and the poor, who often rely on unpredictable, expensive (relative to income), uncomfortable, slow and, sometimes, unsafe public transportation.

Developing low-cost housing is a political process (I will come back to this argument in Chapters 9 and 10). As such, it is a process in which different—and usually divergent—interests must be arbitrated. It is loaded with decisions that might result in winners and losers. It is therefore hard to imagine that individual *interests* do not motivate decisions in low-cost housing initiatives. If, however, it is easy to envisage that politicians, bureaucrats and professionals act according to self-serving interests, it is more difficult to prove so. But this is exactly what Canadian architect Graeme Bristol succeeded in doing when analysing land management issues in the aftermath of the South-Asian tsunami in 2004.

Bristol's study (published in the book *Rebuilding after Disasters* that I co-edited with Colin Davidson and Cassidy Johnson)[6] shows that several decision-makers found an opportunity in the tsunami to pursue changes in land occupation that benefitted certain people and organizations—but that worsened the housing and economic conditions of thousands of families. Buffer zones that restricted residential use near the sea were set in Indonesia, Thailand, Sri Lanka and other affected places just after the disaster— apparently to protect people from future tsunamis. In reality, these buffer zones were used to legitimize the displacement of households (notably fishing communities) which had for decades benefitted from the proximity to the sea for their livelihood. Many of them did not have legal titles and, thus, lost their land in forced evictions or legal courts. However, to add insult to injury, recreation activities and tourism were allowed in coastal areas in Tamil Nadu, Sri Lanka and Banda Aceh in which local communities were displaced or evicted. Bristol wonders:

> Like most traditional cultures and communities, [fishermen and local households] were there before the concept of the com-modification of land had taken hold— before there was a ministry of forest or parks or tourism. Does their right to be where they are—held prior to any notion of property rights—take precedence over any subsequent legal constructs?
>
> (p. 141)[7]

He notes that multiple injustices were conducted in South Asia after 2004 and—in the form of an answer to the previous question—suggests that communities must rather be prepared for the aftershocks that follow disturbing events (he calls them a second tsunami) in which developers, politicians and agencies are ready to implement their own plan and pursue their own interests. Land—he reminds us—is a powerful tool they will use to achieve their aims.

FIGURE 4.4   Low-cost housing projects in South Africa have favoured detached units built in relatively large plots, such as this one in Mfuleni in the Cape Flats.

Underused Land

Urban land is very expensive, even the untitled and often unstable or muddy land underneath slums and informal settlements. Results of a study that David Root, Mark Massyn and I conducted on the Cape Town townships in South Africa serve as an example.[8] We found that land in South African townships is disproportionally expensive when compared to the costs of building a low-cost unit. A 230m^2 serviced plot in an area close to Freedom Park (about a 1.5-hour ride using public transport from the city centre) costs R65,000 in 2006. The cost of building a 36m^2 subsidized unit in that plot was approximately R25,000. Of course, the prices are even higher in townships located closer to the city centre such as Khayelitsha, where a 167m^2 serviced plot was valued at R598 per m^2 in 2006.

Despite the elevated costs of land in the low-cost housing equation, governments and NGOs in many countries still favour low-density projects (see Figure 4.4). This is the case of the subsidized projects in Netreg, Mfuleni, Freedom Park and Wallacedene (all located in the periphery of Cape Town, South Africa) that David, Mark and I studied. These projects follow certain common patterns with regards to the use of land: large plots that range from 81m^2 to 120m^2, low densities that range from 54 to 64 units per hectare, a predominant use of semi-detached and detached units and low ratios of occupation of land, in which only 36% to 51% of the plot's area is occupied by the original house. Why is land so often wasted? I believe that in order to know *why* these decisions are made, it is necessary to know *how* they are made. Let's consider the example of Netreg, on which we recently published an article in the *Construction Management and Economics* journal.[9]

Decision-Making in Netreg

Since 1986, shack dwellers in Netreg (an informal settlement in the outskirts of Cape Town) aimed at developing both economic opportunities and housing solutions for their community. Ten years later, though, community members had not mastered the bureaucratic manoeuvres necessary for obtaining public subsidies offered by the post-apartheid government. The community, therefore, requested the collaboration of the Development Action Group (DAG)—a well-known South African NGO acting as a support organization for local communities. DAG was committed to "building people's skills, integrating social and physical development processes and enabling communities to be involved in their own development" (p. 6).[10] Unsurprisingly, the involvement of DAG turned this local initiative into a project of "community participation." DAG's contribution permitted unlocking the process of land acquisition—a prerequisite for obtaining the subsidies. A piece of land in the settlement, surrounded by a railway on the one side and highway connectors on the other, was ultimately selected for housing development.

Nevertheless, various political and administrative barriers further delayed the project. Three years were required to identify the owner of the plot (it belonged to the municipality) and to transfer the land title to the community. The land was subdivided into 192 parcels of 81 m², and was sold to the beneficiaries at a sum below the market price.

The project adopted the People's Housing Process (PHP), a model of procurement of subsidized housing in South Africa that promotes community involvement; thus, a community steering committee was formed in 2003. One of its initial tasks was to supervise the construction of infrastructure, which began in 2004. The following year, the Niall Mellon Foundation (NMF)—an Irish NGO—became interested in the project and decided to inject additional resources, which allowed the community to upgrade the conventional 36 m² PHP house to 42 m². These extra resources also allowed for additional features, which are not standard in PHP units. These include cement roof tiles instead of corrugated sheets, electric outlets inside the house, indoor sinks, hot water geysers and roof insulation. With these new quality standards, the construction of the houses started in January 2006 and finished in October of the same year (you may note that this was 20 years after the community started the initiative).

The involvement of an international NGO was not required within the framework of the PHP strategy. In fact, according to the PHP policy, projects have to be always driven and managed by the beneficiaries themselves. The community was well aware that the participation of the NMF could dilute its decision-making power in the project. However, an international partner was perceived as an opportunity to improve the quality of the houses, a feat that could not be obtained from the subsidies alone. Ultimately, the NMF assumed a leading role in the architectural design and in the construction of the project.

Defenders of community participation argue that it is important to use local labour and resources in housing projects. In the case of Netreg, a number of informal construction enterprises operate in the area. However, these enterprises were not employed on the project. One of the first decisions made by the NMF was to appoint a private officer to procure the materials and subcontractors required for the project. Yet, some of the subcontractors engaged in the Netreg project (for example, roof trusses providers) were not from the area, or even the province. This was a decision that reduced costs in construction but unfortunately created several negative outcomes. Not only were local suppliers ignored in the process, but some external distributors were late in delivering the products and local subcontractors had to be trained in the use of external technologies.

Another early and important decision made by the NMF was to modify the housing typology and thus the potential density of the project. The community members agreed in the early meetings of the steering committee to build row-housing. This housing type was already used in the rest of the settlement and was seen by the residents as being economically efficient. The NMF, however, proposed to adopt semi-detached and detached units. After consultation, the steering committee agreed on this change. The NMF later reported that beneficiaries were involved in the design of the semi-detached houses.

Wasted Land and Decisions That Prevent Future Development in Netreg

In a conventional low-density layout, the 81 m^2 plots were ultimately occupied by 42 m^2 units located in the middle of the lot (note that this translates into a 51% usage factor). The low occupation of the plots was aggravated by the fact that the remaining unbuilt area cannot be used for future additions. As such, the design of the units does not take advantage of the common process of incremental construction that we will explore in the next chapter. The remaining space around the detached units in Netreg is not big enough for building extra rooms of a reasonable size. In the case of the semi-detached units (see Figure 4.5), the backyards are just large enough to allow one additional room; however, the windows of the bedrooms have not been properly positioned to accommodate future additions. If built, the new room will suppress the natural ventilation and lighting of the existing bedrooms. The additional door of the living room duplicates the main entrance of the house and creates a diagonal circulation that fragments this social space. This same door, located in the back of the unit, could have permitted access to future spaces that could be rented or used for economic activities.

The future vertical expansion of the units with a second floor (a common practice among informal dwellers) was also compromised by using roof trusses that span the two adjacent units. Residents willing to undertake additions in the future are thus obliged to coordinate their improvements with the neighbour, and to ensure that they happen at the same time and pace—something, of course, rather difficult to achieve.

At the urban scale, no attempt was made to allow for a variety of housing solutions and plot sizes (see Figure 4.6). With the exception of a few corner plots, all the plots are identical in size (5.4m front). The same applies to the housing units. Except for a few detached units, all houses are a rubber-stamped version of the semi-detached model. They all have two bedrooms and the same built area (provisions were only made for disabled residents). This repetition does not correspond to the level of variety and multiplicity that exists among the residents of Netreg, particularly considering that residents have a large variety of economic activities, jobs and occupations that range from industry workers to scrap collectors. The decision to homogenize the designs also ignores the fact that household sizes in Netreg vary from less than five members to more than ten, and that households have different priorities and economic levels.

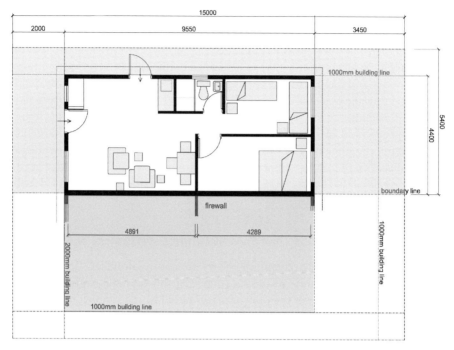

FIGURE 4.5 Layout of a semi-detached unit in Netreg.

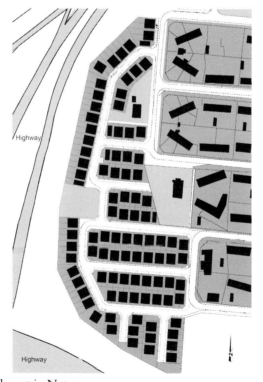

FIGURE 4.6 Urban layout in Netreg.

Arguably, the design of the houses does not respond to the original objectives of the Constitution of the Netreg Housing Project. It was then decided that the main objective of the project was "fostering local economic development initiatives to create income-generating opportunities for all."[11] This was particularly relevant considering that 65% of households in Netreg were headed by women—who are likely to work while taking care of their children and carrying out domestic activities. However, the low density of the new project and the poor design of the units' front façade discourage the development of home-based economic activities. There is no shadowed front in which commercial activities such as a store or a workshop can be developed. Besides, the possibility of later building a porch or a veranda for these activities is compromised by the shape of the roof (the slopes run parallel to the front façade and not perpendicular to it). Similarly, the small size of the windows in the front prevent the connection of the interior of the house with the street, a prerequisite for commercial activities that require capturing the attention of pedestrians and motorists. For households to ever transform these opaque façades to accommodate commercial activities will prove difficult and expensive.

The Causes and Consequences of Low Densities

There are two significant consequences of low densities. First, the long-term sustainability of the settlement is significantly challenged. Lower densities increase both the upfront investment and maintenance costs of open areas, roads, sidewalks and public lighting, as well as the construction and maintenance costs of infrastructure required for sewage, water, electricity, internet, gas and telephone provision. They also make the delivery of transportation-dependent, and thus distance-sensible services—such as police patrolling, fire department response, ambulances, waste collection and postal services—more expensive. Second, a significant number of low-income households rely on informal economic activities, many of which are conducted within homes (see Chapter 2). Most of these businesses are only viable when densities are relatively high, and thus when there is the critical mass of people buying a soft drink, having lunch, making photocopies, purchasing a cell phone card, etc.

Whereas the consequences of low densities are easy to identify, their causes are sometimes unclear. It can be argued that the tendency to propose low densities is linked to deep-rooted *ideology*. In many cultures, people still associate the concept of a house with a freestanding unit surrounded by green areas—an image even depicted by children in graffiti in the townships of Gugulethu, South Africa (see Figure 4.7). However, the decision to adopt low densities is probably also driven by *ignorance* about the long-term negative consequences in the sustainability of home-based economic activities, infrastructure and services. Unfortunately, long-term assessments of costs (energy and water consumption, maintenance costs, etc.) are rarely made when deciding which urban or architectural designs will be adopted in low-cost housing projects.

Yet other motives might also exist. When we interviewed officers responsible for the projects in the four South African townships and officers responsible for the project in Choluteca, they showed pride in explaining that the choices made in housing typologies were led by their interest in satisfying users—who apparently demanded detached units. This sounds like a noble choice. But deeper analysis in our research showed that

FIGURE 4.7 The idea of a "house" is closely related to a freestanding unit—even among urban children (certainly talented artists) raised in this township in Gugulethu, South Africa.

in the Netreg project, the community members agreed in their early meetings to build row-housing. Besides, our study also highlighted that beneficiaries wanted many things that were not granted in the projects: public services in Choluteca and better materials in Cape Town. Nonetheless, low density was a desire that NGOs were more willing to concede to than others. Why? The underlying reason (partially admitted by some of the interviewees) is that building identical freestanding units has at least three advantages for the organizations responsible for implementing the project.

First, one-story units require simple architectural plans, which reduce the time and resources required during the design phase. Our research results suggest that the NGOs working in Netreg sought to cut design-related costs. In fact, they hired a recent graduate architectural intern (in her twenties) who had no previous experience of design and construction in South Africa. This junior intern was responsible for designing housing solutions for hundreds of highly vulnerable low-income households—largely determining the fate of them and their families.

Second, unlike most mid-rise buildings, standardised one-story units can be easily built through self-help. NGOs typically underscore their interest in community participation. "We work through community participation" has become a mantra and cliché for NGO officers worldwide. However, research conducted by our team in Honduras, El Salvador, Colombia and South Africa, along with studies conducted by anthropologist Alicia Sliwinsky, have found that this community participation rarely involves power in decision-making. Most often, community participation is limited to users' contribution in sweat equity organized around self-help construction. For most NGOs, it implies laying bricks, mixing mortar, transporting sand bags, etc. Using unskilled labour is easier in small one-story units than in complex structures, or for that matter, in two and three-story buildings that require special skills, safety measures and equipment.

Third, unlike more complex constructions, a simple model of a one-story unit can be easily repeated. Providing identical units gives the impression that the organization is being equally fair with all beneficiaries. This, however, is a strange way of perceiving equity and fairness, because all families do not have the same needs and do not have the same resources to maintain their properties. Yet distributing equal products to all beneficiaries—regardless of family size, economic conditions, desires, etc.—is a principle that few NGOs and public institutions are ready to abandon.

In sum, opting for low-density solutions is a strategy that facilitates the work of the organization responsible for the project. It is one, however, that does not necessarily correspond to the long-term performance of the settlement and the needs of low-income households.

Fragmented land

Inefficient use of land is not the only planning mistake made in Netreg. The project also exacerbates the fragmented character of most townships in the Cape Flats. The project enlarges an enclave settlement that has one single access point and is surrounded by high-speed highways (see Figure 4.6). If anything, its urban design gives the impression of a gated community. It probably contributes to the consolidation of the neighbourhood and the community itself but does very little for its integration in the city fabric. This fragmentation has negative implications for its own residents. A document produced by DAG notes that the residents of Netreg are socially isolated from the surrounding communities, and are often regarded by their neighbours as "dirty" and prone to being money lenders, drug lords and bar owners. Unfortunately, the urban design adopted will do very little to combat these prejudices and generalizations.

Isolating the Netreg Community

With limited available resources, DAG attempted to achieve ambitious objectives of social development, including community empowerment, development of social skills and social capital, and leadership training. In order to do this, DAG conducted several workshops in 2002 and 2005, which resulted in the establishment and empowerment of the community executive committee in which many women participated. Giving considerable importance to community ties and a solid governance structure consolidated the residents' skills and community affiliation. These results can make households less dependent on external aid and more autonomous in the future. This community-based approach is well-intended and common practice among NGOs; yet it does not actually respond to the development needs in Netreg. The major problem that was initially recognized in the area was not little representation (remember that the community was active ten years before the involvement of NGOs) but the isolation of the Netreg community from its larger neighbour, Bonteheuwel. A study conducted by DAG in 2002 concluded that "strained relationships between the communities of

Netreg and Bonteheuwel further prevent the Netreg community from accessing the health and educational facilities located in Bonteheuwel they desperately require to enhance their livelihood opportunities."[12] It was then argued that the failure to integrate the settlement would relegate future generations of Netreg inhabitants to the periphery of society.

Unsurprisingly, the community involvement decreased when the NMF assumed leadership of the project. Contrary to the spirit of conventional PHP, the NMF officers acted as construction managers and project managers in fieldwork meetings. In the last phase of the project, the participation of community members was limited to attending the steering committee meetings, helping with the security of the site and painting housing façades. However, even convincing the residents to paint their houses as a sweat equity contribution proved to be difficult and had to be enforced by the NGO. Community participation became deceiving in Netreg; but by focusing almost exclusively on this end, organizations in charge of the project missed the opportunity to tackle the real problems that affected local residents. Consequently, they exacerbated the fragmentation that had afflicted the community for years.

Isolating the Freedom Park Community

The Netreg case shows that urban fragmentation might occur as an unintended result of land management and urban design. Nonetheless, it also occurs as a deliberate decision of space occupation. Take the case of Freedom Park, a housing project aimed at informal dwellers who occupied a parcel of land located between two well established low-income settlements in the township of Mitchell's Plain, South Africa. The two established neighbourhoods were, for many years, in constant conflict, which often involved violent disputes between gangs. In order to respond to the needs of the informal residents, the urban design of the project (developed by an urban design firm based in Cape Town) gave priority to security in the new settlement. The residents did not want to get involved in the disputes between the two rival communities, and thus it was decided to create an enclosed settlement for the new residents. The layout has only four entries, and roads are not connected to the regular urban fabric, limiting the possibilities to enter and exit the neighbourhood other than through supervised access points (see Figure 4.8).

Architects, urban specialists and other decision-makers often forget that a strong emphasis on the short-term benefits of the community (security and independence, for instance) might have relevant negative consequences in the long-term development of the city. Urban fragmentation facilitates the stigmatization and marginalization of social groups. It also interrupts the flows of traffic, thereby increasing commute times and distances. Disconnected settlements make it difficult for residents to enjoy public facilities and services offered in other (richer or poorer) areas, increasing deprivation for marginalized citizens. Additionally, enclosed settlements reduce the chances of success of several home-based commercial activities, which rely on a critical mass of pedestrians and traffic.

FIGURE 4.8   The urban layout in Freedom Park deliberately creates an enclosed community, aiming to avoid social conflicts with neighbouring communities.

Too Much Focus on Communities?

There is little doubt that responding to the needs of a group of residents is a sound approach in most urban interventions. Action at the community level and community development have become so widely accepted in poverty alleviation, disaster management and urban studies that arguing that there can be "too much focus on communities" might sound like a contemporary heresy. Nonetheless, when it comes to the relationships between land, housing and economic development, an excessive focus on a community-based territory—to the detriment of its integration in the city—can have significant negative effects.

Motivated by well-intended *ideology*, organizations tend to define housing problems and their solutions at the level of communities. They therefore tend to ignore the fact that the well-being of urbanities depends as much on the prosperity and security of their social groups as on the efficiency and integration of neighbourhoods and settlements within the city. *Ignorance* about the negative consequences of fragmented urban development has become one of the main barriers to integrating poor communities in cities in developing countries. Our study also suggests that there is an *interest* among organizations in avoiding problems derived from multiplicity of social groups and their integration in the same settlements. It is easier for organizations, for instance, to emphasize the community level and its needs, rather than to try to respond to broader urban or regional problems and solutions. Finally, it is easier for them to deal with social groups as homogeneous communities and to provide equal outputs for all. This avoids seemingly uncomfortable discussions and debates about the different desires and needs of families and individuals.

However, this is a weak approach. Households within communities have different needs and expectations, and communities are not composed of homogeneous individuals. Having a finished or large house, for instance, is not a priority for all residents—even within the same community. Empirical evidence shows the strength of this claim. A study conducted by researchers Bruce Boaden and Aly Karam emphasizes that ownership is not always a priority for low-income families.[13] They found that many low-income families in the townships of South Africa sell their homes and plots "when Christmas approaches and people urgently need cash." Others sell their subsidized units at a fraction of the real replacement costs in order to pay for family funerals or to pay debts. Another study, conducted by DAG, demonstrates that residents of Netreg are three times more likely to stop paying rent during bad times than stop paying funeral insurances and funeral savings. The study concluded that more than 40% of households skip rent payments during bad times. If ownership and finished units are not an equal priority for all, it could be expected that different solutions are required for different types of users—even when they share common problems.

Implications for Rethinking and Designing Low-Cost Housing in Developing Countries

Stakeholders' decision-making in housing and urban development is frequently led by *ideology, ignorance* and (selfish) *interests*. Ideology leads stakeholders to make decisions based on prejudices or the desire for continuity, and for maintaining the status quo. However, it can favour outputs that are not consistent with households' real needs and expectations and urban solutions that threaten the viability and sustainability of cities. Ignorance about the long-term effects and trade-offs that result from certain decisions can have important effects in the sustainability of initiatives and the future feasibility of infrastructure and services. Selfish interests deviate attention from the real necessities of vulnerable and marginalized groups, and reduce the capacity to implement policies and programs that benefit those who have an insufficient voice and influence in the public realm. Unsurprisingly, ideology, ignorance and interests are manifest in the management and planning of land development. This is linked to the fact that land is a powerful instrument to guide development and economic growth. Accordingly, it becomes an important political resource that can be used to benefit the poor and to improve the well-being of society at large or to benefit a small group of influential political and economic elites.

Land is an instrument that affects and is affected by numerous political, economic and legal mechanisms that go beyond the scope of housing development. However, it is one of the most influential variables in the low-cost housing equation. Land distribution, urban layouts and plot design make household livelihoods feasible or not, make housing extensions possible or not, segregate or integrate communities and enhance or halt the development of community ties and cohesion. It is therefore necessary to understand the reasons that motivate development in city outskirts and remote areas, layouts that favour low densities and freestanding units, as well as the strong emphasis placed on community needs and expectations. Nonetheless, avoiding housing development in distant, underutilized and fragmented land must be a priority for policy and decision-makers.

Projects need to recognize the multiplicity of needs and expectations that exist among households within communities, and the heterogeneous character of contemporary urban social groups. While doing so, designers, planners and other decision-makers need to consider the importance of different plot sizes and housing types. They must also consider the trade-offs and unexpected outcomes that result from implementing low densities and from enclosing communities. Integrating low-income communities in the urban fabric is a prerequisite for reducing marginalization and exclusion. An appropriate and efficient use of expensive urban land is the first step towards the sustainability of both low-income settlements and cities at large. The planning and designing of land is one of the most powerful instruments that architects, urban planners and other design professionals have for rethinking housing solutions in developing countries. This requires carefully considering the evolution of settlements and plots over time. Let's examine now how informal housing development processes can inform policy, programs and projects aimed at low-income families.

Notes

1 FUNDEMUN-USAID. "Estudio socioeconómico y censo de población y vivienda, Ciudad Nueva, Choluteca." Unpublished, 2001.
2 CECI. *Projet de reconstruction de maisons au profit des sinistrés de l'Ouragan Mitch: rapport narratif final*. Montreal: CECI, 2001.
3 Ibid.
4 Banerjee, A.V. and E. Duflo. *Poor Economics: A Radical Rethinking of the Way to Fight Global Poverty*. New York: PublicAffairs, 2011.
5 Bouraoui, D. and G. Lizarralde. "Centralized Decision Making, Users' Participation and Satisfaction in Post-Disaster Reconstruction: The Case of Tunisia." *International Journal of Disaster Resilience in the Built Environment* 4, no. 2 (2013): 145–67.
6 Lizarralde, G., C. Davidson and C. Johnson, eds. *Rebuilding after Disasters: From Emergency to Sustainability*. London: Taylor & Francis, 2009.
7 Bristol, G. (2010). "Surviving the Second Tsunami: Land Rights in the Face of Buffer Zones, Land Grabs and Development." In G. Lizarralde, C. Davidson and C. Johnson (Eds.), *Rebuilding After Disasters: From Emergency to Sustainability* (pp. 133–148). London: Taylor & Francis.
8 Lizarralde, G. and M. Massyn. "Unexpected Negative Outcomes of Community Participation in Low-Cost Housing Projects in South Africa." *Habitat International* 32, no. 1 (2008): 1–14; Lizarralde, G. and D. Root. "Ready-Made Shacks: Learning from the Informal Sector to Meet Housing Needs in South Africa." Paper presented at the CIB World Building Congress Construction for Development, Cape Town, South Africa, 2007; Lizarralde, G. and D. Root. "The Informal Construction Sector and the Inefficiency of Low Cost Housing Markets." *Construction Management and Economics* 26, no. 2 (2008): 103–13.
9 Lizarralde and Root, "The Informal Construction Sector and the Inefficiency of Low Cost Housing Markets."
10 Lizarralde and Massyn, "Unexpected Negative Outcomes of Community Participation in Low-Cost Housing Projects in South Africa."
11 Netreg Committee. Constitution of the Netreg project. Unpublished document, 2003.
12 DAG. Swot. Unpublished document, 2002.
13 Boaden, B. and A. Karam. "The Informal Housing Market in Four of Cape Town's Low-Income Settlements." In *Working Papers*. Cape Town: University of Cape Town, 2000.

5

INVISIBLE INFORMAL PROCESSES

About the Way Land is Occupied and Houses are Produced, Purchased, Installed and Enlarged

> Those who arrive at Thekla can see little of the city, beyond the plank fences, the sackcloth screens, the scaffoldings, the metal armatures, the wooden catwalks hanging from ropes or supported by sawhorses, the ladders, the trestles. If you ask, "Why is Thekla's construction taking such a long time?" the inhabitants continue hoisting sacks, lowering leaded strings, moving long brushes up and down, as they answer, "So that its destruction cannot begin".
>
> *Invisible Cities*, Italo Calvino (p. 115)

Occupy land

Cité Lajoie, the shantytown on the seashore of Port-au-Prince that we visited in Chapters 1 and 3, did not exist before the 1990s. In the beginning there was water, so to speak. The national road (now called *route nationale 2*) followed the curves of the seashore, with only a few amenities—notably an open-air fish market—standing between it and the sea. But land was reclaimed from the Caribbean Ocean as rural migration accelerated in the 1990s, and housing demand in the capital city skyrocketed. Rubbish and debris had been used for many years to create the landfill and thus expand the settlement. It is therefore not surprising that a significant increase in construction occurred after the 2010 earthquake that partially destroyed the city and left impressive volumes of debris with no place to be disposed. Today, there are 30ha of unstable land between the road and the coastline, and there are about 2,600 buildings in a settlement that, crossed by many water streams, overflow in the rainy season (see Figures 5.1 and 5.2).

In a constant process of consolidation, most houses in Cité Lajoie start as improvised shacks built with wood sticks and plastic. At different paces, provisional materials get replaced by corrugated metal sheets and wooden panels and, ultimately, concrete blocks. Families and landlords claim property in Cité Lajoie, yet neither hold titles or are close to obtaining them in a city where cadastral records are almost inexistent. Despite the instability of the soil and constant flooding, today it is possible to find home-based

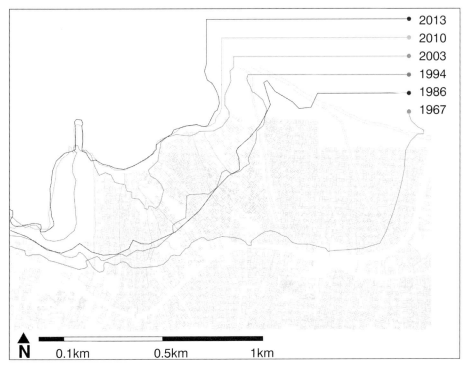

FIGURE 5.1 Cité Lajoie, Haiti, has grown in the past ten years as housing deficits in Port-au-Prince have increased.

FIGURE 5.2 Most housing constructions in Cité Lajoie start with a temporary structure built with wood sticks, fabric and plastics, materials that get quickly replaced by corrugated iron sheets.

commercial activities, two-story houses and—as we saw in Chapter 3—units for sale and rent. This is housing in the making in the informal world.

Occupying vacant land—public or private—through collective invasion and creating landfills in water shores, swamps and open-air waste deposits are frequent strategies to start an urban informal settlement. However, sometimes informal land development stops being a survival strategy of the poor and becomes a lucrative illegal activity—a pirate business as we shall now see.

Purchase Land—Pirates *in* the Caribbean

On the morning of January 19, 2012, eight houses were still on fire in Marruecos, a neighbourhood in the outskirts of Bogotá, Colombia. Flames started in the evening and spread rapidly. When journalists arrived, hundreds of residents had already been rioting for more than 24 hours against evictions enforced by the police. But this did not interrupt the visit and improvised press conference by Marta Bolivar, the mayor of Localidad Rafael Uribe Uribe, the borough that ordered the eviction. Amidst angry residents and busy bulldozers, Ms Bolivar explained that Marruecos was an *urbanización pirata* (local jargon for an illegal neighbourhood) that did not respect urban regulations and thus was to be demolished. Even though unauthorized subdivisions and illegal developments are common practice in Colombia, very few of their houses are actually demolished. Ms Bolivar learned just a few hours after the press conference the underlying reason for this. To her surprise, residents had already obtained a writ to defend their tenure rights. Very quickly, the *Corte Constitucional* (a high court that protects constitutional rights) ordered the immediate stop of the evictions in Marruecos, arguing possible violations to citizens' rights to housing. The Municipality later showed evidence that Marruecos was designed and built by "*Los Tierreros*" (literally, the landlords), a sophisticated criminal band operating in various areas of Bogotá and with infiltrated members in the municipal planning offices and other public organizations. But it was too late to bring back the bulldozers.

Urbanizaciones piratas, in which developers create illegal land subdivisions that do not respect regulations and later sell land titles or houses to poor families, exist in many other developing countries. Fake developers often benefit from connections with politicians and technocrats who, in the best of cases, turn a blind eye to their activities and, in the worse cases, even act as shareholders in their operations. This form of housing development does not embody the romanticized view of informality sometimes portrayed in housing literature and the "community participation" paradigm. If anything, illegal developments are the ugly face of informality. Very often, homebuyers lose purchase deposits, houses are poorly built, infrastructure is missing and informal contracts (when they exist) are full of fine prints and are sometimes fraudulent. But despite their illegal nature, these developments provide housing solutions for residents that cannot afford any other alternative. Furthermore, in cases such as Marruecos, illegal developments typically provide a certain level of tenure security to homebuyers. According to a study conducted by Nora Aristizabal and Andrés Ortíz in Colombia, this security is due to the fact that plots are typically "sold by the real owners of the land in a technically illegal, but socially legitimate manner" (p. 251).[1]

After land occupation or purchase of a plot in a pirate development—and once a certain level of tenure security is perceived—the process of construction of top structures starts. We already know that it employs a combination of self-help strategies; but we will now discover that it sometimes includes purchasing ready-made units.

Purchase Components—Innovation in the Townships

Khayelitsha Shacks has three employees and more than seven years' experience on the market. The company delivers an average of 25 ready-made shacks per month. Patrick, a former informal builder (pictured in Figure 5.3), is the owner and manager of the enterprise. Like many other innovators, he realized that he could obtain price reductions by purchasing larger quantities of recycled and new material, and standardizing a production of prefabricated units obtaining economies of scale. The strategy paid off. Patrick now owns a truck, a *shebeen* (an informal canteen in the townships) and a house in a well established, middle-class neighbourhood. The business is based in Khayelitsha, a shantytown in the Cape Town area, but it also serves other townships (including Mfuleni, Mitchell's Plain, Gugulethu and Hout Bay), even in areas as remote as Stellenbosh—a 1.5-hour drive from Khayelitsha.

But Patrick is not alone in the South African business of ready-made housing units. Township Shacks, another enterprise based in Khayelitsha, now has several satellite selling points, including one in Mfuleni in which the salesman pictured in Figure 5.3 is in charge. These informal construction enterprises have slowly grown over the last ten years despite no access to formal contracts and financial products. They create jobs, train local employees and bring capital to the informal settlements. Besides, in the case of South Africa, in which the government enforces through legislation an affirmative action to empower historically marginalized groups, the fact that both enterprises are owned by a black person becomes relevant and inspiring for many other slum dwellers.

The core product of both enterprises is a 3×2.6m shack made of corrugated metal sheets and a timber structure. The unit has a small window, a sloped roof and a wood door. It is sold for R1,900 (roughly US$280 when David Root and I obtained the prices in 2007) with a compulsory deposit of at least R500. But one can also purchase a double shack (3×5.2m) for R3,900 or a customized unit through special orders. All the products include transportation to the site and installation. The single shack is installed in less than 30 minutes by nailing together four panels and the roof (see Figures 5.4 to 5.6).

Like many other informal shacks, the units do not include a slab and are instead installed directly on the ground without foundations and connections to infrastructure. When asked about the lack of proper flooring and foundations, the owners of the enterprises explain that some clients move their shacks up to three times in one month, and that having a permanent "solid" floor is therefore a wasted investment for many of them.

The shacks combine different types of corrugated iron sheets and new and recycled materials. But the best sheets are often used for the roof in order to avoid water leaks. Only the front façade of the shack is usually painted, and no internal insulation is provided for the units. Nevertheless, the light wooden structure easily allows the residents to add an internal wall (usually in cardboard or wood sheets) and to add roof insulation. The same profile of wood (1x2″) is used for both vertical and horizontal structural elements. This avoids complications in the purchasing of materials, and permits the managers of

FIGURE 5.3 Despite their success in providing solutions for the poorest households in Cape Town, South Africa, the managers of the informal enterprises Khayelitsha Shacks (top) and Township Shacks (bottom) are largely ignored by government-funded housing projects.

FIGURE 5.4 This exhibition of prefab shacks in Lansdowne, a main road in Khayelitsha, becomes a sales point for informal construction companies.

FIGURE 5.5 The core product of Township Shacks.

FIGURE 5.6 Transportation means used by Khayelitsha Shacks.

the enterprise to negotiate good prices by buying large quantities of the same product. However, more than one profile of wood is required for the corner studs and main "beams." In this case, two or three profiles of wood are nailed together to produce the required structural support. The structure permits maximum flexibility for later additions and modifications of the basic module. In fact, the core-units are often later enlarged with extra rooms or additional space for income-generation (a shop, rental accommodation, etc.).

Gimme Shelter—Informal Business Operations

Patrick buys recycled and new materials according to the opportunities of the market. He stocks corrugated sheets, spare sheets and wood in a storage site in Khayelitsha. Some panels are then built and assembled to simulate a finished house in the exhibition area in the sidewalk of the main road, where seven other enterprises also display their own units. Although only minor differences exist between the products and prices of different enterprises, the proximity of them and their unit exhibition permits clients to compare quality and prices and select their provider. Colourful prototypes help to attract clients in the absence of signs and advertisement, and guarantees visibility and recognition.

When clients arrive, they are ushered over to the assembled prefab units. If a deal is sealed (and a deposit is paid) then Patrick uses the deposit to buy the materials required for the roof, the window and the door. These "more expensive" components are not usually stocked in large quantities. This strategy minimizes the costs of holding stock. The employees then deliver the product and assemble the units on site. Township Shacks has a pick-up car for transporting large materials. However, it also uses a modified shopping trolley to transport small components across short distances (see Figure 5.5). Employees in Khayelitsha Shacks and Township Shacks do not receive formal training, yet the company owners acquire management skills. I do not really know how, but there are surely communication channels and knowledge transfer that go undocumented.

It is never easy to run an informal construction enterprise. Informal companies face frequent evictions, crime and general exclusion from formal contracts. As discussed in Chapter 2, one of the most important barriers for informal business growth is lack of financing. Limited access to credit, unsurprisingly, undermines Patrick's capacity to keep more materials in stock and to take advantage of reduced prices that can be obtained by purchasing large quantities during sales. Patrick's predicament is not an isolated incident. Insufficient or expensive credit is also a significant barrier for potential buyers. Prefabricated shack enterprises are frequently affected by default payments.[2] However, paying a deposit and the remaining balance during several weeks or months is one of the few options of credit that households in South Africa have for acquiring housing.

The Invisible Construction Enterprises

It is difficult to estimate the number of informal construction companies in South Africa (figures from the year 2000 ranged from 2,500 to 40,000). In fact, there is so little knowledge about informal construction companies—not only in South Africa but in many other developing countries—that their modus operandi is one of the most unexplored aspects of low-cost housing in developing countries. They have become invisible to most decision-makers and academics. But are they actually as different from formal companies as we naturally tend to believe? Probably not, according to some studies. In fact, about 91% of construction companies formally registered in South Africa are classified in the two lowest levels on a scale from 1 to 9, which means they are small companies with limited capacities.[3] Much like their informal counterparts, these small formal companies find it difficult to develop large housing projects through which profits can be obtained by economies of scale. Similarities seem to emerge in other contexts too. Researchers R.S. Mlinga from the University of Dar es Salaam and Jill Wells, from the ILO[4] found that in Tanzania, the profile of unregistered contractors was very similar to that of small registered contractors. The primary difference between both types of companies is that the registered ones sometimes have access to contracts introduced by the public sector.

Despite the prominent role of small-scale producers in the supply of different components, their businesses should not be automatically associated with informal settlements. Builders who sometimes work informally also do repairs and maintenance work in high-income areas of the city.[5] Subcontracting and increased fragmentation of construction work (this is what specialists call the "unpackaging" of the construction process) has enhanced the spread of informal construction in many Sub-Saharan countries.[6] Wells explains that there has recently been a "movement in many countries towards greater casualization of the labour force, with the subcontracting of general labour as well specialized skills" (p. 270).[7]

Despite these similarities, our research in South Africa shows that both public and private (non-profit) organizations systematically ignore the role of the informal sector. There are at least six ways in which the procurement and design of low-cost housing marginalize and exclude informal construction companies. First, materials are supplied from formal construction companies, including from other provinces, even when local providers are available (remember procurement practices in the Netreg project). Second, users are encouraged or forced to demolish their informal constructions once they receive formal houses. The explicit objective of the NMF (the international NGO that got involved in the Netreg project) is to "eradicate shacks," unfortunately by means of substitution rather than economic development of households and communities. Third, labour is often hired on an individual basis, but informal companies are not directly appointed. Fourth, housing designs do not frequently anticipate later additions and modifications to the basic units—which are often conducted informally. Fifth, even though the construction of informal backyard dwellings is a current pattern in South African townships, formal housing units and plots do not anticipate the future construction of backyard shacks and, in some cases, they are explicitly designed to hinder their construction. Finally, even though subsidized units provided by the induced formal sector are small (from 36 to 50m²), they are rarely treated as core houses with available options for incremental growth, or in which basic features (roofs and floors) can be finished by users or informal companies.

Invisible Decisions by Owner-Builders

We know now that informal housing is most often the result of a progressive system of housing production that starts with land occupation (sometimes by invading vacant land) and that continues, almost perpetually, with incremental construction.[8] The informal construction sector facilitates an intimate relationship between homeowners and building labour. Since the seminal work by British architect John Turner in the 1970s,[9] it has also become widely known that informal housing engages owners and (paid and unpaid) self-employed construction workers.[10] This is hardly surprising, given that the informal sector brings several advantages to both owners and less-skilled workers.

For workers, it is a doorway to generating income with very few complications. As well, it involves almost no paperwork and administrative requirements, little need for training and no need for initial capital.[11] For owners, the informal sector provides an opportunity to hire affordable, local—and most often—flexible labour. Incremental construction not only accounts for 70% of housing investment in developing countries,[12] but also allows some poor residents to gradually "climb" the housing ladder.[13] Incremental construction by owners is a process of progressive adaptation, by which housing solutions respond to the availability of resources and the needs and priorities of individual users.[14] This process typically includes horizontal and vertical expansion of the units and the integration of space or facilities for income-generation activities.[15] As I discussed in previous chapters, it is also a savings mechanism for the poor. Through later enlargement of the units and self-help improvements, it becomes a natural strategy to invest capital.[16]

But do poor people make good decisions during this process? This is a contentious issue in development studies and among economists. We do know that—contrary to common belief—self-help construction is not produced in a spontaneous or random manner. It rather responds to rational decisions that often anticipate long-term development, community well-being and economic and physical upgrading.[17] There are many examples of this argument, but I will focus on one that I hope will be sufficiently convincing.

FIGURE 5.7 A common pattern of land occupation permitted women to conduct domestic activities while overseeing open and public areas in Mfuleni.

New Houses and Crime in Mfuleni

By 2001, Mfuleni—a township in the outskirts of Cape Town—had 12,000 residents, about half of them living in land occupied informally. Between that year and 2005, thousands of residents of Mfuleni received a piece of land with a latrine from the government, and enjoyed access to running water, electricity and sewage (many of them for the first time). Beneficiaries were free to build or install their own self-help dwellings wherever they wanted on their plots. However, by 2006, when we conducted fieldwork research in Mfuleni, a common pattern of land occupation had emerged. Residents had not installed their shacks in a random manner, as one might expect without having expert knowledge. Instead, they had opted for installing corrugated-sheet modules of 3×3m (some of them purchased from informal prefab companies such as Khayelitsha Shacks) in the back of the plots, leaving the front unoccupied. As more space was needed, most families added additional 3×3m modules creating an L-shape plan in the plot (see Figure 5.7). About half of households in Mfuleni were headed by women. It was therefore not surprising to find that many of the shacks also included one or two modules for income-generation activities (a shop, a canteen, a workshop) that allowed them to work from home.

This deliberate occupation of the lots helped create a supervised space for conducting outdoor activities such as laundry, drying clothes, child caring, BBQ cooking and other social roles. It provided a shadowed area for women to wash clothes and for children to play, and a protected area for parking a motorcycle or a car in the evenings. These open spaces also played a fundamental social role in the community. They provided the opportunity for neighbouring women to talk, oversee the street, meet and exchange goods while doing domestic chores. There were, of course, some problems in Mfuleni. Shacks, for instance, lacked proper foundations and thus they became humid in winter, causing respiratory problems among children and vulnerable adults. But Mfuleni was a dynamic neighbourhood where six- and seven-year-old children walked alone to and from school (incidentally, in perfectly clean and ironed uniforms). It was a place where a foreigner like me could wander around talking with residents, having a soft drink and playing with children.

But a few local and international NGOs thought that this was no decent place for people to live. They considered that shacks were not secure enough and were demeaning for residents. In 2006, organizations such as Habitat for Humanity and the Niall Mellon Foundation started an ambitious plan aimed at replacing informal shacks with what they considered "decent" houses—this is NGO jargon for detached, $36m^2$, one-story masonry units. By 2008, they had replaced almost all shacks with their rubber-stamp solution of concrete block detached units that occupied almost the whole plot and left very little space in the front of the house.

And then, a significant change occurred in Mfuleni—but not quite the change NGOs were expecting. Crime skyrocketed in 2007 and 2008. From 61 murders reported in 2006, figures rose to 109 in 2008, while murder attempts more than doubled in the same period. Burglary almost tripled in these two years. Sexual crimes increased about 25% from 2006 to 2007. Neglect and ill treatment of children rose about 40% between 2007 and 2008. Cases of robbery became normal. All of this happened in a period in which crime was generally receding in the province of the Western Cape. So, what happened in Mfuleni?

Undoubtedly, housing and infrastructure investment resulted in a significant increase in population. In fact, it is estimated that the population of Mfuleni tripled between 2001 and 2011. Nevertheless, population levels were also rising in other townships that did not follow the same drastic increase in crime and violence. In terms of per capita occurrence of criminal activities, Mfuleni became the most murderous settlement in the Southern Cape Flats in 2007 (more dangerous than neighbouring townships such as Mitchell's Plain, Gugulethu, Delf, Phillipi, Nyanga and Khayelitsha). Per capita sexual crimes became about twice as frequent as in Phillipi, Nyanga, Khayelitsha, Mitchell's Plain and Gugulethu. By 2009, there was more residential burglary per capita in Mfuleni than in any of these other settlements. Per capita theft occurrences also rose in Mfuleni, while this type of crime was receding in Khayelitsha, Nyanga and Gugulethu[18] (see Figure 5.8).

It is very difficult to isolate causes of crime in low-income settlements. Fluctuations in crime are sometimes the result of largely invisible changes in gang leadership, mafia businesses, illegal trade agreements, etc. Nonetheless, given that the frenetic and rapid replacement of shacks by new houses did not occur with the same intensity in other areas, it is hard to imagine that spatial changes are not responsible for (at least) part of the crime increase in Mfuleni. A local study conducted at the University of the Western Cape confirms this hypothesis. The study concludes that:

> Urbanization has seriously eroded communal life in Mfuleni characterised by a loss of family functions, broken homes and illegitimacy [...]; erosion of natural

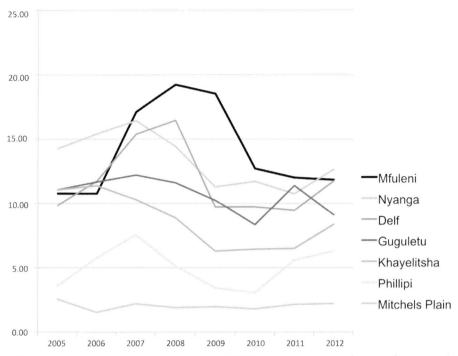

FIGURE 5.8 Murder incidents per capita (1:10,000) in various townships in the Cape Flats (source of data: Institute for Security Studies, South Africa).

> rules of order and conduct due to urbanization, implies that youth are no longer regulated by laws and customs of earlier pre-urban stage of life. Sanctions have lost their force.
>
> (p. 51)[19]

But, what was the change that "eroded communal life"?

New houses built in Mfuleni entirely neglected the importance of outdoor activities that used to take place in the front yards of informal shacks. In fact, in most new houses, kitchens were often located far from the façade, areas for laundry and clothes drying were located in the backyard, and indoor spaces had little contact with the street (see Figure 4.4). Before the construction of new houses, women could conduct several household activities outdoors, which guaranteed surveillance over the street. In fact, when I asked residents whether having small children walking around by themselves in the afternoon was dangerous, they replied that women were usually busy in the front yards (cooking, peeling fruits, washing dishes, etc.), but they knew the neighbours' children and watched for them as they made their way home from school. The study at the University of Western Cape echoes this argument and found that more than 70% of rape and other attacks were taking place in the dark corners of the streets. The study concluded that "lack of family or parental supervision is also one of the major causes of conflicts in Mfuleni" (p. 52).[20]

To be clear, arguing a connection between households' capacity to oversee both public and open private space and crime control is hardly a new idea. Back in 1972, architect and writer Oscar Newman demonstrated this connection and popularized the concept of *Defensible Space*.[21] In his most recent book, Newman examined several housing typologies and concluded that when there is "a close juxtaposition of the street to the private front lawn of each dwelling, residents are concerned about ensuring its safety and act to maintain and control it." (p. 19).[22] I had the unfortunate opportunity to see how women's control of crime works in South African townships when I was conducting voluntary work in a project in Wallacedene, a settlement located between Cape Town and Stellenbosch. One of the Cape Town University students I was working with was mugged in Wallacedene and she had her sunglasses stolen. Soon after the incident, we innocently reported the story to one of the community leaders, a chubby matron in her forties. About 30 minutes later, we saw a group of five or six women pulling a man rather violently to the back of a house. They beat him repeatedly, and he was ultimately let free a few minutes later. One of the women who had beaten the man came back to the group and returned the sunglasses to the horrified student. This was women-led, socially accepted crime control in Wallacedene.

Blinded by their obsession with eliminating informal shacks, decision-makers ignored the benefits that informal patterns of land occupation had in Mfuleni. By rapidly and drastically altering the use of collective and open space, new houses in Mfuleni modified social behaviours with regrettable consequences in terms of crime incidences.

Growth—Housing Improvements and Adaptations in Choluteca

Incremental construction emerges as a natural response to the lack of affordable, finished, solutions. Nevertheless, it can also emerge as a process of adaptation of formally produced housing units. As such, it becomes a form of adaptive capacity to inadequate units, demonstrating the resilience of poor households in the face of adversity. This response appears whether original designs have anticipated modifications and additions or not. Unplanned incremental construction appeared in infrastructure-deprived Choluteca (the project we visited in Chapter 4) as beneficiaries' response to NGO-produced housing units that were too small and uncomfortable.

When I visited Choluteca four years after the construction of original units had finished, self-help incremental construction had already taken place, and additions and improvements to housing units were common. But interventions were not random; instead, much like in the case of shack installation in the Cape Flats, common patterns could be observed (see Figure 5.9). If anything, these patterns revealed the real priorities that people had regarding their living environment. The following are some observations.

Almost all households had—in one way or another—created boundaries on their plots. Some of them (solidly built in masonry or with iron mesh and metallic tubes) were decidedly aimed at improving security, while others, made of wood sticks, trees or chicken wire, aimed at defining the property or producing shadows over the façade. Particular attention was paid to personalizing the rubber-stamped units provided by NGOs. In order to do so, most families painted the front façades, sometimes with bright colours. Furthermore, several families extended the roof over the front façade in order to provide a shaded area and improve the thermal comfort of the units. Common interventions also included building a space for bathing, and a space for cooking in

FIGURE 5.9   Transformations to housing units in Choluteca followed a common pattern. The original units (top left) were often modified to increase privacy and personalize the houses.

the back of the units. Finally, a great number of households created additional space in the front or extended the roof in the front façade in order to include income-generation activities (see Figure 5.10). Structural mistakes were, however, often found in extensions, including lack of structural joints between materials, reduced sections for columns and beams, insufficient bracing or reinforcement of the structure and insufficient attachment of the envelope and partitions to the structure.

Implications for Rethinking and Designing Low-Cost Housing in Developing Countries

Several forms of land appropriation and occupation exist in the informal sector, and multiple types of housing typologies and upgrading mechanisms are put in place. The cases shown in this chapter do not provide an exhaustive typology of strategies used in the process of informal construction of housing units. If anything, they must be taken

FIGURE 5.10 Frequent transformations to housing units in Choluteca aimed at integrating productive activities (top left and right, bottom left) or building additional rooms for extended families (bottom right).

as examples that do nothing more than illustrate some of these strategies, and highlight the vast ignorance that still exists about them. No doubt, more work is still required in the housing industry in order to understand how people acquire land, build their units, hire labour, obtain materials, upgrade units and save the money required for hiring labour and purchasing components. Yet, these examples illustrate several valuable lessons for people who have a hand in housing programs and projects.

The case of Cité Lajoie brings into light the relationships that often exist between land scarcity and households' trade-offs. Families and landlords that reclaim land from the furious Caribbean Sea make a radical, but deliberate and rational, choice. They suffer constant floods and are in the front line of seasonal tropical storms; but they value the proximity to services, transport and markets that Cité Lajoie provides. It is futile for decision-makers and academics to try and decide from our comfortable desks and offices whether this is a good or bad choice. Instead, we are responsible for recognizing the reasons behind this trade-off, and addressing their importance in low-cost housing projects.

The case of Marruecos provides a quick look at forms of informality that do not correspond to the romantic view of the informal sector typically portrayed in academic literature. It serves as a reminder of the delicate boundary that exists between resourceful informality and illegality, and thus as a cautionary message to decision-makers about the difficult challenge of embracing and integrating the informal sector in housing development.

By resorting to a simple module and process, a specialized service and efficient delivery, informal construction companies (like the South African ones) have proved to have competitive advantages to respond and adapt to the hostile conditions of the lowest-income housing market. Through increased innovation, these companies demonstrate the entrepreneurial capacity to generate local jobs in the townships. These cases remind us that production linkages such as subcontracting between the poor/small-scale builders and larger-scale firms should be encouraged. They can help integrate formal and informal areas of the city and economies, and create income opportunities for the poor.[23]

The Mfuleni case illustrates how some decisions made by households in informal settlements are far from being chaotic or spontaneous. They sometimes respond to deliberate choices in the use of space and consider long-term consequences and collective well-being. Ignoring these occupation patterns and their causes in low-cost housing projects can disturb the social mechanisms that permit communities to face hostile conditions (for example, women's daily gatherings in the front yards) and exacerbate common social problems (crime, for instance).

The Choluteca case illustrates how little attention is often paid to the role of stakeholders during the post-occupancy phase. Yet, it is precisely during that phase that households make additions, upgrade and customize their units. It becomes therefore of prime importance to integrate stakeholders *after* the project. More often than not, beneficiaries have the capacity to make decisions regarding the upgrading, customization and enlargement of their own units. However, smart choices frequently require training and education on disaster-resistant standards and a clear understanding of the consequences of physical vulnerabilities associated with poor construction practices.

Sometimes, households in developing countries are not used to buying a fully finished house. Building a house is, for them, a long self-help process, which may even last various generations. In this way, houses "grow" according to the dynamic needs of the family, expectations and availability of resources. Instead of focusing too much on the delivery of completed units, central and regional governments can increase efforts to make information accessible, train workers, provide subsidies and create low-interest loans for the upgrading of housing units. Municipalities need to provide supervision and assure the respect of disaster-resistant standards for additions and upgrades. I probably do not need to dwell on the fact that rather than being ignored, the informal sector needs to be considered as an important (also unavoidable) partner in housing development. Its participation in post-occupancy upgrading and housing completion can—and must—be designed in advance.

Incremental construction is a natural process that can be enhanced by providing basic infrastructure. Let's now examine the limits to this claim and also other benefits of providing infrastructure for housing development.

Notes

1 Aristizabal, N.C. and A. Ortíz Gómez. "Improving Security without Titles in Bogotá." *Habitat International* 28, no. 2 (2004): 245–58.
2 Hawker, D. "Riding Wave of Shack Business Boom." *Cape Argus News*, 2006, 3.
3 Construction Industry Development Board (CIDB). *Annual Report 2004–2005*. Pretoria: CIDB, 2005.
4 Mlinga, R.S. and J. Wells. "Collaboration between Formal and Informal Enterprises in the Construction Sector in Tanzania." *Habitat International* 26, no. 2 (2002): 269–80.
5 Werna, E. "Shelter, Employment and the Informal City in the Context of the Present Economic Scene: Implications for Participatory Governance." *Habitat International* 25, no. 2 (2001): 209–27.
6 Wells, J. "Construction and Capital Formation in Less Developed Economies: Unravelling the Informal Sector in an African City." *Construction Management and Economics* 19, no. 3 (2001): 267–74.
7 Ibid.
8 Gough, K.V. and P. Kellett. "Housing Consolidation and Home-Based Income Generation: Evidence from Self-Help Settlements in Two Colombian Cities." *Cities* 18, no. 4 (2001): 235–47.
9 Turner, J.F.C. *Housing by People: Towards Autonomy in Building Environments*. New York: Pantheon Books, 1977.
10 Choguill, C.L. "The Search for Policies to Support Sustainable Housing." *Habitat International* 31, no. 1 (2007): 143–49; Datta, K. and G.A. Jones. "Housing and Finance in Developing Countries: Invisible Issues on Research and Policy Agendas." *Habitat International* 25, no. 3 (2001): 333–57; Keivani, R. and E. Werna. "Modes of Housing Provision in Developing Countries." *Progress in Planning* 55, no. 2 (2001): 65–118; Keivani, R. and E. Werna. "Refocusing the Housing Debate in Developing Countries from a Pluralist Perspective." *Habitat International* 25, no. 2 (2001): 191–208.
11 Werna, "Shelter, Employment and the Informal City in the Context of the Present Economic Scene."
12 Ferguson, B. and J. Navarrete. "New Approaches to Progressive Housing in Latin America: A Key to Habitat Programs and Policy." *Habitat International* 27, no. 2 (2003): 309–23; Gilbert, A. "Helping the Poor through Housing Subsidies: Lessons from Chile, Colombia and South Africa." *Habitat International* 28, no. 1 (2004): 13–40.
13 Strassmann, P. "The Timing of Urban Infrastructure and Housing Improvements by Owner Occupants." *World Development* 12, no. 7 (1984): 743–53.
14 Bhatt, V. and W. Rybczynski. "How the Other Half Builds." In *Time-Saver Standards for Urban Design*, edited by Watson, D., A. Plattus and R. Shibley, 1.3.1–1.3.11. New York: McGraw-Hill, 2003.
15 Kellett, P. and A.G. Tipple. "The Home as Workplace: A Study of Income-Generating Activities within the Domestic Setting." *Environment and Urbanization* 12, no. 1 (2000): 203–14.
16 *The Economist*. "Slumdog Millions." *The Economist*, March 24, 2010; Ferguson, B. and P. Smets. "Finance for Incremental Housing; Current Status and Prospects for Expansion." *Habitat International* (in press) (2009); Lizarralde, G. and M.-F. Boucher. "Learning from Post-Disaster Reconstruction for Pre-Disaster Planning." In *2nd International i-Rec Conference 2004. Planning for Reconstruction*: 8-14–8-24. Coventry, England: Coventry University, Coventry Centre for Disaster Management, 2004; Lizarralde, G., C. Davidson and C. Johnson, eds. *Rebuilding after Disasters: From Emergency to Sustainability*. London: Taylor & Francis, 2009; Morado Nascimento, D. "Auto Production Housing Process in Brazil: The Informational Practice Approach." In *Sustainable Slum Upgrading in Urban Area*, edited by Santosa, H., W. Astuti and D.W. Astuti: 51–62. Surakarta: CIB, 2009.
17 Lizarralde, G. and C. Davidson. "Learning from the Poor." In *3rd International i-Rec Conference 2006. Meeting Stakeholder Interests*, edited by D. Alexander … [et al.], 14 p. Florence, Italy: Firenze University Press 2006; Lizarralde, Davidson and Johnson, *Rebuilding after Disasters*; Lizarralde, G. and D. Root. "Ready-Made Shacks: Learning from the Informal Sector to Meet Housing Needs in South Africa." Paper presented at the CIB World Building Congress Construction for Development, Cape Town, South Africa, 2007.

18 Institut for Security Studies. "Crime and Justice Hub." South Africa: Institut for Security Studies, 2013.
19 Louis, M.N. "The Effects of Conflict on the Youth of Mfuleni." University of the Western Cape, 2006.
20 Ibid.
21 Newman, O. *Defensible Space*. New York: Macmillan, 1972.
22 Newman, O. *Creating Defensible Space*. Washington: Diane Publishing, 1966.
23 Werna, "Shelter, Employment and the Informal City in the Context of the Present Economic Scene."

6

INVISIBLE INFRASTRUCTURE

Housing is Not Actually About Delivering Houses, But About Developing Infrastructure, Collective Services and Economic Activities. But, Where?

> It has nothing that makes it seem a city, except the water pipes that rise vertically where the houses should be and spread out horizontally where the floors should be: a forest of pipes that end in taps, showers, spouts, overflows.
>
> *Invisible Cities*, Italo Calvino (p. 42)

Shine a Light

A comprehensive analysis of the challenges and opportunities of infrastructure construction in the developing world is the subject of a book on its own—or probably, of a collection of books. I do not pretend to do so in a short chapter. We know that lack of infrastructure in several countries continues to be simultaneously one of the most important causes *and* consequences of underdevelopment. One figure might just act as a reminder of this: it is estimated that in India, 700 million, or more than half of the population, have unreliable or no connection to the national grid of electricity.[1] Most of the poor thus resort to the use of paraffin lamps, which typically produce both respiratory problems and very dim light that hampers income-generation activities and school homework. I need not emphasize the obvious benefits of traditional public services (water, sewage, electricity, roads) in improving public health, reducing child mortality, enhancing productivity and learning as well as preventing environmental degradation, or the positive effects of new services (Internet and mobile phones) in small and micro-business efficiency, agricultural production and access to knowledge and education. It is easy to get the picture.

Let's instead focus our attention on the contentious side of things. Infrastructure development is often affected by lack of political will—which should not be taken for granted, even in richer, more developed nations. It is also largely affected by implementation challenges, including lack of managerial and financial skills among public entities in developing countries, inadequate legal frameworks to facilitate project development, corruption in the use of resources, inadequate contracts and procurement practices, and other inhibiting factors. However, even if political will exists and implementation practices are being considered, decision-makers must face an additional challenge that is worth discussing here: given the limited resources available and infrastructure needs across almost every sector (water, environmental protection, telecoms, education, transport, and so on), what choices need to be made? And more specifically, where should infrastructure projects be built?

This is an open-ended question with almost infinite answers, depending on the context and local conditions. But I am surprised at how often the debate about where to invest boils down to a decision about developing infrastructure in empty land or in existing informal settlements. There are many alternative choices and, probably, middle grounds. Yet, arguably, almost all housing programs and NGO interventions in developing countries are, at one moment or another, confronted with the following dilemma: given the scarcity of resources, should infrastructure provision be prioritized in slums (where, many people think, nothing seems to work "the right way") or else in new settlements, where things can be done "right" from scratch?

In order to explore the elements at stake, I will present here—much like a live debate—two opposing arguments and their "pros" and "cons." Instead of proving or disproving the arguments, I will provide an example for each of them highlighting their merits and limitations. In doing so, you will be able to draw your own conclusions before I share my own point of view at the end of this chapter.

Better to Build Infrastructure in Empty Land

There are several reasons that justify the choice of prioritizing infrastructure for new developments rather than for existing slums. The first, and probably most fundamental one, is that it is cheaper. Several recent studies have found that building infrastructure in existing slums is up to three times more expensive due to long legal procedures required for expropriation and compensation, technical difficulties and administrative barriers.[2] The second fundamental reason is that it effectively halts slum formation. Defenders of this approach usually criticize that while bulldozers and excavators are working in one slum in order to introduce infrastructure, another slum is often in the making as a natural response to demographic pressures, thus perpetuating the problem of slum creation. Increasing the supply of new formal housing, they argue, is the only real solution to stop the emergence of informal settlements. Given these arguments, Ferguson and Navarrete conclude that the best way to deal with urban slums is "to decrease or stop their formation, and thereby avoid fixing them retroactively at high cost" (p. 204).[3]

One of the most seductive reasons—even for observers who do not know the technical aspects of the decision—is that by creating new settlements through infrastructure development, it is possible to do things "right" from scratch, rather than trying to fix settlements that will be perpetually affected by the original lack of proper planning. International NGOs and defenders of this approach are often enthusiastic about, among other things, the possibility of building wide roads, of planning green areas in advance and of deciding on appropriate zoning beforehand—separating non-compatible uses such as polluting industry and residential.

Another common argument is that developing infrastructure in vacant land facilitates achieving economies of scale and mass production. Unlike laying down construction work in a dense slum, new components (including electric posts, pipelines, sidewalks, urban furniture and lighting) can be installed at large with small variations allowing time and cost efficiency. Consequently, building infrastructure "from scratch" is faster. There are fewer delays in expropriation processes, and the project phasing can be planned according to technical needs and not externalities (such as legal procedures or negotiations of land).

It is probably naïve not to recognize that generally, developing new settlements provides better visibility for politicians, NGOs and bureaucrats. Cutting a ribbon in a new settlement that respects regulations and housing standards enhances reputation for politicians and NGOs, something more difficult to achieve when the project concerns laying down infrastructure (especially if it concerns underground pipes, drains and cables) in slums. There is finally another procedural advantage in building infrastructure for new settlements. Intervening in empty (often previously agricultural) land in the outskirts of cities or in distant places for housing development generally faces less opposition from pressure groups and residents than intervening in dense urban areas where multiple interests collide and project visibility is high.

Better to Build Infrastructure in Existing Informal Settlements

There are also good reasons to prioritize building infrastructure in existing, informal, urban areas. Laying down infrastructure often provides a form of tacit tenure. In this regard, Smets writes: "The provision of basic facilities by a public body already creates the impression that people will not be removed" (p. 598).[4] Another relevant argument— typically connected to the previous one—is that it accelerates housing consolidation. *De facto* or formal tenure, mixed with access to public services, encourages residents to invest in finishing, beautifying and upgrading their own houses. After a comprehensive survey of housing in Lima, Peru, in which he compared informal settlements with core-housing developments, Paul Strassman found hard evidence that confirms this argument. He concluded that in low-income settlements in Lima, a sewerage system connection more than doubles the probability that residents conduct six or more improvements to their own dwellings.[5]

Infrastructure accelerates economic development in informal settlements, notably because it facilitates the development of home-based income-generation activities. A study conducted by the Development Planning Unit of University College London and local researchers in Colombia showed that about 50% of houses located in informal settlements in Bogotá and Medellín have spaces that are devoted to income-generation activities (these activities generate about 60% of family income). When the informal settlements get consolidated, and infrastructure therefore improves, the fraction of housing units that include spaces for income-generation rises to 75% (it must be noted, however, that the impact of these activities on family income decreases).[6] Besides, roads permit efficient transportation of people and goods, bringing economic advantages to micro-, small- and medium-size enterprises. Public lighting and proper sidewalks often reduce crime and deter individuals from conducting vandalism.

Unlike the development of new settlements in which housing units can easily filter up to wealthier households, this strategy also brings better possibilities to target the very poor and most needy families. Besides, by concentrating on existing built areas, slum upgrading and infrastructure development within settlements reduce urban sprawl, which has obvious environmental benefits and advantages for production efficiency, while also avoiding long and expensive commuting times for residents. In this way, it keeps families close to jobs and services. Finally, bringing infrastructure to existing settlements, instead of bringing people to live in a new place, avoids the numerous negative consequences usually associated with displacing poor communities.

Drawn-Match Arguments

There are several contexts in which it is more difficult to determine an obvious "winner" between the two approaches. This, for instance, is the case for disaster prevention. Developing new settlements can be an efficient and proactive risk-reduction approach, notably because the supply of new housing reduces the chances of families invading land in risk-prone areas. However, after the disaster occurred in Haiti in 2010, upgrading infrastructure in existing urban areas in Port-au-Prince proved to be an opportunity for reducing disaster risk, particularly in areas such as Martissant where public service provision was accompanied by cleaning sewerage and drains, and building water channels that reduce the risk of flooding.

One of the most important challenges in both approaches is the maintenance of infrastructure. Once the ribbons have been cut and the photographs with politicians have been taken for electoral purposes, finding the resources for cleaning pipes, replacing broken light bulbs, fixing vandalized furniture or cleaning open areas becomes difficult. Priorities shift to new areas, attention is given to other "urgent" problems and maintenance budgets (if they exist at all) diminish. Let's explore an example of how infrastructure and core-housing were developed in a recent project in Colombia.

Infrastructure for New Housing in Juan Pablo II

Before 2004, Facatativá—the city where Mr Ruben Sanchez (who you read about in the beginning of Chapter 1) found a place to live—was relatively inactive. Like many other Colombian cities, Facatativá (a city with 100,000 inhabitants) had a significant housing deficit, and hundreds of residents were living in illegally occupied land and dangerous conditions. By that time, it was estimated that 5,800 people were living in substandard housing, and an additional 1,000 families in disaster-prone locations. However, unlike many other municipalities, in 2005 Facatativá designed and executed an ambitious strategic housing plan. About 18ha were required for this plan; yet, the only large plots available were in the outskirts of the city. In response, the municipality opted for purchasing a piece of land as close as possible to public infrastructure, residential areas and commerce. The project was called Juan Pablo II, in honour of the charismatic Pope. In the next phase, the city authorized a specific urban development plan defining zoning and regulations that allowed for housing development, commerce and community services.

The design included developing six consecutive phases for a total of 1,262 row-housing units clustered around green areas, basketball courts and a central park, all located on a natural hill. The final phase was completed in 2007, that is, only two years after the beginning of construction. The settlement has only one vehicle road, which connects to parking spaces and a network of pedestrian paths. All houses are located less than 100 m from a parking space and a green area, giving priority and space to children and pedestrians and not to cars (Figure 6.1). A school and a library were also built in the middle of the settlement. Though commercial space and a technical education centre were initially proposed, they were never completed.

The financial plan—albeit largely subsidized—was as solid as the urban design. The project mobilized roughly US$1.2 million in subsidies for land, US$1.7 million in subsidized infrastructure and US$44,600 in subsidies for plans and design, for a total of almost US$3 million (about 6,027,456,948 Colombian pesos). These resources were eventually transferred as upfront subsidies of US$2,371 offered to each beneficiary through the *Cajas de Compensación Familiar*—the private, non-profit, welfare funds in Colombia. However, following existing regulations, only households that held permanent jobs and that followed a "Programmed Savings Plan" could apply for these subsidies. Unemployed households living in unsafe and illegally occupied land were not eligible. In response, the municipality created the *Valor Unico de Reconocimiento* (VUR), a mechanism to expropriate these households from their illegally occupied land while compensating them with from 1 to 12 million pesos (US$500–6,000). In July 2006, The *Fondo Nacional de Vivienda*, a national fund that administers public subsidies, gave 103 VURs to an equal number of families living in disaster-prone areas.[7]

Through a fiduciary duty, the city then established a partnership agreement with a general contractor, who acted as a private residential developer responsible for administering both the land and the resources, building infrastructure and ultimately transferring the houses to the beneficiaries with full-tenure rights. Officers knew that the available resources could not fully match the expectations of the beneficiaries, and thus opted for a core-housing strategy allowing for owner-driven incremental construction during the post-occupancy phase. This strategy combined the benefits of a contractor-driven project (providing standard public services, appropriate infrastructure and general urban coherence) with the benefits of owner-driven interventions—notably the freedom to adapt the housing unit and develop it according to household needs and resources.

Each family obtained a 4×10m plot with a core-unit in the front—adjacent to another core-unit on each side, much like the form of row-housing. The 37m² core-units were two stories high, including a living area and a kitchen on the first level, and two bedrooms and one bathroom on the upper level. It was anticipated that the 20m² original backyard of the core-unit was to be built by the beneficiaries as the house grew. All core-units had running water, electricity, sewage and a telephone connection. The scope of additions—including use, subdivisions and size—was largely defined by a pre-established plan and a booklet of guidelines that were provided to each beneficiary. The booklet, animated with diagrams and drawings, prescribed materials to be used in the case of additions, provided the general layout, the structural elements required and the accepted connections to existing infrastructure. It also emphasized that beneficiaries who did not follow the guidelines would lose the five-year guarantee provided by the contractor. This was seen at that moment as a way to enforce quality standards, and guarantee that additions respect disaster-resistant regulations.

What happened after infrastructure and core-housing had been built? Since 2006, we have conducted more than six fieldwork studies in which we have examined the evolution of the settlement. Our results show that, as expected, post-occupancy additions

FIGURE 6.1 Urban designers in Juan Pablo II proposed a central park in the middle of the settlement (from where the top image was taken), sport facilities, reduced roads for cars and efficient pathways for pedestrians (bottom image).

and modifications to the basic units were managed and developed directly by end-users. They certainly used their freedom to make decisions regarding funding, design, procurement and construction. Various residents had construction skills and worked directly on the construction themselves. Others opted for hiring informal contractors to build the additions. A great number of households opted for a mixed approach in which they bought and supplied the materials and hired only labour force for the construction. Each family followed its own pace according to the resources available. Extensions usually started with improvised materials such as plastics and sticks. In a second step, the foundations and floor were built. Walls and roof for the first floor followed, and the second floor appeared later, only when resources were available (see Figures 6.2 and 6.3).

However, various families opted for additions and alterations to the original dwelling that differed from the ones proposed by the original residential developer in the booklet. These included changes to the location of the kitchen, the patio (often covering it with a transparent roof in order to use this area for domestic interior activities), the distribution of bedrooms and the openings towards the patio, the installation of the elevated water tank, the bathroom located on the first floor and the distribution of electric switches and sockets.

Temporary structures used in the first stages of housing upgrades were mostly conducted by users themselves, whereas a good part of permanent construction was undertaken by paid workers, or completed with the help of unpaid labour (mostly friends and relatives of the beneficiaries). Informal workers contributed to the designs of both changes to the existing unit layouts and changes to the pre-established addition designs. Common upgrades included interior and exterior painting, tiled flooring in the bathroom and kitchen, new internal partitions, demolition of internal partitions, plastering internal walls and building fences and security grids (Figures 6.4 and 6.5).

The availability of infrastructure allowed residents to include income-generation activities within their homes rather quickly. By December 2007, 12% of the units were already mixed use (residential and commercial). Commercial uses included convenience stores, childcare places, movie rental stores, hair and beauty salons, Internet cafés, cafeterias, and stores for shoes and clothing repairs. Several families were already renting space within their homes.

The provision of infrastructure in Juan Pablo II became an excellent opportunity for including attractive urban features, such as the park on the existing hill, green areas within clusters of houses, sports courts and a network of pedestrian paths. It also allowed for anticipating future community facilities, such as a school and a library. But more importantly, it became an excellent opportunity to make appropriate decisions regarding the density of the settlement, avoiding expensive streets for cars and obtaining a proper balance between open and built areas. The settlement managed to reduce the growing pressure of housing demand in Facatativá, and successfully resettled families that were living in disaster-prone areas.

Income-generation activities within homes were not initially anticipated in the core-housing project. However, appropriate density and urban design, coupled with universal access to public services, facilitated the rapid emergence of these activities. By being able to produce additional income, families were able to complete and upgrade their houses more rapidly than project decision-makers had anticipated. This created a process of positive feedback in which families could take advantage of additional space (often rented or used for production), and thus could continue to invest in their own properties.

FIGURE 6.2 Extensions built by homeowners in the backyards of the core-units (pictured above with a difference of six months) appeared very quickly in Juan Pablo II. Additions started with temporary materials that were later replaced with concrete structures and masonry.

FIGURE 6.3 After occupation, residents of Juan Pablo II personalized the unit façades (see the changes in windows) and created playground areas in open spaces.

FIGURE 6.4 Upgrading of the units often included plastering interior walls and laying ceramic tiles on the floors.

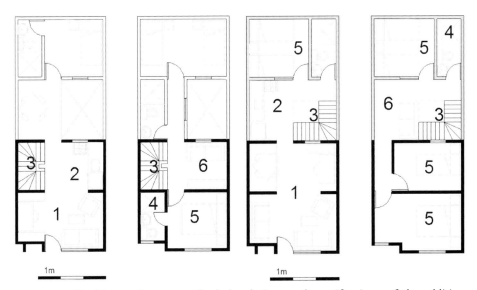

FIGURE 6.5 Decision-makers prescribed the designs and specifications of the additions to the core-units. On the left, the plans of the first and second floors with the original walls of the core-unit filled in black. On the right is an example of a house transformed during the post-occupancy phase. Legend: 1: social living room, 2: kitchen, 3: stairs, 4: WC, 5: bedroom, 6: living room.

Infrastructure in Favela Santa Marta

On May 30, 2013, the American Vice-President Joe Biden toured Favela Santa Marta in Rio de Janeiro. Followed by journalists and local officers through the urbanized hills of the Brazilian slum, he stopped at one of the local stores to eat ice cream with a group of neighbourhood children. It was certainly an uneventful, relaxed visit.[8] Not many people abroad know about Favela Santa Marta. But Mr Biden was not the first well-known American to visit the settlement. In the 1990s, Michael Jackson filmed the video for his famous song "They Don't Care About Us" in the favela. Santa Marta was a different place then. Though controversial at that time, this shantytown was an appropriate background for filming a video that condemned segregation and violence. Today, it might not be an appropriate place to belt out the lyric, "Tell me what has become of my rights. Am I invisible because you ignore me? All I wanna say is that…" In fact, Santa Marta is now one of the safest favelas in Rio and one of the most integrated with the formal structures of the city; it has an enviable cable car that transports residents (free of charge) to the top of the hill. It has clean sidewalks and pathways, garbage bins, public lighting and hundreds of shops that sell products to both locals and visitors.

A comprehensive and long-term plan of police intervention—which included incorporating a police station on top of the Santa Marta settlement—transformed security issues in the slum, making it safer for residents and more accessible to outsiders. Santa Marta's physical transformation is also largely due to the infrastructure upgrading conducted over the last ten years (see Figure 6.6). This upgrading has included building the cable car and cantilevered side walks, and introducing lighting, urban furniture,

FIGURE 6.6 In the infrastructure of Favela Santa Marta, cantilevered sidewalks create a network of safe pathways that facilitate access to the upper units on the mountain.

electricity, running water and a waste disposal PVC tube that rests on the mountain like a hungry snake. Given the importance of soccer in Brazilian culture, the construction of a community soccer field on the slopes of the mountain (see Figure 6.7) represented a significant achievement for the residents of Santa Marta.

Favela Santa Marta's transformation has not been all positive, however. Along with building new infrastructure also came building the concrete retaining wall I described in Chapter 2 (see Figure 2.5). But, there is little doubt that Santa Marta has become an overall positive example of slum upgrading in Brazil. Having foreign politicians and celebrities visiting slums is hardly a structural solution for the problems of poor households. Yet, sufficient examples of successfully introducing public services and collective facilities exist in the slums of Medellín (Colombia), Johannesburg (South Africa), Rio de Janeiro (Brazil) and other cities in the developing world. These examples permit us to claim with confidence that infrastructure does in fact help informal settlements better integrate into urban functions, fabric and networks. Infrastructure thus becomes a powerful tool for improving living conditions for the poor. Projects that facilitate mobility, access to health care, culture, education, recreation and safety against natural hazards have the potential to transform human settlements. These transformations occur not only because of the functional improvements that come along with improved roads, pipes and facilities, but also because of the symbolic benefits that come with recognizing human rights, redressing social injustices and integrating informal dwellers in the systems and structures of the city.

FIGURE 6.7 Defying all expectations, a soccer field was constructed on the steep mountain, providing an important recreational facility for residents of Favela Santa Marta.

Infrastructure Processes

The main argument of this book is that housing is about creating the conditions in which people can live lives that they have reason to value. Chapter 8 will show that this implies a considerable decentralization of decision-making power, transferring it to individuals and households. Only in this way, the argument goes, can individuals and households create living environments that respond to their own values, needs and aspirations. However, we will also see that this argument faces an important challenge: the need to develop urban infrastructure. Urban infrastructure cannot be efficiently developed through individual interventions at the household level. Infrastructure is clearly both more efficient and cheaper when developed as a collective service for a group of housing units. It thus requires planning, design, construction, finance and management at a collective level (a social group, a neighbourhood, a city).

Public services and collective facilities are projects of public interest, in which divergent or opposing interests and expectations must often be arbitrated and mediated. This raises the issue of project governance, the subject of Chapter 9. Governance is to infrastructure projects what individual decision-making is to housing units. Consequently, project governance mechanisms for collective decision-making are for infrastructure what individual decision-making mechanisms are for housing unit development. Unlike other common terms such as "governability" and "govern," governance relationships do not necessarily depend on hierarchical structures. Instead, governance implies project management mechanisms between several stakeholders that share decision-making power. In other words, governance is the structure that sets common objectives and establishes the means to achieve them. The key issue of infrastructure development is, therefore, the design, implementation and monitoring of appropriate scenarios and mechanisms for participation and collaboration between heterogeneous stakeholders.

But this raises a fundamental question: how do we reconcile short-term needs and expectations with long-term ones? Although resources may be insufficient in the short term (or present), they can become progressively available in the future, or over the long term. Besides, households can obtain resources at different pace, and thus they can achieve better standards at different moments in time. Progressive development of infrastructure is therefore one of the most promising strategies to deal with short-term needs and long-term expectations. It is also a suitable approach for reconciling individual decision-making with collective efforts. Strategies in which basic (collective) infrastructure can be (individually or collectively) upgraded become potential solutions for reconciling the different timing of individual and collective decision-making and opportunities. This includes latrines that can be later connected to septic tanks and then to sewerage, or propane gas systems for cooking and water heating in which individual tanks can be later replaced by city networks. Unfortunately, incremental infrastructure remains a largely unexplored area of housing research and public agendas.

Implications for Rethinking and Designing Low-Cost Housing in Developing Countries

So, what about the initial dilemma proposed in this chapter? Should we prioritize building infrastructure on empty land or on existing settlements? Surely the right response is that both strategies must be conducted simultaneously, and that the advantages and disadvantages of each approach depend on the context. Fair enough. Given limited resources, however, choices have to be made, and the argument for stopping slum creation through the creation of new housing stock is of great importance. It certainly sways the balance towards developing infrastructure on empty land. But not too far; developing infrastructure in existing informal settlements can be accompanied by a densification and consolidation of the existing housing stock—notably, because it encourages households to complete and enlarge their dwellings and thus, very often, to offer rental space or space for sale. As such, this approach can also become a tool for creating new housing supply while consolidating and upgrading existing informal settlements. There is obviously no single solution that fits all housing needs in developing countries, but given the double advantages of this strategy, it becomes, in some places, a potentially solid approach to the simultaneous reduction of qualitative and quantitative housing deficits.

As we saw in the case of Choluteca, houses without infrastructure lead to the deterioration of living conditions. Developing infrastructure is often more relevant and sustainable than building houses, particularly because it accelerates the process of housing consolidation (conducted, anyhow, quite effectively by the informal sector) while creating the conditions for urban integration, economic development and public-health improvement. Solutions that develop new infrastructure but leave room for incremental construction replicate the natural response of the informal sector to incremental housing development. Core-housing projects such as the ones exemplified in this chapter show that lower housing standards can be (and are) accepted by users if alternatives for incremental upgrading are available and properly planned in advance. Infrastructure and proper densities that encourage and support income-generating activities are the engines behind core-housing completion and upgrading.

However, these post-occupancy interventions need to be properly supervised and controlled in order to reduce physical vulnerabilities related to, for example, disaster risk. They require careful planning of project stakeholders' roles. The informal construction sector presents several advantages that can be used in the design of top structures and in the completion of core-units. It has an increased capacity to adapt to hostile economic environments, deliver customised and affordable solutions, and adapt work and objectives in the project life cycle, following the pace of available resources and partial commissioning. However, it also presents several limitations that need to be addressed while considering urban infrastructure development. It often has limited access to financial solutions and competitive interest rates, limited capacity to respond to disaster-resistant standards of construction, and limited capacity to develop technically sophisticated and interconnected public services.

Nonetheless, strategies that integrate contractor-driven construction of basic infrastructure and core-housing can optimize the advantages of both the formal and informal sectors. Incremental upgrading of infrastructure can then create proper spaces for individual decision-making, particularly if it allows residents (or the community at once) to reach higher standards over time. All of this is still challenged by the fact that decisions of public interest require consensus. The collective decision-making necessary for the efficient construction of infrastructure demands appropriate project governance scenarios and structures, allowing for effective participation and collaboration between stakeholders. Before we discuss the importance of freedom and governance in detail, let's first consider the importance of the relationship between housing and disasters.

Notes

1 *The Economist.* "Lighting Rural India: Out of the Gloom." *The Economist*, July 23, 2013.
2 Dávila, J., A. Gilbert, N. Rueda and P. Brand. "Suelo urbano y vivienda para la población de ingresos bajos. Estudios de caso: Bogotá-Soacha-Mosquera; Medellín y área metropolitana." *Development Planning Unit, University College of London* (2006); Ferguson, B. and J. Navarrete. "New Approaches to Progressive Housing in Latin America: A Key to Habitat Programs and Policy." *Habitat International* 27, no. 2 (2003): 309–23; Ferguson, B. and J. Navarrete. "A Financial Framework for Reducing Slums: Lessons from Experience in Latin America." *Environment and Urbanization* 15, no. 2 (2003): 201.
3 Ferguson and Navarrete, "A Financial Framework for Reducing Slums: Lessons from Experience in Latin America."
4 Smets, P. "Small Is Beautiful, but Big Is Often the Practice: Housing Microfinance in Discussion." *Habitat International* 30, no. 3 (2006): 595–613.
5 Strassmann, P. "The Timing of Urban Infrastructure and Housing Improvements by Owner Occupants." *World Development* 12, no. 7 (1984): 743–53.
6 Dávila, Gilbert, Rueda and Brand, "Suelo urbano y vivienda para la población de ingresos bajos."
7 Lizarralde, G. "Stakeholder Participation and Incremental Housing in Subsidized Housing Projects in Colombia and South Africa." *Habitat International* 35, no. 2 (2010): 175–87.
8 The White House. "The Vice President Visits Favela Santa Marta." (2013), http://www.whitehouse.gov/photos-and-video/video/2013/06/11/vice-president-visits-favela-santa-marta.

7

VISIBLY VULNERABLE, INVISIBLY RESILIENT

On Why Disasters Are Not Strictly "Natural" and Reconstruction Projects Sometimes Represent a Different Type of Disaster

> Beware of saying to them that sometimes different cities follow one another on the same site and under the same name, born and dying without knowing one another, without communication among themselves.
>
> *Invisible Cities*, Italo Calvino (p. 26)

The Disaster Strikes Back

On January 13, 2001, an earthquake with a magnitude of 7.6 on the Richter scale occurred off the El Salvador coastline. A month later, a second earthquake with a magnitude of 6.6 struck the country again. Aftershocks continued for the following weeks, largely affecting the region of La Paz and the capital city, San Salvador. Landslides, and floods caused by debris damming the rivers and channels, soon followed. There were in total 1,159 deaths and 8,122 injuries. It is estimated that about 1.5 million people were affected and 186,444 houses were destroyed. In San Salvador alone, 929 houses collapsed, and about 5,000 units were partially damaged.

The Salvadorian government was not prepared to create a central fund for supporting reconstruction initiatives, and could hardly increase its debt with additional loans. While several units of the government, at all levels, were asked to participate in reconstruction efforts, the strategies and mechanisms for funding these initiatives were never clearly determined. President Francisco Flores' administration found it difficult to implement a comprehensive reconstruction plan. Consequently, fragmented and dispersed initiatives, largely supported by international donors and humanitarian aid, emerged. Much like in the case of post-Mitch Honduras, a "tsunami" of NGOs and international humanitarian agencies followed the disaster.

Hector Silva, the mayor of San Salvador, concentrated on disaster relief immediately after the earthquake. A specially appointed commission conducted the assessment of damages. However, collecting and processing the information took over four months. The Municipality then created a Reconstruction Committee (*Comité para la reconstrucción*) to lead reconstruction initiatives. The first obstacles appeared when the

Municipal Council decided not to participate in the committee, seemingly because representatives of the Council proved to be more interested in their political activities than in administrative or technical initiatives. The Reconstruction Committee was ultimately composed of staff of the Department of Planning and Projects, a few representatives of industry and reputed researchers with experience in the field of low-cost housing. Given the high profile of its participants, the committee seemed to be well equipped for the challenge. It defined an ambitious agenda, which included the construction of more than 6,000 housing units and both "hard" outputs such as infrastructure reconstruction, and "soft" ones such as a comprehensive mitigation plan, risk reduction and risk mapping. Plans and construction documents for a prototype house were soon ready to begin construction.

The (Literally) Invisible Houses in San Salvador

Whereas cities were given the responsibility for housing reconstruction, the municipality of San Salvador was no better equipped to deal with the disaster than it had been to deal with the mounting (but considered "regular") housing deficits. Alas, a singular political circumstance made urban reconstruction in the capital city even more difficult. The national government of President Flores was formed by the right-wing party ARENA (*Alianza Republicana Nacionalista*), whereas the ruling party at the municipal government of San Salvador was formed by the opposition FMLN (*Frente Foribundo Martí para la Liberación Nacional*, the leftist political representation of the disarmed guerrilla movement) in coalition with the USC (*Unión Social Cristiana*, a centre-left party). The historical and ideological opposition of these two groups created tensions that rapidly affected the reconstruction process.

Hurdles started to appear in the search for funding (the initial target was US$2 million). The director of the program explained, in an interview:

> Private loans are extremely expensive (13% interest rates) and even though the interest rates of international institutions are lower (5.5%), the requirements of international Banks are very strict. Not even the World Bank would have given us money because we do not have any more debt capacity.

A national ban on the transfer of large funds coming from international aid to municipalities without passing through Congress made matters worse. Not only did the municipality not have the funds to reconstruct, but it did not have the flexibility to collect its own resources without risking corruption and deviation of funds in Congress. Unable to obtain loans or credits, the municipality's only chances for funding came from its own "functioning" budget, humanitarian aid and donations by supporters of the Mayor's political party.

With limited funds, the municipality could only accomplish the maintenance of water channels, the purchase of tents for temporary housing and the provision of a few housing subsidies for its own employees. The housing project was abandoned without any single unit built. The Reconstruction Committee was later on removed from the duties of execution and transformed into a consultant role. Finally, with little chance of providing any additional help, it was definitively dissolved in April 2002.

A New Slum in Tonacatepeque

Eighteen months after the disaster, reconstruction was no longer a priority and the municipality was working on "other important issues." Given that the Urban Development Master Plan (or POT, for its acronym in Spanish) proposed by the city was rejected by the National Congress, very limited planning and structural prevention was being conducted. Very little had changed in the city; squatter settlements kept growing, as did most urban risks. In the meantime, the national government was trying to implement a relocation project for 928 families in the capital city. Beneficiaries were given materials (wood and corrugated metal sheets) for building a temporary shack in a settlement called Tonacatepeque, near San Salvador. Even though the settlement was still in its early phases of development, by June 2002 it was already recognized as one of the most dangerous areas of metropolitan region; it did not have infrastructure and access to it was risky, even for the local police. Tonacatepeque was yet another area notorious for its urban slums. In the meantime, San Salvador was, once again, waiting for the next disaster to happen.

The case of reconstruction (or lack of it) in San Salvador exemplifies several common challenges in urban low-cost housing, including political tensions, administrative barriers, insufficient political will and lack of resources and expertise. However, before we discuss other challenges facing reconstruction projects, let's first explore the connections between housing and disasters. In order to do so, we need to rely on two apparently contradictory theories: vulnerability and resilience.

Vulnerability, or Why Disasters Happen

Vulnerability theory sustains that disasters are partially the result of man-made (thus, socially built) conditions that emerge from root causes and dynamic pressures—that is, historic and more recent social settings that put people at risk.[1] It contends that social, economic and political vulnerabilities increase the risks of disasters triggered by either natural events (such as earthquakes, floods, tsunamis, etc.) or man-made events (such as wars, industrial pollution, technological accidents, etc.).[2] The underlying consequence of this concept is that disasters are not strictly "natural" but created by unsafe circumstances that societies develop and institutions tolerate—natural events (sudden or incremental) only trigger the devastation that results from the dynamic pressures. These unsafe conditions include physical characteristics such as construction in disaster-prone areas (see Figure 7.1) and weak buildings (see Figure 7.2), but also less tangible characteristics that put people in fragile situations, such as unreliable information about disaster response measures, lack of property titles or insurance and limited education.

Let's explore the concept of vulnerability by returning to the Salvadorian case and asking the following question: Why did the disaster happen in the first place?

To be clear, the 2001 earthquakes were not the only recent disasters in El Salvador. In retrospect, their dramatic effects seem like a repetition of the 1986 earthquake. Major landslides, the collapse of weak infrastructure, thousands of units reduced to uninhabitable conditions and a huge number of deaths and wounded were, for a second time in two decades, the price that low-income communities paid due to several forms of vulnerabilities.

FIGURE 7.1 Housing construction in flood-prone areas, such as this one in Yumbo, Colombia, put people at risk and exacerbate the effects of disasters.

FIGURE 7.2 Where is the missing column? Weak structures such as this one in an informal settlement in Cali, Colombia, contribute to create physical vulnerabilities.

Historical causes and political decisions contributed to creating physical vulner-abilities in the country.[3] These causes must be traced back to political factors as well as the 12-year civil war (1980–1992) in which the government and leftist guerrilla groups were opposed. This was one of the most violent Latin American wars of the twentieth century (it took over 75,000 lives in a country with a population of 6.5 million). The war had significant effects on the economy, on society and, obviously, on politics. When, during the war, leftist rural insurgent groups gained both enough public support and military power to seriously challenge the government, concern about the stability of the region mounted in the United States. The response was ambitious economic and military support (worth US$6 billion) to the Salvadorian right-wing government. The effect of the American help was that the two armed parties (the government and the guerrilla movement, FMLN) found their forces balanced enough to decide, in 1992, to sign a peace agreement.

Talks between the United States and Salvadorian governments were tainted with political pressure to modernize and reform Salvadorian public institutions following neoliberal principles.[4] To be precise, El Salvador was not alone in this process. In order to compensate for the danger perceived from socialist movements, and the fragility of unstable governments in the region to drift towards leftist extremes, a strict political plan, based on the advantages of the private sector, was proposed by the United States for most Latin American nations.[5] Neoliberal policies were widely implemented by the World Bank, the Inter-American Development Bank and through political persuasion. For many Central and South American nations, this pressure also included putting conditions on the delivery of international aid, loans and commercial agreements, and implementing structural reforms.

These policies attempted to overcome the traditional limitations to development—as they were seen from Washington and London—by reducing the responsibilities and influence of the State (neoliberal thinking associates the State with inefficiency, high levels of corruption and extreme bureaucracy). It was expected that, by reducing the influence of the State, decentralizing the government and transferring responsibilities to the private sector, and its organic market forces, corruption and bureaucracy could be minimized, resulting in a more efficient system overall. Simultaneously, government downsizing and privatization of public functions were instruments to reduce the increasing financial deficits. Unsurprisingly, a process of eliminating public jobs quickly ensued.

The new model challenged the need for public departments or units responsible for housing and infrastructure development.[6] It was believed that traditional duties of the government during the 1960s and 1970s, such as building housing for the poor, were no longer needed if transferred to the "more efficient" private sector. In fact (as we saw in Chapters 1 and 3), this sector was expected to respond appropriately to the forces of supply and demand with better quality products. Public units in charge of developing housing were reduced or eliminated, ministries of housing were replaced or transformed into ministries of "public works" and many other national and regional units responsible for housing and planning were abolished. In El Salvador, many of the responsibilities for housing issues were transferred to municipalities, which, suddenly, were forced to take on new responsibilities.

But municipalities in El Salvador—and for that matter, many other developing countries—did not have the economic means, staff, technical equipment and administrative capacity to deal with the new challenges. Reforms were rarely accompanied by capacity-building initiatives, stronger budgets or plausible ways of increasing resources. In housing alone, the challenges became enormous, and the causes and consequences of the problems extremely complex. This led to an unbearable situation where municipalities did not have the legal, economic and administrative capacities to attract funding, enforce plans and develop sufficient projects.[7] In this context, the experience of previous disasters was not enough to create a political and social culture of prevention and risk reduction. The lack of a comprehensive housing policy, rapid migration to urban centres and lack of urban planning and enforcement of standards exacerbated physical risks, notably in ever-growing informal settlements. By 1999, 27% of housing in metropolitan San Salvador was inadequate, almost 40% of squatter settlements were built in illegally occupied land and 13% of the population of the city lived at risk of landslides or flooding.[8] In terms of infrastructure, the situation was not any better; in 1994, 25% of urban residents in El Salvador did not have regular potable water service, and 43% of urban housing presented risks associated with weak structures and inappropriate construction.[9]

When the earthquakes occurred, landslides destroyed hundreds of houses and clogged rivers and water channels, weak roofs and structures killed thousands of people, roads were fractured and important buildings collapsed. Much like in previous disasters, there was a momentary sense of anger towards the authorities and a phase of searching for responsibility and accountability among public officers just after the destruction. But these feelings dissipated with time and a return to "normality" was soon felt again. Arguably, the coupled natural events hit an ill-prepared country still navigating democratic consolidation through radically implemented political reforms.

If disasters occur when natural triggers meet physical—but also social, cultural and political—vulnerabilities (as vulnerability theory suggests), the opposite effect can potentially also occur. Societies and communities can develop capacities that allow them to avoid, cope with or mitigate the effects of natural hazards. This is precisely what the concept of resilience suggests. According to resilience theory, communities can develop adaptive capacities that allow them to avoid and/or withstand a disaster or to recover and re-establish themselves after a disruptive event.[10] The metaphor of resilience works relatively well in theory. However, as seductive as the concept may be, there is still insufficient hard evidence to explain how communities or societies become resilient.

I had the privilege of recently working with a group of researchers (including Andrés Olivera, Lisa Bornstein, Arturo Valladares, Kevin Gould and Jennifer Duyne Barenstein) who explored, and subsequently published on, a particularly interesting case of resilience in Cuba, a small Caribbean country with a long-lasting communist government.[11] Reporting this case just after I presented the negative effects of neoliberal policies in Latin America might seem like an ideologically charged argument in favour of socialism; but, it is not. Instead, I hope that exploring two significantly different political contexts will shed light onto some of the structural issues that are at stake in the relationships between housing and disasters.

Resilience: How Do Communities Avoid Disaster, Adapt and Cope?

Like many other Caribbean countries, Cuba is frequently hit by meteorological events and seismic activity. Its successful risk mitigation strategies have become so widely known[12] that it is often said that when tropical storms and hurricanes travel through the Caribbean on their way to the United States, they kill hundreds of people in Haiti, affect dozens in the Dominican Republic, cause huge economic losses in Florida but kill or injure almost nobody in Cuba. This perception is largely backed up by data. PreventionWeb, a database supported by the United Nations International Strategy for Disaster Reduction, reports that 57 hazards caused 200 deaths between 1980 and 2010 in Cuba, while during the same period, 59 events caused 15,838 deaths in Honduras, and 118 events killed 27,943 people in Colombia.[13]

The renowned Scottish geographer Neil Smith[14] once pointed out that Cuba defies common expectations about vulnerability to disasters. He explained that we tend to believe that "the poorer a country or community, the more vulnerable it is to the loss of life associated with disaster"; but, he contended, "this nostrum of disaster researchers is turned on its head by Cuba" (p. 780).[15] Why? Resilience in Cuba is attained through a series of actions and programs that simultaneously depend on, and feed, a well-coordinated network of organizations capable of developing both preventive and reactive measures at the local, municipal, regional and national levels.

Let's consider prevention. Key elements of the model are the adequate use of land, the appropriate location of settlements, the construction of resistant structures and the enforcement of building regulations, tasks that are conducted by the Physical Planning Institute, typically in coordination with the Cuban Institute of Meteorology. Generally, priority is given to safety over economic development. The Civil Defence (with branches at the national, provincial and municipal levels) collaborates with local governments and civil society organizations to implement risk mitigation plans.

Let's examine now disaster reaction. The National Direction Centres for Disasters direct and implement disaster response in coordination with the Cuban Institute of Meteorology. Together they are responsible for an efficient early warning system, which is trusted by the population. Governmental units at all levels, from national to municipal, train regularly in disaster simulations under *Meteoro*, a local disaster response program. The National Housing Institute, the Civil Defence and the Ministry of the Economy share other responsibilities for providing assistance to the population when disasters occur.

Innovation in Institutions: Arquitectos de la comunidad

Prevention also relies on a very particular stakeholder: the Community Architect Offices (*Arquitectos de la comunidad*), a unique Cuban institution that emulates the role that traditional community doctors play in health care systems but in the field of housing.[16] These offices are the result of an ambitious program initiated in 1994 to support self-help housing construction (see Figure 7.3). A Community Architect Office acts as a consultant within a neighbourhood or settlement. According to Arturo Valladares, a researcher at McGill University, these offices generate valuable interactions between architects and households to help residents "articulate their spatial needs and help them make informed decisions about the building processes they are about to undertake" (p. 19).[17] Working closely with households, these offices provide technical guidance to self-builders, and contribute to implement best practices and disaster-safe structures, over time, creating a more resilient housing stock.

FIGURE 7.3 Community Architect Offices (like the one pictured here in Sagua) contribute to create a resilient built environment in Cuba, providing guidance and support to households in the community.

Undoubtedly, Cuban Civil Society organizations, such as the Federation of Cuban Women and the Revolutionary Defence Committees, are closely linked to political action. But they play a key role in risk mitigation activities too. For instance, the Revolutionary Defence Committees contribute to identifying buildings that are particularly vulnerable as well as those that can act as disaster shelters. Provincial and Municipal Assemblies of People's Power constantly collaborate with the Civil Defence to implement risk mitigation plans. These organizations meet regularly to discuss local issues and, while doing so, develop intense social networks and bonds within the community, as well as social capacities to respond to disaster situations.[18]

Other relevant assets include accurate information and communication about meteorological activity,[19] proper coordination at all levels of government[20] and trust between authorities and the civil society.[21] Information campaigns and citizen participation rely on a strong human and social capital. Some figures illustrate the extent of this capital: an average Cuban spends ten years at school, free of charge. Over 16% of the workforce has university education, and over 53% has the equivalent of a high school certificate. A widespread network of clinics and universal "free-of-charge" access to health care has facilitated high life expectancy (76 years for men and 80 years for women),[22] and has kept childbirth mortality rates at about 43 per 100,000 (all labours in Cuba benefit from medical attention).

Despite all its merits, the system still has room for improvement, as the rather surprising devastation caused by Hurricane Sandy recently demonstrated. Challenges include a large stock of old, insufficiently maintained and weak buildings and infrastructure. Increased participation from civil society and municipalities in planning and action is, arguably, still required. Furthermore, the country has an increasingly aging population. Whereas the nation is adopting a more open economy that accepts private business, structural policies have already produced positive results in terms of resilience. Investment in rural areas has prevented massive and rapid rural–urban migration (particularly when compared to other Latin American countries). The government has heavily invested in education—risk mitigation is, for instance, a subject of study in the education system. Is has also put resources and efforts into developing locally appropriate construction technologies and components in partnership with local universities. From an organizational standpoint, these successes are largely based on the interdependent networking between institutions, in which organizations act locally and in close relation with households, while depending on a centralized and coordinated structure.

Beyond Shelter

The Cuban case shows that resilience results not only from access to shelter but also additional factors such as construction industry development, systemic urban and regional planning, early alerts and evacuation plans. Despite this, there is a tendency in most contexts to associate post-disaster reconstruction and vulnerability reduction to mere shelter construction. In fact, major disasters in developing countries are almost always followed by a plethora of architects, engineers and designers proposing the latest, fastest, cheapest, lightest and strongest solution for shelters. I presume that almost all these professionals are well intended, but most of their solutions largely overlook the complexity of the housing problem, and tend to focus almost exclusively on the technical aspects of construction. Most of their solutions are quickly forgotten (fortunately, given the extreme oversimplification of variables such as capacity building, education and information, and their focus on immediate sheltering over mid- and long-term solutions), and only a few reach the level of prototype development. However, building shelters is one of the most visible ways for agencies, NGOs and governments to show that resources from donors are being invested,[23] and thus, some of these solutions are in fact built. This, naturally, leads us to ask: are emergency shelters always needed after a disaster? There is a paradoxical answer to this question (a "yes and no" answer). As we shall now see, some type of transitional housing solution is often needed, but whereas some temporary solutions do help resume daily activities, others have significant (long-term) unintended consequences.

Temporary Housing: Dear Architect—What Can You Do for $50?

Permanent housing reconstruction is most often subject to the same challenges faced by regular housing construction. As such, it frequently takes a long time, notably due to slow procedures to obtain financing, land and permits, and to lay down infrastructure, finalize contracts and transfer titles. Living with family members or friends for a long period of time is not an option to all disaster-affected households, and thus transitional

FIGURE 7.4 Hundreds of tents and temporary units were quickly installed in the Champ de Mars and other public spaces of Port-au-Prince after the 2010 earthquake. Authorities have faced numerous obstacles to remove these shelters and reclaim public spaces.

modes of shelter are sometimes required in order to resume domestic and income-generation activities as quickly as possible. Common solutions include emergency sheltering (for instance, plastic tarps) and temporary sheltering, such as the provisional use of facilities as collective shelters. It can also include the temporary use of tents, such as the ones installed in Champ de Mars and public squares in Port-au-Prince after the 2010 earthquake in Haiti (see Figure 7.4).

Transitional solutions can also include the use of rudimentary shelters built with local materials that can be dismantled. Consider the case of the over 100 camps of temporary units that were built by affected households and contractors in the city of Armenia after the 1999 earthquake in Colombia (see Figure 7.5). The camps included a total of 6,300 rudimentary temporary units made of wood and corrugated metal sheets. Despite the large number of units, all of them were dismantled after a couple of years, due to the efficient work of an unlikely stakeholder: The National University of Bogotá. This organization efficiently managed the camps and the transfer of residents to permanent housing.[24]

However, temporary solutions also include more controversial outputs such as high-tech temporary units, ready-made shelters, transportable houses, industrialized housing solutions and other post-disaster creations that are—most often than not—associated with at least six negative consequences.

First, they typically become permanent. One of the recurrent and most regrettable outcomes of temporary units is that they are difficult to dismantle, notably in urban

FIGURE 7.5 Rudimentary temporary units built in Armenia, Colombia,, after the 1999 earthquake. These units were all dismantled a couple of years after the disaster.

areas where "regular" housing deficits are already high and where there are logistical, legal and operational difficulties to evict residents. Given that they often lack standard infrastructure and community services, the not-actually-temporary camps are typically seen as new slums. A practitioner who worked in the post-disaster reconstruction in Armenia, Colombia, once told me that ideally, temporary housing units should be made out of cotton candy, so they can "melt" after the reconstruction process is over. Thus, they would leave neither permanent scars on the city nor the politically sensitive difficulties of vacating and dismantling the units.[25] A similar effect can also occur in rural areas. The temporary units that were installed by the local NGO FUNDASAL in the rural region of La Paz after the 2001 earthquakes became permanent (see Figure 7.6). In many cases, even when permanent solutions were given to residents, they preferred to keep the temporary units (see Figure 7.7).

Second, temporary camps facilitate urban sprawl. Cassidy Johnson, a lecturer at University College London, has judiciously reported the long-term effects of temporary shelters in Turkish cities. She reports that the majority of the 47,000 prefabricated temporary units provided by the government after the 1999 earthquake in Turkey became permanent, perpetually increasing the footprint of cities and settlements.[26]

Third, temporary solutions divert resources that could otherwise be used on permanent solutions. Building temporary housing is a pragmatic way of showing that efforts are being deployed without necessarily overcoming all the barriers that building permanent housing faces. Besides, acting in the emergency phases (just after the disaster) allows organizations to show donors that their financial contributions are being invested to alleviate the shock caused by the disaster and to respond to the pressure of media and commentators who typically want fast results on the ground.

FIGURE 7.6 Temporary housing solutions were built by the local NGO FUNDASAL in rural areas of El Salvador after the 2001 earthquakes. However, most of these units became permanent and were used by residents as an extension of their units.

FIGURE 7.7 Pressed to act quickly after the disaster, FUNDASAL, a local NGO, built thousands of temporary and permanent units (like these ones) in the region of La Paz, El Salvador. However, no sewerage solution was implemented.

Unsurprisingly, there is a disproportionate amount of resources devoted to "Band-Aid solutions" that do not necessarily produce structural resilience in the long run.[27]

Fourth, they are too expensive when compared to producing permanent solutions. I am often surprised to notice the number of professionals and construction companies that repetitively (and rather seriously) propose the use of ready-made shelters made of containers that "only" cost US$4,000 each (and can be transported by using "just one" helicopter!), or high-tech insulated tensile structures "affordable for only US$10,000 each," Lego-style prefab units that can allegedly be built in just four days and for "just" US$15,000, and other post-disaster fantasy solutions. Most of these inventions miss two main points:

- The cost of construction materials is only a fraction of the overall budget required for housing development. Other important costs include land acquisition and preparation, infrastructure development, connection to public services, labour, legal procedures, administrative activities, etc. Frenetic inventors of post-disaster housing rarely have a convincing plan for dealing with these aspects of the housing equation.
- In many developing countries, one can buy local construction materials (even after a disaster, when prices have increased due to exceeded demand) to build a full permanent house for the amount of money that most temporary, prefab, industrialized and imported units cost.

Considering the disproportionate solutions that some housing inventors propose after disasters, Graham Saunders, the head of the Shelter and Settlement Department of the International Federation of Red Cross and Red Crescent Societies[28] once asked architects what type of solution they could produce for US$50. The figure was not arbitrary, he explained. It corresponds to the actual resources that are devoted by his institution for individual post-disaster sheltering solutions. Graham's challenge should motivate architects and design professionals to explore innovative—but also real—strategies.

Fifth, they are generally offered too late, when permanent reconstruction has already begun. The construction phase is not actually the phase that significantly delays reconstruction processes. It is the phases before construction (when negotiations, financing, legalization, land development, infrastructure, obtaining permits and contracts are conducted) that usually take a long time. After the Haitian disaster in 2010, for instance, several Canadian construction companies promised that they could produce, ship and install prefab units in Haiti in two to three weeks. They overlooked, however, the fact that clearing customs in Haiti after the disaster was an activity that, alone, could take several weeks. The promise was just unrealistic. Similar experiences have occurred in many other contexts. Mahmood Fayazi, an Iranian researcher associated with my research group, reveals that close to 1,400 high-tech units, imported from Turkey, Japan and South Korea, were installed in the outskirts of the city of Bam, Iran, after the 2003 earthquake. However, these units arrived about 15 months after the earthquake, when temporary shelters were no longer needed and reconstruction activities had been largely conducted.[29] These units also became permanent.

Sixth, they deviate resources away from local organizations and builders. By investing in imported or high-tech solutions, resources are transferred to companies that seldom reinvest in local subcontractors, manufacturers or suppliers. In this way, financial resources obtained for reconstruction end up having a small effect on the local economy, and thus on the recovery of affected families and businesses.

Permanent Housing Reconstruction

Every reconstruction project is different. However, the analysis of recent housing reconstruction projects in developing countries suggests that common mistakes are constantly repeated in different contexts, often leading to another disaster. There are common contingency factors that influence the approaches adopted by local and national governments, and by local and international NGOs involved in low-cost housing development. Let's consider now some of these factors.

Relocation

Local, regional and national authorities often face heavy pressure to respond quickly and alleviate the housing needs of affected families. However, as we saw in Chapter 4, one of the most difficult challenges in housing provision concerns the availability of—and capacity to use—land. Thus, pressure typically leads public organizations and NGOs to favour the development of low-cost housing projects in areas that are far from services and infrastructure. One of the reasons is that previous locations are perceived to be too dangerous for residential use, and thus it is often believed that affected residents are better off relocated to "safe" locations. Other reasons include the fact that land is usually scarce and expensive when in close proximity to services, infrastructure, transportation and jobs. Likewise, it is often less expensive in less desirable locations on the periphery of cities and towns. Additionally, organizations tend to favour the search for economies of scale, which leads to prioritizing the development of large pieces of land instead of the development of dispersed projects in small plots.

However, relocation to remote areas, such as the one implemented in Nueva Choluteca (see Chapter 4), often causes major negative effects on the social structures that are required for income-generation, recovery and development of low-income families.[30] Relocated families typically lose social connections and the proximity to friends and services, which constitute the social structure through which they can have access to credit, child care, services and affordable transportation, security, labour, recreation, etc. Too often, unemployment rates increase, public services are insufficient or too expensive for both beneficiaries and municipalities, maintenance costs are unsustainable and commercial activities do not succeed easily. Furthermore, projects developed on the periphery of cities, and poorly integrated with the urban fabric and public transportation, are usually at risk of being "ghettoized" and stigmatized. It is therefore not surprising that relocation is often considered one of the most important causes of users' dissatisfaction in reconstruction projects.[31]

The Bulldozer Strategy

Both governmental and non-governmental organizations typically tackle post-disaster housing deficits by developing a process that brings a considerable amount of responsibility into the hands of one entity (and few people) that collect and use the available information. In this process, decisions are often made based on limited information collected by one or a few organizations. The natural response is, most often, to design a unique housing model that responds to needs assessed with the very limited information available to organizations.[32] Once this model unit is designed, organizations proceed to demolish affected units and to repeat the unit in order to offer it to as many beneficiaries and affected families as resources will allow. However, this approach overlooks two important elements. First, it overlooks the fact that the needs and expectations of affected families vary significantly (they have different sizes, resources, obligations, etc.). Thus, residents sometimes dislike the housing units provided—to the point that many of them do not even occupy them. Second, in many cases, houses are not fully destroyed by the disaster. Several construction components that are still useful (think of toilets, sinks, kitchen counters, and others) are not reused in the new projects, wasting resources in the process.

Avoiding the Informal Sector

Very often, the informal sector resumes construction very quickly after the disaster—faster than formal companies and agencies. This was clearly exemplified in the recent disaster in Haiti. While high-tech temporary units were still clearing customs and governmental units and humanitarian agencies were solving administrative barriers, informal builders and suppliers started rebuilding affected houses in most of Port-au-Prince's slums. The unfortunate consequence of this is that substandard construction practices implemented by informal builders and companies before the disaster (for instance, insufficient reinforcement in concrete structures, inappropriate construction joints or inadequate foundations in structures) are often replicated after the disaster, perpetuating the physical vulnerabilities that led to the destruction in the first place.

This should not be the case. A disaster (though very unfortunate) is a prime opportunity for implementing training programs and educating informal builders on disaster-resistant standards and best practices. In other words, a disaster provides an opportunity to make informal builders aware of the importance of appropriate construction techniques. It is also an opportunity to provide them with financial solutions and with training in managerial and financial skills that can eventually help them integrate the formal sector. In this way, the disaster can not only become an opportunity to reduce physical vulnerabilities in the built environment, but also can reduce the less visible vulnerabilities of informal workers and companies (notably the vulnerabilities that do not allow them to embrace formality). However, this strategy implies that the informal sector be recognized as an agent of change and action in the construction process, something that almost never occurs. Two reasons explain (but do not justify) why the informal sector is significantly ignored in post-disaster action.

The first is related to corruption. Project initiators—notably central authorities, regional governments and municipalities—often transfer large reconstruction contracts to a reduced number of companies and organizations. Sometimes they do it for partisan reasons and because of favouritism, benefitting lobbyist and companies that support political parties. Sometimes they do it for the opposite reason: to seek to minimize the risks of corruption and mismanagement. Several examples in this book have shown that housing provision implies significant financial risks and is often affected by high levels

FIGURE 7.8 Part of the problem or part of the solution? Concrete blocks produced by informal companies in Delmas lie in a temporary camp after the 2010 earthquake in Haiti. Informal construction is repeatedly accused of causing disasters; yet it can be part of the solution for reconstruction.

of corruption,[33] political pressure and legal constraints. It is therefore not surprising that organizations sometimes resort to hiring companies that they consider "reliable." In both cases, this concentration of investments in just a few contracts reinforces the centralization of decision-making. Investments rarely benefit local companies, informal workers and businesses, missing the opportunity of accelerating the recovery of the local economy.

The second reason is that informal practices—more specifically, the substandard quality of structures built by the informal sector and the location of informal housing units in disaster-prone locations—are often accused of causing the disaster in the first place. The manager of a Canadian construction company willing to enter the reconstruction "business" in Haiti claimed in 2010 that the technology developed by his own company should immediately be used to replace the concrete block technology largely used in housing in Haiti (see Figure 7.8). "These concrete blocks are killing people," he shouted in an international conference in Montreal, waving an example of the hollow, grey blocks that informal manufacturers produce in Port-au-Prince. His argument, however, fails to acknowledge that if it weren't for the informal construction sector, millions of Haitians would have died long before the 2010 earthquake. It falsely accords blame to the informal construction sector for causing the disaster. Disasters are caused by the accumulation of physical, social, economic and political vulnerabilities. Indeed, concrete block producers and other informal entrepreneurs are a crucial part of the solution for housing deficits before, during and after disasters.

Implications for Rethinking and Designing Low-Cost Housing in Developing Countries

Despite the obvious differences between project contexts, there are common patterns in the strategies adopted by public and private organizations that intervene in post-disaster situations. Unfortunately, several of these patterns also correspond to characteristics that are associated with reduced project performance. However, these characteristics (or mistakes) can be avoided if some strategic and tactical decisions are made. Central governments can contribute to improving housing strategies by regulating the participation of NGOs in reconstruction and development, by creating financial mechanisms that allow for a decentralization of investment, and by promoting participatory programs and subsidized programs based on owner-driven procurement and/or cooperative housing (see Chapter 10). Municipalities can contribute by enforcing construction codes, regulating land titles and facilitating processes so that land can be developed for low-cost housing construction in areas close to services, infrastructure and jobs. Finally, (private) local and international NGOs can contribute by adopting participatory approaches (notably owner-driven or cooperative mechanisms when appropriate), by delegating decision-making to individual families and social groups, by involving informal labour and informal construction companies, by avoiding closed construction systems based on industrialized components and, finally, by guaranteeing that housing projects include infrastructure, services and the appropriate conditions for developing income-generation activities.

Unreliable governance, political fragmentation, partisan interests and administrative inefficiency are the major barriers for the adoption of these strategies. Together, these barriers exacerbate, rather than reduce, vulnerabilities. However, previous experiences remind us that these strategies are indispensable for the built environment's long-term sustainability and for the prosperity of the local population. Low-cost housing can play a crucial role in moving communities from a state of vulnerability to a state of resilience. However, this implies the consideration of housing as a process that goes beyond the mere provision of shelters and implies considering the full implications of "freedom of choice." Let's now consider the extent of this particular argument.

Notes

1 Blaikie, P.M., T. Cannoon, I. Davis and B. Wisner. *At Risk: Natural Hazards, People's Vulnerability, and Disasters.* New York: Routledge, 1994; Hewitt, K. *Regions of Risk: A Geographical Introduction to Disasters.* Harlow: Longman, 1997.
2 Ibid.
3 Wisner, B. "Risk and the Neoliberal State: Why Post-Mitch Lessons Didn't Reduce El Salvador's Earthquake Losses." *Disasters* 25, no. 3 (2001): 251–68; Lungo, M. and S. Baires. "Socio-Spatial Segregation and Urban Land Regulation in Latin American Cities." Paper presented at the International Seminar on Segregation in the City (Cambridge, MA, USA, 2001); Lungo, M. and R. Martel. "Ciudadanía social y violencia en las ciudades centroamericanas." *Realidad: Revista de Ciencias Sociales y Humanidades*, no. 94 (2003): 485–510.
4 Wisner, "Risk and the Neoliberal State: Why Post-Mitch Lessons Didn't Reduce El Salvador's Earthquake Losses."
5 Ibid.
6 Ibid.

7 Lizarralde, G. "The Challenge of Low-Cost Housing for Disaster Prevention in Small Municipalities." In *4th International i-Rec Conference 2008. Building resilience: achieving effective post-disaster reconstruction*, edited by i-Rec, Electronic publication. Christchurch, New Zealand: i-Rec, 2008.

8 Lizarralde, G. "Organisational System and Performance of Post-Disaster Reconstruction Projects." Ph.D. Thesis, Université de Montréal, 2004.

9 CEPRODE. *Caracterización de los desastres en El Salvador: tipología y vulnerabilidad socioeconómica*. San Salvador: CEPRODE, 1994.

10 Alexander, D.E. "Resilience and Disaster Risk Reduction: An Etymological Journey." *Natural Hazards and Earth System Sciences Discussions* 1 (2013): 1257–84; Manyena, S.B. "The Concept of Resilience Revisited." *Disasters* 30, no. 4 (2006): 434–50; Martin-Breen, P. and J.M. Anderies. "Resilience: A Litterature Review." Rockefeller Foundation, 2011; Norris, F.H., S.P. Stevens, B. Pfefferbaum, K.F. Wyche and R.L. Pfefferbaum. "Community Resilience as a Metaphor, Theory, Set of Capacities, and Strategy for Disaster Readiness." *American Journal of Community Psychology* 41, no. 1 (2008): 127–50.

11 Lizarralde, G., A. Valladares, A. Olivera, L. Bornstein, K. Gould and J.D. Barenstein. "Towards Strategic Resilience: The Cuban Model to Vulnerability Reduction and Reconstruction." *Disasters*. In press (2013).

12 Medicc. *In the Eye of the Storm: Lesson in Disaster Management from Cuba*. Decatour, GA: Medicc, 2005; Sims, H. and K. Vogelmann. "Popular Movilization and Disaster Management in Cuba." *Public Administration and Development* 22, no. 1 (2002): 398–400; Thompson, M. and I. Gaviria. *Weathering the Storm: Lessons in Risk Reduction from Cuba*. Boston: Oxfam, 2004; Rodriguez, C.M. and A.L. Perez. "Componentes de la gestión del riesgo en la prevención de desastres naturales: caso Cuba." In *Jornadas Iberoamericanas sobre el hábitat, vulnerabilidad y desastres*. Santa Cruz de la Sierra, Bolivia: Centro de formación de la cooperación Española, 2004.

13 UNISDR. "Preventionweb." UNISDR, http://www.preventionweb.net.

14 Smith, N. "Disastrous Accumulation." *South Atlantic Quarterly* 106, no. 4 (2007): 769–87.

15 Ibid.

16 Valladares, A. "The Community Architect Program: Implementing Participation-in-Design to Improve Housing Conditions in Cuba." *Habitat International* 38 (2013): 18–24.

17 Ibid.

18 Thompson and Gaviria, *Weathering the Storm: Lessons in Risk Reduction from Cuba*.

19 Gaeta-Carrillo, N. "La incursión de la comunicación en la prevención de desastres: el caso Cubano." In *I Congreso de Salud y Desastres*. Cuba: La Habana, 2011.

20 Sims and Vogelmann, "Popular Movilization and Disaster Management in Cuba."

21 Olivera, A., G. Gonzalez and A. Rodriguez. "Cuba. Por una buena gestion publica municipal en la reducción del riesgo y la recuperación post-desastre." In *Prevención y respuesta a desastres: estudios de caso*, edited by Foro Iberoamericano y del caribe sobre mejores practicas. Rio de Janeiro: ONU Habitat, 2012.

22 Mesa, G. "The Cuban Health Sector and Disaster Mitigation." *MEDICC Review* 10, no. 3 (2008): 5–8.

23 Johnson, C. and G. Lizarralde. "Post-Disaster Housing and Reconstruction." *The International Encyclopedia of Housing and Home*, Elsevier Ltd, 2010. MS number 46 (2010).

24 Lizarralde, G., C. Johnson, and C. Davidson. "Houses of Candied Sugar: Comparative Research on Controversial Temporary Housing after Earthquake Disasters in Colombia and Turkey." Paper presented at the Proceedings from the International Association for Housing Science 31st World Congress on Housing Process and Product, Montreal, Canada, June 23–27 2003.

25 Ibid.

26 Johnson, C. "Impacts of Prefabricated Temporary Housing after Disasters: 1999 Earthquakes in Turkey." *Habitat International* 31, no. 1 (2007): 36–52.

27 Lizarralde, G. "Mythes et réalités de la reconstruction à la suite de désastres." *Revue ARQ N0. 144*, 2008, 8–11; Lizarralde, G., C. Davidson and C. Johnson, eds. *Rebuilding after Disasters: From Emergency to Sustainability*. London: Taylor & Francis, 2009.

28 IFRC. "World Disasters Report 2004." New York: International Federation of Red Cross and Red Crescent Societes, 2004.

29 Fayazi, M. and G. Lizarralde. "The Role of Low-Cost Housing in the Path from Vulnerability to Resilience." *International Journal of Architectural Research*, 2013.

30 Barenstein, J.D., P.M. Phelps, D. Pittet and S. Sena. *Safer Homes, Stronger Communities: A Handbook for Reconstruction after Natural Disasters*. Washington: World Bank, 2010; Lizarralde, Davidson and Johnson, *Rebuilding after Disasters: From Emergency to Sustainability*; Oliver-Smith, A. "Successes and Failures in Post-Disaster Resettlement." *Disasters* 15, no. 1 (1991): 12–23.

31 Bouraoui, D. and G. Lizarralde. "Centralized Decision Making, Users' Participation and Satisfaction in Post-Disaster Reconstruction: The Case of Tunisia." *International Journal of Disaster Resilience in the Built Environment* 4, no. 2 (2013): 145–67.

32 Lizarralde, G. "Project Management and Democracy: Owner Driven Reconstruction in Rural Colombia." Paper presented at the Owner Driven Reconstruction Conference, London, 2009.

33 Murray, M. and M.R. Meghji. "Corruption within International Engineering-Construction Projects." In *Corporate Social Responsibility in the Construction Industry*, edited by M. Murray and A. Dainty, 141–64. New York: Taylor & Francis, 2009; Lewis, J. "The Worm in the Bud: Corruption, Construction and Catastrophe." In *Hazards and the Built Environment*, edited by L. Bosher, 238–63. New York: Routledge, 2008.

8

INVISIBLE FREEDOMS

On an Ethical Position Towards Housing in Developing Countries

> Cities also believe they are the work of the mind or of chance, but neither the one nor the other suffices to hold up their walls. You take delight not in a city's seven or seventy wonders, but in the answer it gives to a question of yours.
>
> *Invisible Cities,* Italo Calvino (p. 38)

A Coffee Break in Rural Colombia

Making ends meet from farming is difficult in most developing countries—as thousands of Colombian rural peasants who make a living from coffee production very well know. Things can only get worse when disaster strikes. And a disaster did affect Colombian coffee workers in 1999 when an earthquake hit one of the more productive agricultural regions in the country. When the earthquake occurred, peasants were vulnerable for many reasons other than just poverty. They had poor access to banking services and health care. The State was rarely present in rural areas, which were instead largely controlled by drug dealers, guerrilla and paramilitary groups. They were also historically marginalized and excluded. Unsurprisingly, the earthquake's impact on housing was enormous: 1,856 rural houses were destroyed and 4,552 were damaged. More than 1,000 buildings used for coffee production in mostly family-based micro-businesses collapsed, and more than 2,000 were partially damaged, eventually leading to losses in the productive sector equivalent to 4.2% of the regional GDP.

Despite these catastrophic damages, coffee growers also exhibited great strengths. To begin with, most of them were landowners. They also had construction skills and organizational capacities for developing their own businesses. For years, they had organized coffee production, marketing and exports through the *Federación Nacional de Cafeteros de Colombia*, a countrywide network of coffee growers organizations (CGOs). The CGOs operate as a rural guild and tight network of cooperatives with influence at the national, regional and local levels.

In response to the disaster, the national government prepared an ambitious reconstruction program and, almost simultaneously, created FOREC (Fondo para la

Reconstrucción del Eje Cafetero), a body mandated to manage the resources available for reconstruction and outsourcing specific housing and infrastructure projects. FOREC was also funded by the World Bank and the Inter-American Development Bank, private donations, resources from the National Budget and new national taxes. The destruction in urban centres such as Pereira, Armenia and dozens of small municipalities was significant, and it soon became clear that procurement could not be handled by one single organization. Instead, FOREC anticipated a first level of decentralization for project operations. FOREC put out a call for proposals, and selected 32 NGOs responsible for executing reconstruction projects in specific urban sectors. By delegating the work to various NGOs, the fund aimed not only at distributing the work and resources among organizations that could best handle them, but also at reducing bureaucracy, guaranteeing transparency in the decision-making process, reinforcing democratic organization and consolidating opportunities for social participation.

Rural reconstruction was delegated to the CGOs. It was a reasonable choice; the organization was deeply concerned and committed to help affected residents in the region; it had its own resources to invest in rural recovery; it also had support and credibility from the community. Furthermore, it had distributed infrastructure throughout rural areas (including a comprehensive database of coffee growers) and a strong administrative and financial capacity to deal with peasants' needs and expectations.

Enhancing Households' Freedoms

Despite their good intentions, the CGOs had neither the personnel nor the knowledge to directly design, plan and build thousands of houses and infrastructure projects. In response, the CGOs adopted a second level of decentralization and opted for an alternative strategy in which they could focus on managing the funds and controlling the quality of construction work. The work was to be undertaken by, or for, households. Instead of providing complete and fully finished houses and infrastructure, the strategy relied on owner-driven procurement. Each affected family was eligible for a subsidy, and households were responsible for making their own decisions about the construction they wanted. Individuals (and their families) enjoyed five types of individual freedom:[1]

1 *Freedom in project-scope definition:* Affected families were invited to apply for the subsidy by proposing one or various reconstruction projects. But these did not have to be exclusively housing projects. Instead, households could choose the type of project they required or wanted. Initiatives included the reconstruction of *beneficiaderos* (a coffee-processing infrastructure), repairs to existing structures, the reconstruction of a damaged house, the demolition and construction of a new house, the construction or repair of septic tanks, stores, workshops and spaces for developing agriculture production (see Figure 8.1).

2 *Freedom in financial management of individual projects:* For a housing project, households had the opportunity to match a US$4,000 subsidy given by the CGOs with a US$1,000 government loan. For infrastructure and production-related structures they could match a US$2,000 subsidy with an extra loan of US$3,000. They also had the freedom to complement these resources with a loan given by the CGOs (amounts varied according to credit capacity), private credit and savings.

FIGURE 8.1   Coffee growers proposed different types of individual projects to the CGOs. Using the subsidies and loans offered by the CGOs reconstruction program, this rural resident (left) repaired the kitchen (right top and bottom) and rebuilt the septic tank of his house.

3   *Freedom in project design:* In order to apply for funding, households were required to present a photograph of the affected structure or infrastructure and to propose a basic design (a simple plan or drawing), which many of them presented on the back of an envelope or scrap paper. If they wanted, they could also hire their own

FIGURE 8.2 Beneficiaries of the CGOs program worked through self-help or hired formal and informal construction companies. Above, a house rebuilt just a few months after the disaster.

engineers or architects. The CGOs appointed a group of structural engineers responsible for receiving the designs, checking the compliance with disaster-resistant standards, and approving them or proposing modifications. Engineers completed, in many cases, the submitted information with structural details and construction specifications.

4 *Freedom in project procurement:* Beneficiaries of the program could also decide their own procurement approach. They could opt to build by themselves, to hire formal or informal construction firms (in a turnkey contract or in several contracts) or to hire labour alone.

5 *Freedom in project construction:* The projects proposed by beneficiaries could be built in any material or technology. It must be noted that the disaster attracted several construction companies and non-profit organizations to the region. Consequently, there were multiple housing products (using a variety of technologies) and programs simultaneously offered to affected residents. Beneficiaries of the CGOs project enjoyed the freedom to repair their houses or build new ones with any of the different choices available (see Figure 8.2).

Concerned about possible speculation in the price of construction materials and indiscriminate use of wood, the CGOs organized a parallel program to promote appropriate technologies and the use of prefabricated components. While doing so, the CGOs opted for a third level of decentralization. Architects hired by the CGOs designed three different prototypes of one-story units largely inspired by vernacular typologies used in the area. Then, the CGOs put together a call for proposals aimed at selecting the most suitable prefab companies (some were NGOs engaged in housing construction). Companies were selected according to certain parameters that included the quality of the construction system, price, production capacity, respect of natural

FIGURE 8.3 Prefabricated houses were presented in the housing exhibition organized by the CGOs. Even though few finished houses were actually sold, the exhibition had other positive effects on the reconstruction process.

resources, socio-cultural acceptability of the technology proposed and scope for the use of local labour force.[2] Given that the government offered tax incentives to businesses operating in the disaster-affected area, the construction companies chosen offered competitive prices. The CGOs built an exhibition area where residents could visit all the prototypes chosen and directly contact the construction companies to finalize a purchase (see Figure 8.3).

The results of this program were mixed. In reality, very few fully finished prefab units were sold. However, the program had an unexpected positive result. Thousands of residents attended the exhibition and purchased construction components (windows, doors, tiles, etc.) directly from the prefab companies in order to construct their own personalized units. In this way, the exhibition became a source of inspiration and information for hundreds of households who could copy the models, or certain construction details, and build them by themselves. The program also succeeded in limiting speculation in construction materials and in avoiding massive deforestation practices.

Freedom Comes with Responsibility

In this process, all beneficiaries were responsible for their own initiatives. There were, however, mechanisms to control the quality of the outcomes and to accompany local residents through their own decision-making process. A financial institution verified the eligibility of households; notably that residents did live in the area, that they were house or landowners and that they had indeed been affected by the disaster. The team of engineers of the CGOs then reviewed all individual projects proposed by the beneficiaries. They specifically validated whether the projects conformed with disaster-resistant principles and with the ecological and environmental principles that were at the core of the CGOs' mission. These standards included responsible use of wood, measures to reduce water pollution and a norm that obliged the construction of a sewage system in all units provided with sanitary services (to prevent soil pollution). After clearance, residents were given a first instalment with which they had to accomplish significant progress on their own project before the second evaluation (about 25% of the work had to be complete). The engineers inspected the projects before authorizing the second instalment, which had to correspond with significant advancement in the work (typically 50% of the project). This process of inspection and approval was repeated as many as four times until total completion of the work.

In order to guarantee that resources were used according to the priorities of the program (local reconstruction and development), subsidies and loans were given under promissory notes bound to a time limit requirement. If construction activities were not complete within the specified time and with the specified standards, beneficiaries had to pay back the amounts.

The program responded not only to the "hard" (or physical) needs of local residents (shelter, money, food, etc.), but also to "soft" and process-related factors such as social organization, education, information, employment opportunities and economic reactivation. Two construction manuals were printed and distributed among peasants: one explained best practices in the use of *guadua*, a type of bamboo, and the other concerned best practices in masonry construction. Several messages about disaster awareness and disaster-resistant standards were frequently broadcasted on television and radio. Information about available resources, construction best practices and other practical solutions was periodically published in printed media. Furthermore, a counselling program was offered to survivors.

"Hard" results included 9,800 rural houses rebuilt (including almost 2,000 units for non-coffee growers), 4,700 structures for coffee production and 2,131 individual infrastructure projects for agricultural production, sewage, water and electricity. Some families conducted more than one project; for example, some of them rebuilt the house and built a road, or repaired a sewage system and built a *beneficiadero*, or repaired the house and the septic tank (see Figure 8.4). It is estimated that about 10,000 direct and indirect jobs were created in the region. Nonetheless, the best indicator of performance was to be perceived on January 17, 2004, when an earthquake of magnitude 5.2 on the Richter scale hit the region again. This time no deaths, destruction or physical damages occurred, suggesting that vulnerabilities among rural residents were significantly reduced.[3]

Making Sense of Owner-Driven Approaches in Housing

The CGOs project illustrates several merits of owner-driven approaches to housing construction—and reconstruction. Similar approaches based on a transfer of decision-making power to households have recently captured significant attention among scholars and practitioners. For instance, owner-driven approaches to housing construction and reconstruction have been successfully applied on a large scale in Gujarat, India, in the last decade[4] (see Figure 8.5). Furthermore, interest in adopting these approaches in the context of post-disaster housing reconstruction led to an

FIGURE 8.4 Beneficiaries of the CGOs program enjoyed the freedom to choose the type of project they wanted, and needed, to build. Here a *beneficiadero* rebuilt just a few months after the disaster.

FIGURE 8.5 Owner-driven approaches have been successfully implemented in Gujarat, India, in the last decade. Here, a unit rebuilt within the owner-driven reconstruction program launched by the Gujarat Government after the 2001 earthquake.

international conference in the UK and the subsequent publication in 2009 of the book *Building Back Better: Delivering People-Centred Housing Reconstruction at Scale*.[5] Supported by successful examples of owner-driven or freedom-based projects conducted in Sri Lanka, Pakistan, India, El Salvador and Peru, among others, the conference and book argued for a significant increase in decision-making power among households. This enthusiasm for owner-driven approaches is hardly surprising. I have argued throughout this book—and the CGOs project demonstrates this as well—that the best way for dealing with the complexity of housing development is to decentralize decision-making power. This means that more people (notably households) must have the capacity to make decisions regarding the conditions in which they want to live. This approach leads us, inevitably, to consider individual freedoms to make decisions, and relevant ways to increase these freedoms.[6]

Housing and Freedom

To be clear, the linkages between housing and freedom are hardly new. Back in the 1970s, John Turner stressed the importance of recognizing freedom of action by households.[7] In their crucial publication *Freedom to Build: Dweller Control of the Housing Process*, Turner and co-editor Robert Fichter argued that "households should be free to choose their own housing, to build or direct its construction if they wish, and to use and manage it in their own ways" (p. 154).[8] "Fulfilment," in Turner and Fichter's reasoning, depends on "personal responsibility for making decisions that shape one's own life" (p. 153).[9] In his many influential publications, Turner saw housing as much more than just a commodity. In his accounts on freedom, he argued housing should be seen not for what it *is*, but for what is *does* (or can potentially *do*) for households.

At that time, Turner was concerned with making a case for a stronger role for households against significantly centralized governmental initiatives that rarely included active roles for the poor.[10] Alexandre Apsan Freidani, a researcher at University College London, notes that freedom in Turner's approach focused on what is called the "negative aspect of liberty." It was concerned, he argues, with "absence of impediments and freedom from something" (p. 6).[11] Turner was in fact concerned with freedom from centralized and mass-produced authoritarian initiatives.

Turner's message, however, was manipulated. Distorting his original defence of the marginalised and excluded, neoliberals incorporated his approach into their policies, finding in Turner's work an argument for reducing the government's influence on market-oriented housing. But the freedom discourse had more to offer. Partly in response to the inequalities resulting from market-oriented and neoliberal policies, a more sophisticated case for individual freedom in development (and, indirectly, poverty alleviation) emerged: The Capability Approach. Largely elaborated on by Amartya Sen, an economist and Nobel laureate, the Capability Approach became more recently an influential theory of social justice.

Sen's theory, based on a multi-faceted and comprehensive consideration of the role of individual liberty, is probably one of the most influential recent contributions to social studies. Some observers claim that it has also become one of the most important recent contributions to human rights[12] and to economic theory at large.[13] The approach has attracted fervent followers, to the point that a kind of capability "cult" has emerged in some academic circles (journal special issues, for instance, have celebrated Amartya Sen's birthday,[14] and conferences are devoted to studying his legacy in various fields). The enthusiasm for Sen's work is understandable. The Capability Approach constitutes a new normative framework that suggests a more nuanced and sophisticated way of assessing a nation's development level.[15] It rejects narrower views of development focused on certain metrics that have become largely contested by social scientists and a group of economists. These contested metrics include the growth of gross national product (GNP), rise of income, industrialization, technological advances, social modernization and increased access to material means.

Sen's theory is also a response to John Rawls' approach to justice.[16] Rawls, an American political philosopher, saw justice (notably distributive justice) as a result of an abstract social contract in which freedom of choice played a significant role. Michael Sandel, another American political philosopher and a Harvard professor, notes that much like Immanuel Kant had done almost 200 years earlier, Rawls adopted a liberal conception of justice in which people are seen as "free, independent selves, capable of choosing their ends for themselves" (p. 242).[17] However, Sen's book, *The Idea of Justice*, went even further, putting individual freedom of choice at the very heart of the concepts of justice and fair development; this, in a contemporary world in which poverty among billions contrasts with the disproportionate wealth of just a few. This new way of understanding justice eventually developed into a way of assessing deprivation and judging and approaching development interventions, policy and human rights.

The Capability Approach defines development in terms of a "process of expanding the real freedoms that people enjoy" (p. 3).[18] It emphasizes the importance of choice but also the *process* of freedom to choose. Thus, in this new version of social justice, expansion of freedoms becomes both a primary end and the principal means of development. "Commodities are analysed," according to Frediani's reading of Sen, "by what they do to people's lives and not by what they are" (p. 2).[19] Capabilities serve to assess the overall advantages of people.[20] They are, according to Sen, "the substantive freedoms that [an individual] enjoys to lead the kind of life he or she has the reason to value" (p. 87).[21] In this way, the approach shifts the focus from the *means* of living to the actual *opportunities* a person enjoys.[22] Capabilities become "attainable outcomes," which are the result of "environmental opportunities and a person's abilities" (p. 350).[23]

Much like in a Kantian account of ethics, freedom to choose and act upon self-imposed objectives has a crucial importance in the Capability Approach. Freedom, from this perspective, makes individuals accountable for the choices they make and their outcomes. But capabilities are not just final outcomes. Instead, the approach considers individual advantages in four "spaces." The first two, well-being achievement and well-being freedom, correspond to the individual's attainable life alternatives.[24] The other two, agency achievement and agency freedom, account for the futures attainable by the individual. In Sen's perspective of freedom, an agent is someone "who acts and brings about change, and whose achievements can be judged in terms of her own values and objectives, whether or not we assess them in terms of some external criteria as well" (p. 19).[25] Agency here is related to "one's ability to pursue goals that one values."[26] By considering agency, the Capability Approach emphasizes that the agent's action and the *process* of choosing and decision-making are just as important as the choices themselves.

The Capability Approach: Beyond Community Participation

From a conceptual lens, how much do individual decision-making, freedoms and agency in low-cost housing in developing countries matter? A lot, I believe. Let's consider the most significant reasons. First, a freedom-based approach provides a poverty-sensitive filter to observe urban dynamics, revealing different advantages and disadvantages between urbanities. Frediani, for instance, considers that the Capability Approach in urban development avoids a "dualistic perception of cities (formal and informal, included and excluded) to one based on freedoms, interactions, multiplicity and diversity" (p. 139).[27]

Second, it permits bridging the conceptual gap between housing processes and outputs. The Capability Approach, believes Frediani, "incorporates an examination of the physical attributes of the product output of design as well as processes affecting its use and appropriation by individuals and groups" (p. 204).[28] He contends that—unlike Turner's approach to freedom—Sen's approach goes beyond the elimination of barriers to encompassing choice, ability and opportunity. Looking at housing through this lens requires, therefore, that we consider not only a household's *opportunity* to make decisions but also that they have effective *choices* to make (alternatives to choose from) and the *ability* to make these choices.[29]

Third, the Capability Approach helps us make sense of the success of housing projects that are based on an increase of a household's decision-making capacity (such as the CGOs project presented earlier). In this way, it provides a conceptual lens for understanding the merits and challenges of owner-driven approaches. Furthermore, it proposes a new language that is capable of bridging otherwise fragmented knowledge about vulnerabilities, resilience, freedoms and values.

Fourth, an approach to housing from the freedom perspective provides an accurate way of assessing development objectives by broadening the scope of considerations required to assess people's needs and expectations. In this way, it facilitates an assessment of a person's living standards *before, during* and *after* housing interventions.[30]

Fifth, adopting the Capability Approach as proposed by Sen (but also by other authors such as Nussbaum[31]) contributes to understanding the role of housing in creating social justice by connecting housing interventions with an unavoidable ethical engagement with human rights.

The following advantage of a freedom-based approach is a bit more controversial, so I will try to put it in subtle terms. A freedom perspective helps us understand strategies, human narratives and social behaviours that are difficult to explain through the alternative, widespread paradigm of community participation alone. The community participation paradigm, widely adopted in the fields of human development, urban policy, city management, post-disaster reconstruction and housing, has undoubtedly provided a significant contribution to the involvement of end-users in project development. However, it has also proven to be ineffective in provoking structural improvements to the way projects are created by actors in free markets, by governmental institutions and by development and humanitarian non-profit organizations.

There are external and internal factors that explain this. Some limits to the community participation approach can be explained by factors that are external to the paradigm. Its essential language (communities, participation, empowerment, capacities, etc.) has been hijacked and abused by all sorts of organizations to the point where it is difficult to extract meaningful moral stances and values from it. Its essential constructs (learning by doing, empowerment through participation, capacities to participate, etc.) have also been so widely used to represent so many different things that they hardly mean anything significant anymore.

To clarify, there is nothing new in rhetorical but meaningless uses of the term "community participation." Writing in 1969 about citizen involvement in planning in the United States, Sherry R. Arnstein identified a scale of community participation that she used to condemn morally dubious practices that she defined with distinctive terms: tokenism, therapy, manipulation, etc.[32] Almost 30 years later, Marissa Guaraldo Choguill, a researcher at the University of Sheffield, adapted Arnstein's ladder to the context of developing countries. Much like Arnstein had done before, Guaraldo Choguill found that *empowerment, partnership* and *conciliation* become effective supporting strategies for participation, whereas *dissimulation, diplomacy* and *informing* are common manipulation practices in participatory approaches (she even finds two lower rungs in the ladder, one of which she calls *conspiracy).*

Other limits of the paradigm can be linked to the way in which its own proponents have reasoned about communities and participation.[33] Defenders of community participation (including most international NGOs) often outshine each other, claiming more and more participation by communities. Alas, they rarely question the real definition or composition of communities, the type of participation that is required in specific contexts, the effective impacts of community-based participation in long-term sustainability or urban development and the unexpected negative social effects of this participation.[34] Besides, they have neither condemned the abuses of its core principles nor that it be used to legitimize contentious interests and dubious decisions. Alicia Sliwinski, an anthropologist and professor at Wilfrid Laurier University, reminds us that under the label of "participatory development," community participation has become an *official development policy*. But, she argues:

> After some two decades of experimentation in a variety of contexts, many would agree that participation has, in turn, become almost a dogma, a belief or an act of faith that has not delivered on its promises and that it requires a profound and thorough re-examination.
>
> (p. 179)[35]

This does not mean that we should abandon the principles of the community participation paradigm or that a freedom-based approach should ignore the objective of community participation (in fact, I will later address participation of social groups from the perspective of stakeholder governance). Instead, it means that the freedom-based approach can fill in the gaps of the community-based perspective, which, after numerous abuses, has increasing difficulty in maintaining a theoretical relevance in contemporary debates.

Advantages of Increased Individual Freedom

Now that we have seen the theoretical strength of the approach, let's return to empirical evidence that demonstrates the practical advantages of increasing individual freedoms in low-cost housing projects in developing countries. This empirical evidence relies on cases presented in earlier chapters in general, and three sources in particular: the CGOs project, the Juan Pablo II project introduced in Chapter 6, and previous studies on owner-driven approaches conducted by researchers Jennifer Duyne Barenstein[36] and Michal Lyons.[37]

Increased freedoms provide operational advantages that eventually translate to increased well-being and more liveable environments. An increase in households' freedoms helps to deal with the difficult challenge of acquiring and computing available and dynamic information. We have seen in previous chapters how difficult it is to identify and assess the necessary conditions for achieving economic recovery, well-being and long-term development. These variables—and the information required to consider them—are highly dynamic. Most frequently, organizations tackle this challenge by concentrating decision-making power into the hands of one entity (typically a small group of "experts") that collects, interprets and makes use of the little and incomplete information that is available. In previous publications, I have called this a centralized approach or a "concentrated decision-making process,"[38] and have denounced it in favour of decentralized, individually-driven or owner-driven approaches.[39] As previous chapters in this book have demonstrated, the centralized approach often leads to the definition of *a* housing model that is then rubber-stamped and given to as many beneficiaries as possible (for economies of scale) in distant, subserviced land. Given the lack of information, organizations typically seek to consult residents and beneficiaries about their needs and expectations—often after the land and financial mechanisms have already been decided. But the participative approaches based on consultation, and not necessarily engagement (typically inspired by the community participation paradigm), are rarely successful. Let's examine the most important causes of this.

1   *Reduced scope of decision-making:* Community participation programs tend to focus on sweat equity and self-help construction. Quite often, households are required—in exchange for minimum wages or economic compensation—to carry sand bags, mix mortar, lay bricks, clean construction sites and paint houses. However, these households typically have limited decision-making power over solutions that significantly affect their lives, such as the location of sites, the financial mechanisms to be implemented, the possibility of using the resources on something other than housing, the development of home-based businesses, the capacity to make changes and extensions to their units and the possibility to recycle construction components.[40] In many cases, households are consulted about projects that are already fully designed or considerably defined, and thus their capacity to make decisions over planning, financing, design and logistics is rather limited. Not infrequently, residents are manipulated in order to approve—and thus legitimize— solutions over which they have had very little input.[41]

2   *Unexpected outcomes:* Previous studies have shown that participatory approaches may lead to unexpected outcomes[42] such as:
    • Limited integration of economic activities due to a disproportionate emphasis on residential solutions at the community level rather than on livelihood development at the family level.
    • Low density, due to a strong emphasis on self-help construction and use of unskilled labour.

- Urban fragmentation, due to a disproportionate focus on the requirements and desires of "the community" (sometimes arbitrarily defined) to the detriment of its integration within the city.
- Limited variety and choices offered to households due to the imperative to build standardized (often identical) solutions and to achieve "equity" in the distribution of resources among members of the community.

3 *Difficulties to represent a variety of interests:* By focusing on community participation, organizations frequently fail to recognize that urbanites belong simultaneously not to one, but to multiple communities that can be assembled around faith, ethnicity, labour organizations, recreational activities, political beliefs, unions, etc. By assuming that a "community" is a homogeneous group, participatory approaches tend to misrepresent the multiplicity of interests and needs that exist among urbanities. Besides, participation approaches frequently rely on "community leaders," who are identified, appointed or provided with a "legitimate voice" on the basis of their fit with the project agenda, a political ideology, a religious belief or economic interests. Yet, they do not always represent the variety of perspectives, requirements and desires that exist among complex urban social groups.

4 *Difficulties to identify attainable objectives:* Low-income urbanities often belong to historically marginalized groups deprived of rights, a political voice and public attention. When consulted in participatory meetings, households do not always find it easy to articulate the scope of their expectations and needs. To make things worse, consultation processes rarely succeed in making residents aware of the long-term consequences (in terms of costs, maintenance and logistics) of some immediate desires and in calculating the trade-offs that result from some choices in density, housing types, construction technology, etc. When this occurs, consultation processes lead to an increase of expectations that cannot be attained by low-cost projects, exacerbating in this way households' frustration with—and disbelief in—institutions.

These patterns should not lead one to underestimate the capacity of the poor to understand their built environment; quite the opposite. My argument is that—contrary to community consultations that occur in the form of a limited number of rather abstract and discursive meetings—households interact with their own environment through consecutive choices and calculations made over long periods of time, within both formal and informal networks. Through direct and constant interaction with human agents and non-human contingencies, households capture and compute information about their needs and expectations and identify, assess and accept the trade-offs that result from their selection of options. However, these narratives are rarely captured in premeditated consultations aimed at identifying needs and expectations. Abstract group discussions in which eloquence is mandatory, and rhetoric is a source of power, do not always permit households to identify adaptive solutions, to exploit the best opportunities, to assess available resources and to mobilize local knowledge. Engagement, time, tests, trial-and-error practices, sharing experiences with other individuals and first-hand involvement do.

Freedom in project procurement, financing and construction gives households the possibility of capitalizing on their own informal networks to obtain materials, labour force and credit. In this way, they are able to reduce costs, personalize their projects, optimize resources and respond to their own needs, expectations and priorities while also promoting the local economy. Take the case of subsidies and loans offered in the CGOs project and in Juan Pablo II. In both cases, financial contributions were lower than the value required to purchase a finished unit in the market. Still, many families were able to rebuild and repair their units—or to extend them in the case of Juan Pablo II. Several reasons explain this success.

First, residents optimized the use of resources by recycling materials. Even when their original units had to be demolished after the disaster, coffee growers recovered useful components such as doors, windows, toilets, sinks, etc. Second, responsibility for the use of resources stimulated residents to search for the best available prices on the market. Conscious about the use of funding, households optimized their constructions by creating flexible spaces that had more than one use. Following a pattern frequently found in informal settlements, residents built units that combined domestic and income-generation activities (living rooms, for instance, were also a workshop or storage space for a home-based business). Third, many residents did not use one single technology or housing model. They instead combined different construction techniques and materials according to their construction skills, the availability of materials, the speed of construction suitable for each technology, and price. Fourth, houses were built in phases, prioritizing immediate needs and postponing certain upgrades and improvements. Finally, being aware of construction costs, many residents who had construction skills worked through self-help. Aging residents and some women, however, opted for hiring labour or having relatives or friends help with the construction. In the CGOs reconstruction project, all the constructions were disaster resistant and responded to individual needs, tastes and priorities. In the Juan Pablo II project, households designed, planned and managed their own incremental projects and assumed responsibility for extensions.

Housing projects are often subject to important risks, such as households not accepting the solutions that are proposed, the refusal to adopt innovative technologies and solutions, the over- or under-estimation of people's needs, corruption in municipal and regional and national governments, construction delays and cost overruns. Contrary to concentrated approaches, which restrict decision-making to a reduced number of participants, owner-driven approaches distribute responsibilities—and therefore some of these risks—among public and private stakeholders (including, of course, end-users and participants from the informal sector).

Given that increased levels of customization can be achieved through direct responsibility for individual projects (rather than through a list of requirements), freedom-based approaches permit progressive adaptation to individual needs, opportunities and expectations. Growing and upgrading of the units, for instance, can be conducted at the residents' own pace and according to the availability of resources. Finally, by focusing on the *opportunity* to make decisions, on guaranteeing that there are effective *choices* for households, and that they have (or develop) effective *abilities* to make these choices, projects can transcend a materially-based view of housing to encompass what housing represents to people.

The Limits of a Freedom-Based Approach

At this point you are probably wondering, is an individual-freedom approach enough to create sustainable, rich, resilient and functional living environments and to rectify social injustices? Fervent defenders of the Capability Approach seem to believe it is. They attempt to make sense of social improvements through the combined lenses of decision-making, freedom and agency. They defend the approach and argue that any criticism results from a poor reading of Sen and Nussbaum's work. However, the principle of "when what you have is a hammer, everything looks like a nail" seems to apply here. Considering how defenders use the approach to explain desirable improvements in almost all social dimensions, I argue that they go to unnecessary lengths; it is wiser to accept the limits of the approach than to force it to explain all ethical concerns. So, let's now consider some limitations to the approach.

Approaches to freedom in housing—as proposed by Turner—have been criticized by social scientists such as Rod Burgess,[43] who see them as a way to exacerbate exclusion, inequality and market dysfunctions. Critics note that transferring responsibility for housing to the most vulnerable does not tackle the real causes of poverty, segregation and lack of political representation and public voice. They argue that instead of dealing with the structural causes of housing shortages, freedom-based approaches use households to advance the disengagement of the State, thereby exacerbating the drawbacks of neoliberal policies.

Similarly, the Capability Approach has also attracted particular criticism about its form and content. The arguments exposed by Amartya Sen to explain the causes of famine (a central subject in his book *Development as Freedom*) have been questioned on methodological and conceptual grounds.[44] Other analysts, including Flavio Comim, a lecturer at Cambridge University, have argued that it is unclear how the Capability Approach can be "operationalized" (his term).[45] Comim and his colleagues reason that "understood as an evaluative framework," the Capability Approach is "a limited structure" (p. 30).[46] Critics also sustain that the capability concept concerns attainable opportunities represented by what could happen in the future, leaving time unspecified. According to Des Gasper, a professor at the International Institute of Social Studies in The Hague, the concept lacks an explicit time-dimension; notably because well-being freedom refers to an agent's life, and agency freedom refers to the rest of history.[47] Finally, Ingrid Robeyns, a professor in Practical Philosophy at Erasmus University Rotterdam, has also claimed that the Capability Approach is radically underspecified and could be accused of reinventing the wheel.[48]

Most critics, nonetheless, seem to be unwilling to reject the approach. Reasoning about its advantages and disadvantages, Comim and colleagues conclude that it must be considered as a work in progress. Des Gasper contends that—in reality—the approach contains multiple features that have been explored differently by different authors. He therefore claims that there are Capability *Approaches* rather than *a* Capability Approach.[49] Finally, Robeyns reckons that it is a valid contribution to social and economic sciences particularly because it "opens a truly interdisciplinary space in the study of well-being, inequality, justice and public policies" (electronic document).[50] But, let's leave the common criticism about its lack of definition behind for a while. Ultimately, this is a setback that can be fixed with more reflection on (and notably *within*) the approach.

Let's focus on three (probably the most significant) arguments against a freedom-based approach to low-cost housing, development and justice.

Moral Individualism

The first fundamental criticism has to do with its emphasis on individual action. By highlighting individual choice over anything else, the approach is often seen as "individualistic." Charles Gore, an officer at the United Nations Conference on Trade and Development, elaborates on this argument and condemns the "moral individualism" of Sen's approach. He notes that within the Capability Approach, "the goodness or badness of social arrangements or states of affairs is evaluated on the basis of what is good or bad *for* individual well-being and freedom and is also reduced to the good *of* those individuals" (p. 242).[51] He clarifies that moral individualism consists of giving little importance to institutions, principles and systems of value which are the property of the society and not of individuals, namely "social goods" that include systems of moral norms, modes of discourse and language and modes of government.[52] Critics of the Capability Approach believe that this individualism can deteriorate the community bonds that exist (or are desirable) in many informal settlements.[53]

Fragmented Value

The second argument challenges the notion that individual freedoms alone can naturally lead to the creation of collective value. The argument recognizes that collective services, public space and infrastructure cannot be efficiently built and run from the addition of disconnected individual interventions (see Chapter 6). They require collective decision-making, coordinated planning and agreement. If individuals have increased freedom to choose the way they design and build their own housing solutions, what guarantees that the sum of individual choices creates appropriate, coherent and efficient settlements and communities? Finally, if each family plans, designs and builds according to its own expectations and needs, the addition of these solutions can create a disparate group of solutions that—due to lack of coherence, continuity and efficiency—threaten the quality of life and living conditions of all.

Defenders of the Capability Approach have rejected these two arguments, claiming that individuals make decisions for many more reasons than just self-interest; and, thus, they do reason in their own decision-making process about collective well-being. However, these defenders have hardly explained why individual reasoning about collective well-being is better than collective reasoning and open, engaged debates.

Moral Disengagement

The third argument can be inferred from a contemporary philosophical criticism of a perspective of justice that is based on neutrally arbitrating individual desires and needs. It could be deduced from a Capability Approach to development, or from Turner's view of housing as freedom, that decision- and policy-makers' assessment of freedoms should be morally neutral. In these approaches, it should not be their responsibility to judge or sanction the choices that people make. Some interpretations of the Capability

Approach may suggest that the role of designers and other decision-makers in housing development is not to prioritize one choice over another. If anything, their role must be to give voice to all needs and expectations and—when needed—arbitrate discussions in which stakeholders discuss all positions and ideas with the same relevance. Following this line of thought, the professional's role should be morally neutral, much like a referee of diverging and dissimilar choices. Only in this way, it could be argued, can decision-makers fully respect the rights of all, embrace contemporary urban pluralism, guarantee tolerance in the face of disagreement and avoid imposing a way of living that does not correspond to households' view of "the good life."[54] Morally neutral architects or urban planners would conceal their own moral values. This would protect households from culturally alienated ways of living and dangerous changes in their customs, practices and ways of occupying the space.

Undoubtedly, a prudent approach to preventing cultural alienation, inadequate uses of private, collective and public space and the imposition of foreign practices (based, for instance, on Western standards or misconceptions created by urban elites) is unavoidable. However, some contemporary philosophers, including Michael Sandel and Alasdair C. MacIntyre, remind us that when it comes to issues of social justice, it is not wise to pretend that we can make a neutral reading of freedoms. "The attempt to detach arguments about justice and rights from arguments about the good life is," according to Sandel, "mistaken for two reasons: First, it is not always possible to decide questions of justice and rights without resolving substantive moral questions; and second, even when it's possible, it may not be desirable" (p. 251).[55] Sandel rejects the moral detachment typically associated with liberal accounts of justice and argues that "deciding important public questions while pretending to a neutrality that cannot be achieved is a recipe for backlash and resentment" (p. 243).[56] "A politics emptied of substantive moral engagement," he believes, creates "an impoverished civic life" in which citizens do not sufficiently debate on important values and desirable common goals (p. 243).[57]

Implications for Rethinking and Designing Low-Cost Housing in Developing Countries

The Capability Approach appeared as a sophisticated way to assess people's living conditions and well-being. This, in a moment in which neoliberal policies had hijacked and distorted the "housing as freedom" discourse promoted by self-help defenders, and had prescribed a disengagement of the State. Housing interventions, therefore, have the responsibility for creating capabilities *during* the project, and guaranteeing that people will enjoy capabilities in their living environments *after* the project. Projects can apply various types of individual freedom at various stages of the project: freedom in project-scope definition, financial management, project design, procurement and construction. During the project, freedom-based approaches can deal more easily with the problem of unavailability of information than centralized approaches. They can also help the distribution of risks among stakeholders and the reduction of costs. They also transfer higher levels of responsibility to users who therefore become accountable for their own decisions. Freedom-based approaches increase user satisfaction with the project and increase its performance. But a freedom-based approach can transcend the scale of the project. The second responsibility implies considering a wider time-scale that goes beyond the consideration of immediate benefits to embracing long-term capabilities.

Capabilities are not created when people are left alone to make their own decisions (when they are just given *opportunity*). They are created when people have, or are given, *choices* and when they have *abilities* to make these decisions and act upon them. Let's consider the first condition, that of guaranteeing that choices are available. Institutions need to act in coordination with informal systems in order to increase the choices that are available to the most vulnerable. Let's now consider the implications of the second condition, which requires that end-users have the abilities to make decisions and act upon them. Institutions need to support residents with education and technical assistance in the process of decision-making; including, for instance, help and guidance on legal and administrative procedures. This also implies recognizing informal frameworks and scenarios that allow individuals to make choices in direct interaction with the built and natural environments. Freedom to choose also requires important support in information and education. Households require access to data and knowledge in order to make informed decisions. They also require the support given by formal and informal legal frameworks and formal and informal institutions.

The freedom-based approach also has some limits, including the insufficient moral engagement identified by Sandel. Sandel does not refer to housing in particular. But, if we accept that housing is a political process (I do), then Sandel's view of moral engagement applies to decisions about what is "just" and "right" in housing planning and design. Housing development cannot simply account for a morally neutral arbitration of needs and desires. In particular because housing is more than a human right—it is an expression of collective values and modes of living—and thus, it is a subject of public debate in which moral views may play a crucial role. But this reasoning in turn creates a dilemma. As we saw in previous sections of this chapter, biased visions of how people should live and the manipulation of consultations and participatory processes have resulted in dangerous outcomes for housing. How does one incorporate morally charged representations of housing among decision- and policy-makers without imposing or prescribing specific visions of how the poor should live?

In order to answer this question and to make sense of collective reasoning about value, we have to rely on a different body of knowledge, one that is more closely related to business administration and project management than to development and urban policy. We shall see in the next chapter how stakeholder theory can help us complete a freedom-based approach to low-cost housing.

Notes

1 Lizarralde, G. "Decentralizing (Re)Construcion: Agriculture Cooperatives as a Vehicle for Reconstruction in Colombia." In *Building Back Better: Delivering People-Centered Housing Reconstruction at Scale*, edited by M. Lyons and T. Schilderman, 191–214. London: Practical Action, 2010.
2 Ibid.
3 Lizarralde, G. "Organisational System and Performance of Post-Disaster Reconstruction Projects." Ph.D. Thesis, Université de Montréal, 2004.
4 Barenstein, J.D. "Housing Reconstruction in Post-Earthquake Gujarat: A Comparative Analysis." In *Humanitarian Practice Network Paper*. London: Overseas Development Institute,

2006; Jha, A.K., J.D. Barenstein, P.M. Phelps, D. Pittet and S. Sena. *Handbook for Post-Disaster Housing and Community Reconstruction*. Washington: The World Bank, 2009.

5   Lyons, M., T. Schilderman, T. and C. Boano. *Building Back Better. Delivering People-Centred Housing Reconstruction at Scale*. Rugby, UK: Practical Action Publishing, 2010.

6   Lizarralde, G. and M.M. Raynaud. "The Capability Approach in Housing Development and Reconstruction." In *Post Earthquake Reconstruction: Lessons Learnt and Way Forward*. Ahmedabad, India: Government of Gujarat, 2011.

7   Frediani, A.A. "Amartya Sen, the World Bank, and the Redress of Urban Poverty: A Brazilian Case Study." *Journal of Human Development* 8, no. 1 (2007): 133–52.

8   Turner, J.F.C. and R. Fichter. *Freedom to Build: Dweller Control of the Housing Process*. New York: Macmillan, 1972.

9   Ibid.

10   Turner, J.F.C. *Housing by People: Towards Autonomy in Building Environments*. New York: Pantheon Books, 1977.

11   Frediani, A.A. "The World Bank, Turner and Sen—Freedom in the Urban Arena." *DPU Working Papers*, no. 136 (2009). Developmemnt Planning Unit, University College London.

12   Nussbaum, M. "Human Rights and Human Capabilities." *Harvard Human Rights Journal* 20 (2007): 21–22.

13   Brighouse, H. and I. Robeyns. *Measuring Justice: Primary Goods and Capabilities*. Cambridge University Press, 2010.

14   Anand, P. "New Directions in the Economics of Welfare: Special Issue Celebrating Nobel Laureate Amartya Sen's 75th Birthday." *Journal of Public Economics* 95, no. 3–4 (2011): 191–92.

15   Nussbaum, "Human Rights and Human Capabilities."

16   Brighouse and Robeyns, *Measuring Justice: Primary Goods and Capabilities*.

17   Sandel, M.J. *Justice: What's the Right Thing to Do?* London: Penguin, 2010.

18   Sen, A. *Development as Freedom*. New York: Anchor Books, 1999.

19   Frediani, "The World Bank, Turner and Sen—Freedom in the Urban Arena."

20   Sen, A. *The Idea of Justice*. Cambridge: Belknap Press, 2009.

21   Sen, *Development as Freedom*.

22   Sen, *The Idea of Justice*.

23   Gasper, D. "What is the Capability Approach? Its Core, Rationale, Partners and Dangers." *Journal of Socio-Economics* 36, no. 3 (2007): 335–59.

24   Ibid.

25   Sen, *Development as Freedom*.

26   Alkire, S. "Why the Capability Approach?" *Journal of Human Development* 6, no. 1 (2005): 115–35.

27   Frediani, "Amartya Sen, the World Bank, and the Redress of Urban Poverty."

28   Frediani, A.A. and C. Boano. "Processes for Just Products: The Capability Space of Participatory Design." In *The Capability Approach, Technology and Design*, 203–22. Springer, 2012.

29   Frediani, A.A. "Planning for Freedoms: The Contribution of Sen's Capability Approach to Development Practice." *UCL Discovery* (2008), http://www.discovery.ucl.ac.uk.

30   Sen, *Development as Freedom*; Sen, *The Idea of Justice*.

31   Nussbaum, "Human Rights and Human Capabilities."

32   Arnstein, S.R. "A Ladder of Citizen Participation." *Journal of the American Planning Association* 35, no. 4 (1969): 216–24.

33   Emmett, T. "Beyond Community Participation? Alternative Routes to Civil Engagement and Development in South Africa." *Development Southern Africa* 17, no. 4 (2000): 501–18.

34   Sliwinski, A. "The Politics of Participation: Involving Communities in Post-Disaster Reconstruction." In *Rebuilding after Disasters: From Emergency to Suistainability*, edited by G. Lizarralde, C. Davidson and C. Johnson, 188–207. London: Taylor & Francis, 2010.

35   Ibid.

36   Barenstein, "Housing Reconstruction in Post-Earthquake Gujarat: A Comparative Analysis"; Jha et al., *Handbook for Post-Disaster Housing and Community Reconstruction*.

37   Lyons, M. "Building Back Better: The Large-Scale Impact of Small-Scale Approaches to Reconstruction." *World Development* 37, no. 2 (2009): 385–98.

38   Lizarralde, G., C. Davidson and C. Johnson, eds. *Rebuilding after Disasters: From Emergency to Sustainability*. London: Taylor & Francis, 2009.

39 Lizarralde, "Decentralizing (Re)Construcion: Agriculture Cooperatives as a Vehicle for Reconstruction in Colombia."

40 Guaraldo Choguill, M.B. "A Ladder of Community Participation for Underdeveloped Countries." *Habitat International* 20, no. 3 (1996): 431–44.

41 Sliwinski, "The Politics of Participation: Involving Communities in Post-Disaster Reconstruction."

42 Lizarralde, G. and M. Massyn. "Unexpected Negative Outcomes of Community Participation in Low-Cost Housing Projects in South Africa." *Habitat International* 32, no. 1 (2008): 1–14.

43 Burgess, R. "Self-Help Housing: A New Imperialist Strategy? A Critique of the Turner School." *Antipode* 9, no. 2 (1977): 50–59.

44 Bowbrick, P. "The Causes of Famine: A Refutation of Professor Sen's Theory." *Food Policy* 11, no. 2 (1986): 105–24.

45 Comim, F. "Operationalizing Sen's Capability Approach." Paper presented at the Justice and Poverty: Examining Sen's Capability Approach, Cambridge, 2001.

46 Comim, F., M. Qizilbash and S. Alkire. *The Capability Approach: Concepts, Measures and Applications*. Cambridge University Press, 2008.

47 Gasper, D. "What Is the Capability Approach?: Its Core, Rationale, Partners and Dangers." *Journal of Socio-Economics* 36, no. 3 (2007): 335–59.

48 Robeyns, I. "The Capability Approach in Practice." *Journal of Political Philosophy* 14, no. 3 (2006): 351–76.

49 Ibid.

50 Ibid.

51 Gore, C. "Irreducibly Social Goods and the Informational Basis of Amartya Sen's Capability Approach." *Journal of International Development* 9, no. 2 (1997): 235–50.

52 Ibid.

53 Frediani, "The World Bank, Turner and Sen—Freedom in the Urban Arena."

54 Sandel, *Justice: What's the Right Thing to Do?*

55 Ibid.

56 Ibid.

57 Ibid.

9

INVISIBLE POWER

On Who Does What, When and How—
a New Framework for Understanding
Low-Cost Housing in Developing Countries

> Cities, like dreams, are made of desires and fears, even if the thread of their discourse is secret, their rules are absurd, their perspectives deceitful, and everything conceals something else.
>
> *Invisible Cities,* Italo Calvino (p. 38)

The Port-au-Prince Republic

"*L'anarchie totale*" (total anarchy) is the way many Haitians describe downtown Port-au-Prince. Street vendors occupy the roads while cars often drive on the sidewalks, tap-taps (Haitian colourful buses) stop anywhere, open sewers overflow and stink, the heavy traffic seems to impede any movement whatsoever and heavy trucks zigzag through residential areas, narrowly avoiding the children walking and playing in the street. Driving through the streets of central Port-au-Prince, it is easy to get the impression that the city has suffered from years of a total lack of planning. Yet, that is not strictly true. In the last few years, there have been several urban plans for the central districts of the capital city. A comprehensive master plan was contracted by the national government to a Canadian architecture and urban planning office. A second, rather futuristic, plan was contracted by a former mayor to a local planning practice. A third one (visibly inspired by new urbanism) was supported by The Prince's Foundation for Building Community (previously called The Prince Charles Foundation for the Built Environment) and designed by a Miami-based firm. Other plans exist for the southern district of Martissant and the eastern district of Delmas. Most of the ideas put together in these ambitious, beautification master plans seem significantly disconnected from local realities. However, it has become clear that the problem is not actually about lack of design.

There are other causes of this perceived "anarchy." A rather obvious cause is that master plans do not get built due to lack of resources (they typically over-estimate donors' help and local credit capacity). But another significant reason lies in a deeper analysis of the situation. Neither the plans, nor the stakeholders that propose or design them, interact with each other; this is hardly an isolated case. Lack of collaboration between NGOs, municipalities, ministries, international agencies, donors, credit institutions and other stakeholders is one of the principal reasons for insufficiently coherent urban development in Haiti and many other developing countries. Foreign observers often believe that lack of collaboration in Haiti can be solved by more intense communication between stakeholders (bringing them together in a series of meetings will help align strategies, agendas, plans and projects, they believe). The same observers quickly learn, however, that the problem is more complicated than that. Political tensions and personal quarrels make it virtually impossible to put most of the principal Port-au-Prince urban stakeholders in the same room. Coordination between the capital and peripheral districts is also difficult. The mayors of surrounding districts complain that power is so concentrated in Port-au-Prince that the capital functions as a separate State that they dub "the Port-au-Prince Republic." Paradoxically, the capital and national administrations hardly collaborate with each other.

Creating human settlements is a collective endeavour. But, how can the complex relations that exist between stakeholders (in Haiti and other developing countries) be understood? And how can they be integrated in a way that creates liveable and sustainable human settlements?

A Stakeholders' Approach to Value

As we shall see, interaction is crucial in order to create collective value among heterogeneous stakeholders in the housing sector. This implies that stakeholders must find the appropriate structures and mechanisms to exchange their expectations and needs and make consensual decisions. But let's examine first why stakeholder theory is relevant when thinking about the development of the built environment. There are two fundamental reasons. To begin with, the built environment has a direct influence on the population at large and over the long term. It affects non-consenting stakeholders and residents who have not made decisions during policy, program and project definition and implementation.[1] Second, housing projects are initiatives of public interest in the sense that they bring together a variety of stakeholders with divergent claims and interests. Stakeholder theory provides us some insight about how to tackle these two realities.

First, most proponents of this theory, including American philosopher and business professor Edward Freeman, consider that project stakeholders include both people *acting on* the project and *being affected by* it.[2] Second, they recognize that project stakeholders in many fields (including housing construction) are brought together only temporarily. These stakeholders create temporary groups of specialized organizations, known as temporary multi-organizations or TMOs.[3] Third, stakeholder theory claims that, through their constant and dynamic interaction, stakeholders can both create value in the project and extract value from it. According to this approach, monetary and/or non-monetary value emerges when stakeholders' needs and/or expectations are fulfilled.

There are two consequences to this line of thought. The first one is that given the definition of stakeholders, there can be two types of interactions between them: collaboration (between stakeholders that typically plan and design the project) and participation (of stakeholders that can be potentially affected by the project). The second consequence is that stakeholders can assess the pertinence of choices based on the value (economic, cultural, environmental, organizational and other types) that is created by their interaction. This implies that architects, designers and other decision- and policy-makers can assess the legitimacy of choices (including their own) based on this perceived value.

I believe that we can adopt this logic only if we accept a rather demanding definition of value. First, value should not be seen in terms of commercial or material benefits alone. Building on the ideas of Peer Smets, John Turner and Capability Approach defenders, value should also be defined in terms of what solutions and outputs *mean to end-users* rather that what they *materially are*.[4] Second, different concepts of "what people value" need to be taken into account; this includes different representations of what can be considered just and right. (Philosophers would then argue that utilitarian, teleological and liberal conceptions of value must find a place; religious believers would embrace a variety of moral stands about "what is right to do.") Third, value needs to be assessed at different time scales: short, medium and long term. It must be acknowledged that most decisions imply trade-offs and that short-term benefits can offset long-term benefits, and vice-versa. Finally, value should not be seen as an intrinsic property of a certain choice. It must be seen as a quality that is perceived *by someone* within a certain context and time. This means that the larger the group of people who perceive this value, the more legitimate this choice becomes.

This interpretation leads us to complement the perspective of housing based on individual freedom with a perspective based on stakeholder relationships. This consideration of both individual and collective agency is not just a theoretical proposition. It can be supported by empirical evidence. Discussing the creation of collective infrastructure in Bogotá's *barrios*, or consolidated informal settlements, Hernández-García finds that "the development process of open space is led by the people, through individual and collective actions" (p. 162).[5] He explains: "The agency of individuals gradually gives way to the agency of groups" (p. 161).[6] Community-based institutions, such as *Juntas de acción popular* (Citizen Action Committees), capture individual initiatives and move them forward thanks to community support, negotiating ideas, decisions and resources with other stakeholders (notably municipalities and elected officers). A similar pattern is also found by Mauricio Hernández-Bonilla in the creation of public space in consolidated informal settlements (or *colonias populares)* in Xalapa, Mexico. He finds that originally fragmented and sporadic initiatives eventually benefit from the establishment of "social networks, alliances and partnerships" that bring them to the level of public debate and negotiation with formal institutions (p. 142).[7] Peter Kellett (a specialist on informal settlements) and Hernández-García observe the transformation of informal settlements in Mexico, Egypt, Thailand, Kenya, Mexico, Indonesia and India and reason that "space, both in the city and within buildings, is the place for social, economic, cultural and ideological relationships, and as such it is collectively produced and transformed" (p. 22).[8] They argue that urban space in developing countries is the result of "dynamic political forces and power relations which make evident the symbolic relationships between unevenly positioned actors and agents."[9]

Let's consider what the stakeholder and value approaches tell us about freedom. If we accept that value is created through the engagement (collaboration and participation) of heterogeneous stakeholders, then transferring freedom is not—and should not be taken as—disengagement with responsibility. Institutions, such as cooperatives, funding agencies, banks and public entities played an important role in the Juan Pablo II project and the CGOs reconstruction program that we examined in previous chapters. Their engagement (and not their detachment) was the key to success. Furthermore, their strong commitment to certain values (just distribution of resources, respect for the environment, respect for freedoms, etc.) played a fundamental role. These examples support the idea that decision-makers are responsible for creating the scenarios and project management mechanisms that can favour the emergence of collective value and individual capabilities. In other words, the value and stakeholder approaches lead us to consider governance.

The Rules of the Game

Housing projects are neither conducted nor commissioned by homogeneous or unified organizations. Instead, a number of stakeholders who participate in project commissioning and development (including community groups, financial institutions, end-users, financial partners, pressure groups, ministries, NGOs and municipalities) may have different and divergent interests that can positively or negatively influence the project. Mechanisms and project governance structures are required in these situations, where hierarchical structures that regulate top-down power relations between stakeholders do not necessarily exist. Largely developed in the field of political science, the concept of project governance helps make sense of situations in which heterogeneous actors must share decision-making responsibilities, even when they may have contradictory or diverging interests and expectations.[10] Even though project governance is defined differently in various fields, there is a general consensus that it corresponds to management systems and structures that provide the framework within which decisions are made at the level of policy, programs or projects.[11] Project governance is not a characteristic of the project itself, argues project management specialist, J.R. Turner. Rather, it is "the structure through which the objectives of the project are set, and the means to attaining those objectives are determined."[12] Put simply, it corresponds to "the rules of the game" that determine the way stakeholders interact in a project setting.[13]

The advantage of considering governance in low-cost housing is that the concept considers both formal and informal stakeholder interaction mechanisms, allowing for a more sophisticated reading of the factors that can influence the intervention of people and organizations. It also helps us identify and distribute the roles and responsibilities of different project participants (in other words, it helps us identify *who* does *what, when* and *how*). By focusing on formal structures, we are able to consider the procurement strategy, the internal structure of the client organization, and project management structures and mechanisms that regulate contracts, partnerships, alliances and agreements. By also considering informal structures, we can perceive non-contractual relations *within* organizations (for instance in units and departments) and *between* them. Fellows and Liu, two construction management researchers, explain: "Formal governance provides the framework—organizational model, contractual rights, duties, procedures, etc.—while the operation of the informal system within (sometimes, in spite of) that framework provides the *de facto* governance" (p. 662).[14]

To be fair, informality in the building and urban sectors is not always perceived in a positive light.[15] Some argue that informal relations and exchanges contribute to creating conflicts, making it difficult to solve them, reducing accountability and reinforcing diverging interests.[16] Social interaction mechanisms, informal communication and soft managerial skills, however, also contribute to reducing adversarial relationships, making timely decisions, avoiding long administrative procedures and reducing bureaucratic (expensive) decision-making processes.[17] Even fervent defenders of formalization agree that human characteristics, more often associated with informality such as leadership and trust, play a significant role in establishing constructive relationships between stakeholders.[18]

Following this line of thought, we can identify three stakeholder attributes: the resources they bring (economic or not), their needs and their expectations. The legitimacy of their participation on project or program development or in policy-making depends on the assessment that other stakeholders will make of these attributes.[19] We can also identify two contingencies in stakeholder interaction: authority and responsibility. Both depend on this legitimacy (as perceived by other project stakeholders) and determine the extent of the influence of the stakeholder. Authority and responsibility can be more or less "formalized," determining different forms of trust, communication, task delegation, engagement and accountability. Let's discuss now the specific characteristics of project governance in developing countries.

Understanding Differences in Project Governance in Developing Countries

We know that all developing countries are different (so are cities and regions within them). However, if we, like most authors, accept that patterns can be observed in many of them, would it be reasonable to expect that projects be conducted differently in developed versus developing countries? If so, what are those key differences? These are—I believe—crucial questions that decision and policy-makers in the housing sector must ask; notably because low-cost housing in the Global South has been (and still is) typically constrained by development and financial programs and policies designed in "the North." We must remember that millions of housing units are built by both international NGOs and local stakeholders with the support of financial programs designed by foreign cooperation agencies. As we have seen in previous chapters, however, these programs have rarely produced the expected outcomes and have created unintended negative effects on local populations. This is partly due to a lack of understanding of the way projects are conducted in developing countries. The recognized danger of implementing construction projects in developing countries without a proper understanding of governance issues motivated our research group at the Université de Montréal to conduct a very specific study, which was later published in the journal *Construction Management and Economics.*[20]

The study proposed a simple question: how, and to what extent, does project governance differ between developed and developing countries? Construction projects in the informal sector are, of course, conducted differently than in the formal sector (and multiple "grey zones" between them exist). However, we wanted to know whether there are still significant differences when formal agencies, companies and institutions mandate and execute the projects in developing countries. In order to answer this question, we deployed three strategies over a period of three years. First, we conducted a comparative study between two projects: one in a developing country and one in a developed country. Then we designed a detailed questionnaire survey to assess the perceptions of project stakeholders with respect to project governance differences (respondents in the Global South were located in more than 15 countries including Algeria, Brazil, Peru, Ecuador and Thailand). Finally, we conducted ten semi-directed interviews with experienced design professionals and decision-makers in both developed and developing countries.

The results of our studies were surprising. Contrary to our expectations, we found similar levels of informal communication in both contexts; moreover, we found that professionals perceive this form of communication rather positively in both developed and developing countries. Engineers, architects, clients and urban planners do recognize that it helps to deal with bureaucracy and to lighten administrative tasks. We also observed several key differences, however. In developed countries, informal procedures and relations between stakeholders are seen as a complementary form of governance that enriches formal mechanisms. In developing countries, instead, they are associated with adaptation to changes and harsh (whether unexpected or not) contingencies. Respondents in developing countries explained that less formalized procedures and relations allowed them to adapt activities, resources, schedules and budgets to changes that typically occur during project development. They suggested that rigid plans do not provide the flexibility that they require to navigate the dynamic context in which they operate.

Results also showed significant differences in the exercise of power and authority. Our study found that the client organization's top management plays a more influential role (formally and informally) in projects in developing countries. Leadership styles also tend to differ between the two contexts: leadership is more authoritarian in developing countries (the "boss" or top management, therefore, plays a more decisive role in the success or failure of projects). In this context, hierarchy, adaptation and trust play a more significant role in developing countries. Finally, we found that procurement units, municipalities and users typically play a less significant role in projects in developing countries.

What do these differences mean for low-cost housing? A lot, my colleagues and I believe. We could read these differences as "problems to be fixed," and quickly resort to finding solutions to project challenges in developing countries. This is what most international officers acting in developing countries try to do (they find a problem and attempt to fix it). However, they often jump to conclusions too fast. Before adopting a prescriptive approach to "solve" project governance problems, architects, decision-makers and design professionals can intervene more appropriately in developing countries by understanding these differences, their causes, and their consequences. Let's consider a hypothetical example (yet plausible and based on real evidence) of the gap between the way projects are planned—often following Western methods—and effective results on the ground.

Planning vs. Adaptation

Let's suppose for a moment that you work for an NGO that does international development work, and your organization attempts to build 500 houses in, say, Ghana, with funding from the Canadian International Development Agency (CIDA) (most of the features of this example could also apply to other international agencies). In order to obtain funding from CIDA, you, as a project officer, are expected to plan the project as rigorously as possible following results-based management tools. One of these tools is called a Logical Framework, a mechanistic graphic-based document in which you must anticipate all the resources and detailed activities that the project will require, the outputs that will be obtained and the short-, mid- and long-term impacts of these results. Given that your budget, schedule and financial instalments will all depend on the rigorous anticipation of all these variables, your assessment must be as exact as possible, anticipating the project unfolding during the next four or five years. Forcing plans to change as little as possible, later changes to the Logical Framework are hardly welcomed by CIDA and many other funding agencies (they must be strictly justified, audited and documented). Procurement units, management policies and administrative mechanisms must be rigorously identified in this planning exercise. The principle here is to plan and *fix* processes as strictly as possible, attempting to guarantee efficient use of resources.

CIDA is unapologetic in its use of this approach, which it calls "modern management" and which it considers a necessary standardized mechanism for "achieving outcomes, implementing performance measurements, learning, and adapting, as well as reporting performance."[21] However, given the dynamic nature and volatility of economic, social and political environments in developing countries, it is surprising that internationally funded projects are typically based on these mechanistic management tools. They reflect, arguably, a planning paradigm more appropriate for developed contexts ("what you can't evaluate, you can't control" is often the motto in this management paradigm). However, it is hardly an approach that can work in the context of project governance in developing countries. Whereas our study on project governance found that adaptation to changing conditions is a crucial aspect of project governance in developing countries, results-based management focuses and insists on rigid planning.

This management paradigm hardly accommodates fluctuating political environments in which mayors, ministries (and sometimes even presidents) change before the end of their mandates. It hardly suits economic environments in which inflation, exchange rates, unemployment and other macro-economic conditions are highly dynamic. Neither does it permit adapting to volatile social conditions in which uprisings, protests, leadership changes and strikes can abruptly change the project conditions. Finally, it is a management approach that significantly differs from the way informal settlements usually operate, and thus it may appear foreign to most community-led initiatives. Examining the production of open space in informal settlements in Bogotá, Jaime Hernández-García, an architect and senior lecturer at Pontificia Universidad Javeriana, finds that "the development of open space is not oriented by a fixed plan, but responds to needs and ideas as they arise" (p. 166).[22]

This "modern" management approach (to paraphrase CIDA) seems to overlook governance mechanisms in developing countries, in which informal mechanisms are used to accommodate projects with fluctuating contingencies, in which hierarchy and trust help create business conditions that respond to local forms of human interaction and in which activities must be constantly revised to respond to dynamic new stakeholder needs and expectations. It is certainly inappropriate in volatile situations where local mayors cannot tolerate being in the same room (but the next day can be close friends) or in which the director of the local water provision agency belongs to a different political party than the local governor, and thus government and agency actors are not willing to cooperate.

Strong leadership from the top management of organizations can make foreign observers and workers—used to flat, less hierarchical and more "democratic," institutions—feel uncomfortable. They often complain that the top bosses are hard to reach, hold too much authority and are resistant to criticism from the bottom. Nonetheless, imposing Western managerial practices, while ignoring the way local institutions operate (and why), is hardly a sensitive approach to improving living conditions for the poor. Transformations to make municipalities more efficient, to give end-users a bigger role in projects and to create stronger procurement units that can balance the power of top management can be desirable outcomes in some contexts. However, these outcomes cannot be achieved rapidly or forcefully by imposing foreign policies, programs and project mechanisms.

This argument does not mean that international agencies must comply with the illegal, abusive or "obscure" managerial practices that can arise in developing countries. It certainly does not mean that foreign organizations must support or accept, for instance, corruption, greed and power abuses. Rather, it means that decision-makers (both native and external) are responsible for understanding local practices of project governance and their causes and consequences. They are also responsible for adapting to legitimate governance structures and mechanisms that respond to local conditions. Governance transformation is not sustainable if made abruptly or by imposing foreign models. The legitimacy of transformation in governance practices depends on local stakeholders' recognition of the need for alternative ways of doing things as well as on their progressive adoption of (sometimes very specific) alternative practices. The undistinguished and sudden transfer of Western, "modern" managerial principles is a barrier to effective project implementation in developing countries. Identifying and adopting mechanisms of governance that are both socially just and culturally appropriate is a prerequisite for the fruitful participation and collaboration between stakeholders and, as discussed earlier in this chapter, for value creation.

Now that we have explored a few of the specificities of project governance in developing countries, let's see how we can piece together the numerous themes we have explored in order to create a framework for rethinking and designing low-cost housing in developing countries.

A Framework of Analysis

Chapter 8 provided two fundamental concepts that allow us to understand the fragile relations that exist between the built, natural and social environments. The concept of vulnerability pointed to the economic, social, political and physical weaknesses that affect people, institutions, buildings and infrastructure. We contended that these vulnerabilities are created by societies over time, as institutions tolerate certain living conditions and social injustices. However, we also saw that families, social groups, organizations—and even countries—develop strengths that allow them to cope with difficult situations. We explored this idea through the concept of adaptive capacity, where individuals and households are able to prepare, respond and adapt to harmful events. These events can be permanent, recurrent or sporadic, and include man-made or natural hazards. By understanding both their vulnerability and resilience attributes, we are able to assess the relations that exist, in a given situation, between the built, natural and social environments. Analysing these conditions is the first step to developing a sensitive low-cost housing intervention.

In Chapter 8 we then considered the power of individual agency in the trans-formation of the built environment. This led us to see the merits of individual decision-making based on *opportunity*, the availability of *choices* and the *ability* to make them. We saw how a freedom-based approach to low-cost housing brings us closer to the idea of justice and human rights. It also decentralizes decision-making power, making it easier to capture valuable information from an increased number of stakeholders and transferring a certain level of responsibility to end-users. Despite its merits, we also explored the limits of this approach. In spite of the advantages of individual agency, we explored how sustainable, socially just and liveable human settlements transcend the notion of individual human rights. Living environments are also collective creations in which people engage in the use, co-creation and co-production of space in multiple ways and in which meanings and collective representations are crucial. Low-cost housing interventions require engaged stakeholders and, therefore, constant, transparent discussions and debates about collective desirable outcomes in the short, medium and long term.

This conceptual approach led us to challenge individual agency as the sole basis for a successful intervention, and to recognize that stakeholder interaction is also crucial in the consensual creation of physical space, services and infrastructure. Intense interaction between individuals is also a prerequisite for the creation of collective representations, memory and value. A comprehensive analytical framework, we reasoned, must consider two types of agents of change: individuals (who act through individual agency) and institutions (which can be formal and informal, and which act through stakeholder interaction). The heterogeneous character of urban dwellers, communities and institutions, however, unavoidably means that diverging interests, aspirations and needs are constantly confronted and negotiated. This process requires governance mechanisms capable of integrating institutions in more or less formalized manners.

A comprehensive framework must therefore recognize that stakeholders engage in the creation of social norms, protocols, practices and structures that allow them to make decisions. Yet, these modes of interaction may differ in developed and developing contexts. It is the decision- and policy-makers' responsibility, therefore, to identify, adopt or adapt legitimate structures and project development mechanisms. Respect for freedoms and individual choices should not lead institutions to ignore the heterogeneous principles that are valued by social groups that are *affected* and *affect* housing interventions. Participation and collaboration between stakeholders must therefore lead to the design and implementation of strategies, outputs and services (note the plural) that can be offered to households so that they have multiple choices at the level of design, construction technologies, financing solutions, labour force and project management. Informal institutions can also play a crucial role in offering alternatives for the poorest sectors of society. They have a deep-rooted sense of mutual cooperation, which can help in this process. They can contribute to the identification of collective values and frameworks to guide the project. This led us to the idea of formal and informal stakeholder interaction, and thus to the concept of governance in low-cost housing.

Figure 9.1 illustrates the conceptual model that results from this analysis. It recognizes the importance of assessing both vulnerabilities and resilience attributes in order to identify pre-existing conditions. Then it points to the main intervention tools, including individual and stakeholder agency (on each side of the diagram). Then, the model shows that interventions (centre column) can integrate these two types of agency at three interrelated levels of intervention: housing projects, programs and policy. The model captures the need for *opportunity, choices* and *abilities* in individual agency. Similarly, it reminds us that formal and informal institutions require formal and informal structures and mechanisms to share roles and responsibilities. The model also shows that the development of individual freedom of choice and appropriate project governance requires adequate information, education, and legal and financial frameworks. They are crucial for the effective development of both capabilities and value *during* and *after* the intervention.

The framework reminds us to clarify the use of some terms that are often used arbitrarily. It recognizes that stakeholders bring resources, needs and expectations to the project, and that their interaction is simultaneously constrained and developed by authority and responsibility. It distinguishes participation from collaboration, underlining different ways to engage in decision-making. Finally, the model exemplifies the phases at which decision-making is required: policy and program definition, project scope, financing, design, procurement, construction and upgrading.

This approach distances itself from the current community participation paradigm. It does not reject the merits of its core principles, such as people's empowerment, capacity building and reinforcement of collective synergies. But it questions the too often superficial and deceitful applications of the community participation values. It also challenges the idea of homogeneous (urban) communities in which a few actors represent all members. It critically questions the value of consultation processes and their capacity for obtaining the information required for sustainable housing interventions. It rejects some manipulative practices often promoted by organizations working under the community participation paradigm. It specifically discards participatory approaches in which end-users are indiscriminately forced to provide sweat equity in order to receive project or program benefits, and those in which they are involved in order to legitimize pre-conceived solutions.

By reframing governance issues, this framework puts emphasis on social justice without ignoring practical contingencies associated with stakeholder intervention. By combining two levels of agency (individual and collective), it values the differences that exist within social groups, while also recognizing the importance of collective meanings, objectives, needs, expectations and values. It refuses therefore to adopt a perspective of housing as an economic commodity exclusively ruled by market forces. It sets itself apart from the disengagement of public institutions that characterizes neoliberal thought. Instead, it recognizes that engaged institutions that are open to public debate and tolerant of differences are required in order to produce collective value and to respect human freedom. Finally, the framework captures the notion that

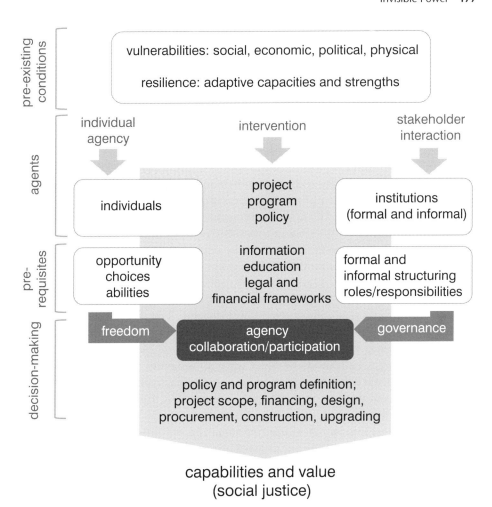

FIGURE 9.1 A framework for rethinking and designing low-cost housing in developing countries, based on an approach to social justice. Individual and collective agency in projects, programs and policy leads to the development of capabilities and value.

the final outcome of interventions is not the production of houses, but, from a social justice perspective, the development of individual capabilities and value.

Implications for Rethinking and Designing Low-Cost Housing in Developing Countries

Is it possible to apply this logic to all housing situations in developing countries? I believe it is, if we accept that this approach provides only a general background against which we can consider specific contexts. At this point, you have probably noticed the paradox of thinking about low-cost housing in developing countries. On the one hand, we have seen that there are several patterns *within* and *across* developing countries in, for instance, housing conditions, the functioning of the informal sector and policy implementation. The framework proposed here suggests that there are several common needs in most developing countries, including the needs to:

- improve access to urban land so it can be used for low-cost housing projects;
- improve subsidized programs to reach the poorest sectors of society with better housing products;
- reduce housing gaps in residential markets;
- increase mobility among the urban poor;
- increase participation of the informal sector in housing and infrastructure projects;
- develop skills and capacities among workers and companies in the informal sector in order to facilitate their progressive integration in the formal sector;
- improve infrastructure in informal settlements and deliver it to subserviced areas;
- reduce vulnerabilities in informal settlements;
- enhance resilience among families, social groups, cities, territories and nations;
- help end-users consolidate their unfinished units and infrastructure.

On the other hand, we know that each context is different and thus every solution depends on contextual, locally specific contingencies. This framework is therefore suitable only if it follows three conditions. First, if it helps us identify local singularities, including the needs and specific conditions that require institutional intervention. Second, if it guides us towards multiple ways of designing and enhancing specific responses. Third, if it helps us understand the tensions that might occur in the decision-making process and the long-term effects of interventions (for instance, if it provides insight on the tensions between monetary and non-monetary benefits and costs, and between individual freedom and collective value). In the final chapter, let's consider some examples of how an approach to social justice in housing development requires the identification, design and procurement of specific characteristics, while recognizing the tensions that might exist in the decision-making process.

Notes

1 Arnstein, S.R. "A Ladder of Citizen Participation." *Journal of the American Planning Association* 35, no. 4 (1969): 216–24; Campbell, S. "Green Cities, Growing Cities, Just Cities?: Urban Planning and the Contradictions of Sustainable Development." *Journal of the American Planning Association* 62, no. 3 (1996): 296–312; Forester, J. *The Deliberative Practitioner: Encouraging Participatory Planning Processes*. The MIT Press, 1999.
2 Freeman, R.E. *Strategic Management: A Stakeholder Approach*, Boston, MA. Pitman, 1984.
3 Cherns, A.B. and D.T Bryant. "Studying the Client's Role in Construction Management." *Construction Management and Economics* 2, no. 2 (1984): 177–84; Mohsini, R.A. and C.H. Davidson. "Determinants of Performance in the Traditional Building Process." *Construction Management and Economics* 10, no. 4 (1992): 343–59.
4 Smets, P. "Small Is Beautiful, but Big Is Often the Practice: Housing Microfinance in Discussion." *Habitat International* 30, no. 3 (2006): 595–613.
5 Hernández-García, J. "The Production of Informal Urban Space: The Barrios of Bogotá." In *Researching the Contemporary City: Identity, Environment and Social Inclusion in Developing Urban Areas.*, edited by J. Hernández-García and P. Kellett, 141–68. Bogotá: Editorial Pontificia Universidad Javeriana, 2013.
6 Ibid.
7 Hernández-Bonilla, M. "People Shaping Public Space: Popular Urban Design Processes in Mexico." In *Researching the Contemporary City: Identity, Environment and Social Inclusion*

in Developing Urban Areas., edited by J. Hernández-García and P. Kellett, 137–50. Bogotá: Editorial Pontificia Universidad Javeriana, 2013.

8 Kellett, P. and J. Hernández-García. *Researching the Contemporary City: Identity, Environment and Social Inclusion in Developing Urban Areas.* Bogotá: Editorial Pontificia Universidad Javeriana, 2013.

9 Ibid.

10 Baron, C. "La gouvernance: débats autour d'un concept polysémique." *Droit et société*, no. 2 (2003): 329–49; Winch, G.M. "Governing the Project Process: A Conceptual Framework." *Construction Management and Economics* 19, no. 8 (2001): 799–808.

11 Bekker, M.C. and H. Steyn. "Defining 'Project Governance' for Large Capital Projects." *South African Journal of Industrial Engineering November* 20, no. 2 (2009): 81–92.

12 Turner, J.R. "Towards a Theory of Project Management: The Nature of the Project Governance and Project Management." *International Journal of Project Management* 24, no. 2 (2006): 93–95.

13 Winch, G.M. "Governing the Project Process: A Conceptual Framework." *Construction Management and Economics* 19, no. 8 (2001): 799–808.

14 Fellows, R. and A.M.M. Liu. "Managing Organizational Interfaces in Engineering Construction Projects: Addressing Fragmentation and Boundary Issues across Multiple Interfaces." *Construction Management and Economics* 30, no. 8 (2012): 653–71.

15 Chan, P. and C. Raisanen. "Informality and Emergence in Construction." *Construction Management and Economics* 27, no. 10 (2009): 907–12.

16 Naoum, S. *People and Organizational Management in Construction.* London: Thomas Telford Books, 2001.

17 Pietroforte, R. "Communication and Governance in the Building Process." *Construction Management and Economics* 15 (1997): 71–82; Emmitt, S. and C.A. Gorse. *Communication in Construction Teams*, Spon Research. London: Taylor & Francis, 2007; Anvuur, A. and M. Kumaraswamy. "Better Collaboration through Cooperation." In *Collaborative Relationships in Construction: Developing Frameworks and Networks*, edited by H. Smyth and S. Pryke, 107–28. Oxford: Wiley-Blackwell, 2008; Kvan, T. "Collaborative Design: What is It?" *Automation in Construction* 9, no. 4 (2000): 409–15.

18 Smyth, H. "Measuring, Developing and Managing Trust in Relationships." In *The Management of Complex Projects: A Relationship Approach*, edited by S. Pryke and H. Smyth, 97–120. Oxford: Blackwell Publishing, 2006.

19 Viel, L., I. Thomas-Maret, F.A. Maherzi and G. Lizarralde. "L'Influence des parties prenantes dans les grands projets urbains. Les Cas du Quartier des Spectacles de Montréal et de Lyon Confluence." *Cybergeo: European Journal of Geography* 604 (2012): http://cybergeo.revues.org/25310 ; DOI : 10.4000/cybergeo.10

20 Lizarralde, G., S. Tomiyoshi, M. Bourgault, J. Malo and G. Cardosi. "Understanding Differences in Construction Project Governance between Developed and Developing Countries." *Construction Management and Economics* 31, no. 7 (2013): 711–30.

21 ACDI Agence Canadienne de Développement International. "Results-Based Management Tools at CIDA: A How-to Guide." ACDI, http://www.acdi-cida.gc.ca/acdi-cida/ACDI-CIDA.nsf/eng/NAT-92213444-N2H.

22 Hernández-García, "The Production of Informal Urban Space: The Barrios of Bogotá."

10

RETHINKING AND DESIGNING LOW-COST HOUSING IN DEVELOPING COUNTRIES

It is Not About Simplifying the Problem, but Rather Committing to Collective Sustained Effort and Embracing Complexity

> Suspended over the abyss, the life of Octavia's inhabitants is less uncertain than in other cities. They know the net will last only so long.
>
> *Invisible Cities*, Italo Calvino (p. 67)

The Case of the Spare Window

It was after dark on a winter's day in the Cape Townships. The community room, a construction office whose furniture was crammed into one corner to make space for about 30 plastic chairs, was full. Several residents who arrived late couldn't find anywhere to sit. Dozens of women and a few men had come to the meeting organized by one local and one international NGO that had, months earlier, assumed responsibility for the replacement of about 100 backyard shacks with an equal number of one-story, finished, "sustainable," masonry houses. There was a full agenda that evening: first, organize resident groups to paint the houses; second, discuss some households' complaints regarding construction finishes; third, debate safety concerns, including one, brought forward by some women, regarding local children's safety being jeopardized by heavy equipment still working in the new urban landscape; fourth, show financial records; and fifth, miscellanea.

Debate was already heated when, in the midst of agenda Item 2, a matronly, black, Xhosa-speaking woman raised her hand. Her point was simple. The NGO had asked her to demolish her backyard shack and had offered her a new house. However, her shack had a 2×2m aluminium window, whereas the new houses had 1×1m wooden windows next to the front entrance. Her question: would the NGO officers allow her to replace one of the small windows provided by the project with the window recovered from the demolished shed?

The question made the NGO officers, seated at the front desk facing the crowd, visibly uncomfortable. They raised some practical constraints—modifying the façade would disrupt the uniformity of the settlement's appearance; the schedule for plastering and painting façades was already tight; it wasn't clear who would cover the expense for the change; would the house's standard guarantee cover the change? Because the meeting was running late, it was thought best not to debate the issue for too long, so the officers accepted the change, hoping to move on to Item 3.

But then the woman in the crowd rose again. If she used her large, aluminium window, she reasoned, she would not need the small standard wooden window, so could she have an extra feature in compensation for the reduced resources that her house would require? This would be fair, she explained, given that her house would not require the standard small window that other beneficiaries would receive.

The NGO officers looked at each other, searching in vain for a mutually acceptable response. There was none forthcoming. Their "sustainable" project had failed to anticipate that construction materials might be recuperated from the demolished shacks. The schedule and budget did not allow for this. The construction plan had been formulated around standard construction methods. Users were supposed to participate in construction and fieldwork activities according to a pre-established plan, not one shaped by their own individual desires. Time was running out; it was late; everyone had to go home. The chairman of the meeting moved on to Item 3, asking the woman to raise the matter later—in private.

Considering Specific Characteristics and Tensions

Chapter 2 showed us that it is difficult, even dangerous, to generalize about people who require low-cost housing. The same principle applies to sites, institutions, settlements and, as demonstrated in the previous example, houses. A housing development approach based on social justice does not involve indiscriminately applying an abstract notion of the "good life." Nor does it mean applying certain standards to reach what was identified in Chapter 3 as a "moral threshold." Instead, it requires that housing policies, programs and projects be able to identify, decode and incorporate existing local, culturally valued, relationships between social, natural and built environments. It is therefore the collective responsibility of institutions (and, for that matter, of architects, urban planners and other design professionals) to recognize the specific characteristics of local informality and learn from them.

Different levels of informality exist in the occupation of urban space. Various sorts of informality respond to different conditions in markets, land, infrastructure, culture and the environment. The case of the spare window highlights the importance of specific characteristics, and questions the meaning of "sustainability" in the particular context of low-cost housing in developing countries.

Low-cost housing is a political process. Although decisions do not necessarily lead to unavoidable trade-offs, some balancing of costs and benefits may be required. It is, of course, impossible to record here the infinite number of specific cases to be considered and all the tensions that can arise in the decision-making process. However, let's consider a few examples of how a housing approach based on social justice can help us determine the specific responses required in certain cases. As we shall see, some of the tensions arising from the decision-making process require that participants simultaneously consider individual rights and collective value, individual capabilities and the common good, short-term benefits and long-term effects.

FIGURE 10.1 Backyard dwellings in South Africa are often seen as part of the "housing problem." If anything, they should be seen as part of the solution.

Uniformity of Standards vs. Backyard Occupancy

Housing policies and NGOs in South Africa and other countries have actively promoted the elimination of backyard dwellings. These rudimentary shacks, typically built in the yards of consolidated houses and rented to poor families, are seen as unacceptable living situations and a threat to neighbourhood uniformity (see Figure 10.1). However, policy seems to ignore the fact that they fulfil important roles for households. They provide housing to the poorest families, who have no access to ownership; they shelter extended families, allowing relatives and friends to live in proximity, while providing privacy for new couples; they facilitate tenant mobility, while furnishing additional (and relatively steady) income to landlords. Finally, by providing landlords with additional income, these shacks contribute to their ability to finish their own houses and secure ownership.

Backyard shacks also offer significant advantages at the urban level. They reduce the need for additional land development and reduce the urban footprint, keeping cities compact and optimizing available infrastructure and services. They also increase the density of consolidated South African townships, which typically have large plots and disproportionately wide streets. Given all these advantages, a social justice approach, committed to learning from informality, would conclude that these backyard shacks should not be eliminated, but rather consolidated. This requires legalizing them, providing them with public services, improving their foundations, slabs and structures and developing effective processes for upgrading and expanding them. These structures can then become an integral part of the solution to qualitative and quantitative housing deficits in South Africa and other countries.

FIGURE 10.2   A slum in the "*cerros orientales*" in Bogotá. Municipal land policies have sent an ambiguous message on the value of environmental protection vis-à-vis profit-driven urban development.

Environmental Protection vs. Housing Development

Land invasion on the periphery of cities is often seen as a threat to agricultural, environmental or protected zones. Authorities tend to restrict or condemn low-cost housing development in these areas. Nonetheless, they often allow, or turn a blind eye to, other uses that have a similar impact. Urban regulations in Bogotá, for instance, had historically restricted development in the so-called "*cerros orientales*" (eastern mountains; see Figure 10.2), while institutions have commonly granted permits to develop upper-class residential buildings and gated communities. Ambiguity concerning the value of protected areas sends an unclear message to institutions and citizens. Socially just land-use policies must be clear and aimed at balancing environmental considerations with protecting the rights and aspirations of the most vulnerable and deprived. As we saw in Chapters 3 and 4, green belts, buffer zones, protected areas, zoning and other land-use policies have a crucial impact on housing supply, and thus on home prices. Public entities (notably municipalities) must constantly foster a transparent debate among heterogeneous stakeholders and institutions that is aimed at identifying a desirable balance between environmental protection and new housing developments.

Security vs. Relocation

The informal occupation of residual urban spaces along rivers, railways and roads generally poses a threat to the safety of both squatters and commuters. While these linear informal settlements are very common in Latin American, African and Asian cities

FIGURE 10.3 Informal housing units get dangerously close to railways, highways and rivers in many cities, including Hanoi (pictured), which sometimes requires the relocation of families. These relocations must, however, be carefully planned and carried out to minimize the negative impact of disrupting livelihoods and valuable social networks.

(including Vietnam; see Figure 10.3), providing titles and infrastructure to squatters is often seen as unacceptable "institutionalization" and acceptance of these risks. When relocation is necessary for safety reasons, a minimum number of households should be relocated and they should be compensated and moved to locations as nearby as possible, so that families can retain their social networks. Take the case of the Juan Pablo II project, which we discussed in Chapter 6. It involved the relocation of hundreds of families living in linear settlements along a river in Facatativá. However, fair compensation for their informally occupied land and relocation nearby guaranteed the families' willingness to relocate and participate in the new project.

Using safety concerns to legitimize beautification plans or selfish interests diminishes institutions' credibility among the urban poor. The legitimacy of socially just interventions lies in the transparency of the stakeholders' interest in the relocation. Institutions can hardly inspire trust when they engage in market-driven negotiations favouring financial profit alone. Instead, they must be engaged and concerned with protecting the rights and interests of socially excluded and marginalized residents.

Accepting Lower Standards vs. Ignoring Informal Builders

We have seen throughout this book that the informal sector is often capable of developing houses for the poorest sectors of society. Shacks made of recycled and rudimentary

FIGURE 10.4 Innovative ideas are required for technical solutions to complement the products and services of the informal sector. This includes floor slabs and foundations for informal shacks.

materials are relatively easy to obtain or are built by unskilled labour and end-users. Over time, these structures are reinforced and upgraded and grow to become complete, fully functional, viable units. They are typically well finished and decorated inside, providing a place where families can conduct regular domestic activities, intimate religious practices and social events. In the case of South Africa (see Figure 10.4) and some other countries, however, the informal sector has failed to produce an appropriate solution for constructing floor slabs and foundations. The lack of solid, water-resistant floors creates humid indoor spaces that lead to respiratory problems in households. Furthermore, without a solid base, shacks are unstable and prone to flooding.

Innovative and affordable solutions that can be adapted to informally produced top structures are required in these situations, yet this is a design area that has been largely ignored by architects, engineers and other design professionals. A housing approach that considers individual and collective agency must recognize the strengths and weaknesses of both formal and informal organizations, seeing them as complementary components of a settlement development system.

Relocating Squatters vs. Informal Income-Generation

The informal occupation of public and open space is a common response to the lack of housing in most developing countries and emerging economies (including China; see Figure 10.5). Squatters, however, are often given little decision-making power in a

FIGURE 10.5 Squatters in public spaces are common in most cities in the Global South, including Shanghai (pictured). When relocated, they are rarely given decision-making power regarding new locations and housing solutions.

relocation process. They are typically allocated a plot, an apartment unit or a house, in a location and of a type previously determined by the authorities. Additionally, often very little is done to improve their livelihoods. In fact, relocation to new settlements or condominiums often takes them far away from job opportunities and informal means of production. A comprehensive intervention in squatter settlements and units must address not only the residential needs of families, but also their income-generation options.

If squatters are given financial and technical assistance and decision-making power, they can make the choices that suit them best, for both their domestic needs and their economic situation. A social justice-based perspective involves trusting them and giving them the decision-making power to identify the feasible alternatives available with financial and technical support from institutions (a new housing unit for rent or purchase, a building plot, an unfinished unit to upgrade and complete, etc.).

Urban Rehabilitation vs. Gentrification of Collective Housing

Owners of multi-family (often multi-story) buildings may have little incentive to renovate and maintain buildings, particularly when their units are rented to low-income families. If demand for rental housing is high and rents are low, landlords have neither the incentive nor the resources to improve housing conditions for tenants.

FIGURE 10.6 Landlords and unit owners can find it difficult to keep up with maintenance and to upgrade multi-family buildings. In urban rehabilitation programs, occupants are at risk of displacement by market forces. Collective value must therefore address the non-monetary expectations of many different stakeholders.

Condominiums in which residents own their own units but lack steady income might also suffer from lack of maintenance, which is the case in some central neighbourhoods in Panama City (see Figure 10.6) and other urban centres. Under these conditions, urban renewal programs can easily lead to neighbourhood gentrification, pushing low-income families into socially stigmatized or peripheral locations. Coherent social networks can be permanently destroyed in this process, making the poor even more vulnerable and exacerbating social segregation within the city.

Urban interventions committed to social justice cannot respond only to the interests of public and private urban elites. Collective value cannot, therefore, be assessed by those with economic and political interests, alone. Interventions need to engage stakeholders in ways that allow local residents to freely decide whether they want to move or not, not based solely on economic variables (whether they can afford to remain in their homes) but on other factors such as feasible alternatives for generating income, proximity to social networks, availability of services and infrastructure, and the monetary and non-monetary costs of moving. Options for low-income condominium owners should include the possibility of upgrading their units with financial support that they themselves manage. Interventions can also benefit tenants by providing landlords with financial incentives and subsidies if they maintain rents at affordable levels for current occupants.

FIGURE 10.7 Market-driven development aimed at preserving the historical value of collective housing structures, such as *inquilinatos* in Barrio Las Cruces in Bogotá (pictured), tends to displace poor tenants. Alternative forms of intervention that are committed to social justice, which take into account capabilities and collective value, are required in these situations.

Traditional forms of collective housing such as *mesones* (in El Salvador), *inquilinatos* (in Bogotá; see Figures 10.7 and 10.8) and *casonas* (in other Latin American cities) experience similar difficulties in balancing upgrades and affordability for tenants. Although they vary in form and density (typically, between one and three stories), these types of collective housing all accommodate several families living in small rooms who share common spaces and services (kitchen, sanitary services, playgrounds, open areas, etc.). Units are often rented, but landlords may or may not live in the building and may own one or more buildings, making it difficult to stereotype them (see Chapter 2). Despite modifications and lack of maintenance, these buildings sometimes have historic value, either because of the building's typology or its contribution to a traditional urban fabric.

Studies have found that urban interventions aimed at preserving this heritage, based on free-market forces alone, tend to displace poor residents.[1] The consequence of these interventions is that rents increase and, thus, renovated buildings are put to other, more profitable uses such as restaurants, hotels and boutiques. In these situations, market-driven, neoliberal disengagement by institutions can hardly achieve social justice, preserve networks and enhance capabilities. Responsible interventions require consensual decision-making among stakeholders based on both individuals' real ability to choose from a variety of possibilities and collective value (monetary or otherwise) in the short, medium and long term.

FIGURE 10.8   Special attention must be paid to guaranteeing that improvements to collective forms of housing, such as *mesones* in El Salvador (pictured), continue to benefit original residents.

Considering Long-Term Effects

Urban Trends

"Be urban. Be cool" reads a residential developer's sign in Shanghai, China (see Figure 10.9). If you accept that "be cool" is marketing shorthand for "increase your chances of having access to better schools, healthcare, a steady income, nearby friends, tolerance for differences and benefitting from serendipity"—then you will probably agree that being urban is cool in almost all developing countries today. Yet, the large number of people who are, or want to be, "cool" is challenging the way we see the future of cities and housing in the Global South.

Besides the concept of vulnerability, there are two paradigms that can help us examine the fragile present and future relationships between humans, nature and the built environment. One of them, the paradigm of resilience (introduced in Chapter 7), focuses on ways to prevent, recover from and adapt to disturbing events. The other, the sustainability paradigm, focuses primarily on improving current performance to provide better environmental conditions in the future. Both share a systemic approach based on a holistic consideration of interrelated variables that takes into account the short-, medium- and long-term effects of neighbourhood, urban and regional interventions. However, both the "blue" and "green" agendas informed by these paradigms in many countries have failed to produce broadly accepted definitions of what is considered to

FIGURE 10.9 Rapid urbanization is challenging the sustainability of human settlements in developing countries. A poster in Shanghai, China, promotes the advantages of urban living in this increasingly urbanized country.

be "resilient" or "sustainable." As a consequence, many analysts believe that green and blue principles must be reconciled in a "turquoise" agenda.[2] Others find that these terms have lost their significance altogether in a sea of heterogeneous interpretations and representations.

In Chapter 8, we explored some of the implications of vulnerability and resilience for low-cost housing, highlighting the importance of organizational networks, institutional responsibility at different levels of government, construction industry development, research, information and communication. Now, let's explore how a social justice-based framework can help endow sustainability with meaning in the specific context of low-cost housing in developing countries.

Invisible "Green"

Part of the problem caused by the lack of clarity of the sustainability paradigm is that its objectives, approaches and tools are generally used interchangeably. The objectives of sustainability (pollution reduction or economic feasibility, for example) are often confused with approaches to achieving them (increasing density, for instance) or with tools to operationalize them (such as community participation). As a result, sustainability is frequently used to refer to things such as energy efficiency, pollution reduction, environmental protection, social involvement, green building, etc.,[3] which are significantly different. To provide some precision, let's consider some specific objectives in each of the three principal dimensions of sustainability—social, economic and environmental responsibility.

Social Responsibility

Thinking about low-cost housing in developing countries has led us to consider social justice, more specifically, the impact of individual agency—which leads to a freedom and human-rights based approach to development—and collective value, which requires intense stakeholder interaction. A sustainable approach to low-cost housing, therefore, is based on developing governance structures that potentiate these two levels of agency. To facilitate trust between stakeholders, governance mechanisms must create transparent decision-making processes in which people have access to information on the arguments for, and consequences of, potential decisions. This approach is not fully sustainable, however, if it is used in the intervention process only. The results of these interventions must enhance the long-term autonomy of individuals and social groups (notably, the marginalized and excluded), progressively reducing their dependency on external aid and welfare. In most cases, it is necessary to permanently redistribute decision-making power so individuals can manage social benefits. Intense stakeholder interaction must be aimed at identifying and preserving collective values. In many cases, consensual decisions on preserving cultural heritage, collective memory and the less tangible capital of traditional construction and local know-how are required. An urban low-cost housing intervention becomes sustainable if it manages to balance individual freedom and the collective good, short-term needs with long-term impacts and local values and identity with regional, national and even global needs and aspirations.

Economic Responsibility

The sustainability of low-income settlements largely depends on households' capacity to generate steady income. Therefore, spaces that can be used for both residential and income-generation activities (including home-based enterprises) must be carefully considered. Projects must anticipate maintenance costs and the expense of future building upgrading, renovation and adaptation. Both types of costs must be carefully considered when calculating present and future economic feasibility.

Construction must aim to reduce waste and anticipate that subsequent unit upgrades and expansion will not necessarily require extensive demolition and, thus, waste. Sustainable interventions are those that optimize the use of locally available resources, including available infrastructures and existing buildings. In many cases, urban interventions must favour the option of repurposing buildings and infrastructure. Investments must be aimed at the target population. In this regard, special attention must be paid to the role of local (informal) construction companies and workers. Decision- and policy-makers must recognize that there is already significant capital invested in informal settlements. In the absence of substantial legitimate cause to demolish informal units, this capital should not be wasted. Instead, projects can take advantage of these structures to increase household capital. In cases where the partial or total demolition of units is unavoidable, initiatives must consider recycling their materials and components.

Environmental Responsibility

Sustainability in low-cost housing requires that the resources used in interventions, particularly those that are non-renewable, be optimized. Particular attention must be paid to optimizing urban land—currently one of the most expensive resources. Stakeholders must, therefore, reach a consensus on the desirable and viable urban density. These decisions cannot be based exclusively on immediate desires, or on adopting a particular construction typology just because it is fast and easy to build (for instance, single-story detached units). Decisions on urban density require that the mid- and long-term consequences of infrastructure construction and maintenance, and the long-term viability of community services, be analysed. The impact of urban sprawl on the sustainability of larger regions must also be considered. Furthermore, stakeholders must also remember that crime reduction and the viability of several forms of home-based enterprise rely on a threshold population density, and on vibrant, animated streets and open spaces.

Environmental targets include the responsible use of energy for building lighting, heating and cooling. In most cases, density decisions must aim to reduce automobile use and reliance on means of individual transportation. Interventions must also consider emission reduction when creating and using energy and technologies. Finally, we should not forget that the long-term sustainability of human settlements depends on structural solutions that reduce vulnerabilities and enhance resilience.

Designing for Specific Characteristics

Responsible interventions in housing policy, programs and projects require design professionals and decision-makers to provide individuals and social groups with a variety of design choices. This means that for every situation (every decision-making process) there must be several, not just one, ideas adapted to local characteristics. This allows individuals and social groups to weigh them and judge which solutions best fit their needs and aspirations. The following examples show, however, that this is unlikely to be feasible by any single institution or organization. Instead, the design and adoption of alternatives typically requires decentralized decision-making.

Dealing with Qualitative Deficits

The enabling markets approach to housing provision is currently the most popular way to alleviate quantitative deficits. Insufficient efforts have been made, however, to solve the qualitative deficits in informal or unconsolidated neighbourhoods. This is an area that needs further attention from governments, scholars, NGOs and international agencies. Creativity and innovation are required to develop interventions that can, through the equivalent of urban microsurgery, reinforce structures, facilitate access to services and upgrade housing units within informal or unconsolidated settlements (see Figure 10.10). This would allow residents to benefit from direct investment, accelerate neighbourhood consolidation, reduce vulnerabilities and optimize existing public services.

This approach is, of course, destined to entail significant challenges. The first is the increased cost of infrastructure, which is disproportionately higher in urban upgrading programs than in new development. The second challenge is creating secure forms of tenure that are well adapted to local conditions, administrative means and resources (see Chapter 4).[4] Another challenge is designing appropriate governance mechanisms and integrating informal institutions into the process. One of the most difficult barriers to overcome is creating financial mechanisms that allow poor families to conduct upgrades

PERSPECTIVE EXTÉRIEURE
Cas B: Ajouter un 2e étage - avant intervention

PERSPECTIVE EXTÉRIEURE
Cas B: Ajouter un 2o étage - après intervention

FIGURE 10.10 Innovative ways of consolidating and improving existing housing are required in developing countries. Here graduate students in architecture from Studio MGPA (Université de Montréal) explore organizational, technical and financial mechanisms for consolidating houses in Martissant, Port-au-Prince, Haiti (students: Stéphanie Boudreau-Chartier and Esther Gélinas).

at their own pace. Examining research results in Mexico and other countries, Datta and Jones conclude that "if formal or informal finance were to become more widely available to low-income households, most would not attempt to move but improve conditions in situ" (p. 350).[5] It should be noted, that, in some countries, initial steps have been taken to address this challenge. Governments in Colombia and Chile, for instance, now offer subsidized programs for housing upgrades and have demonstrated that the method can create positive results.

Designing a Variety of Choices

To supply different levels of the housing pyramid and to fill the housing gap in markets, various products of assorted standards need to be made available to low-income families. This often implies accepting lower standards, and might include, for instance, plots of varying sizes, core-units or units that are small and unfinished. I understand that this argument is contentious and may (although I hope it will not) be used to further deprive the poor, increase low-income families' marginalization and increase institutional disengagement. Controversial though it is, this is not a new idea. Robert Buckley and Jerry Kalarickal, two advisors to the World Bank, explain that decades of studies on housing markets in general, and housing demand in developing countries in particular, have proven "why the units produced could be sustainably financed only if lower and more modest housing standards appropriate to beneficiaries' income levels were used" (p. 236).[6] Let's consider this idea's merits.

Offering housing units of varying standards can benefit the poor for four reasons. First, it can help fill the housing gap, increasing mobility among the poor. Second, if properly planned, it can offer households the possibility of finishing and enlarging their units to meet their own needs and expectations. Third, if settlements include different plot and unit sizes, finishes and features, these differences are likely to attract households of varying social and economic status.[7] This can facilitate the social integration of the poor and reduce the exclusion and stigmatization that characterize low-income settlements. Finally, with multiple housing standards, solutions can more directly respond to the needs and expectations of different target groups. Elevated housing solution standards for the poor sometimes contribute to a process by which the new units "trickle up" in the market and fail to serve the targeted group. Take the case of *Ciudadela Colsubsidio* in Bogotá, Colombia. During the 1990s, a private-fund manager in the Colombian welfare system designed this project hoping to attract low-income families. The results were mixed (see Figure 10.11). A 40 m² subsidized house for the poor in Colombia presently costs 40 million pesos (roughly US$20,000) and is typically charged for public services at Level (or *estrato*) 1 or 2 (public services in Bogotá are billed on a 6-level sliding scale system). In contrast, a 58 m² apartment in *Ciudadela Colsubsidio* costs 135 million pesos and is classified at Level 3. Raising the urban and architectural standards of the settlement created a highly desirable neighbourhood. However, it ultimately did not serve the low-income family target group and instead attracted families with more means.

Most centralized approaches standardize units within settlements and miss the opportunity to tailor solutions to different types of families. Instead, alternatives should be considered for several aspects of housing, including a variety of:

FIGURE 10.11 Whereas steady housing stock upgrades allow households to climb the housing ladder, an abrupt increase in property values might result in housing solutions "trickling up" in the market. The high quality of urban spaces and construction standards in Ciudadela Colsubsidio (a housing project in Bogotá originally intended to attract low-income families, pictured above) has undoubtedly improved living conditions for thousands of middle-class residents, but it also caused the project to bypass the target population.

- plot sizes, shapes and proportions
- configurations—detached, semi-detached or row units
- heights—structures that have one, two or more stories
- materials and construction technologies
- unit sizes
- internal layouts
- urban configurations
- interior finishes.

Core-Units

Core-unit development has several advantages in a social justice-based approach to housing. First, it facilitates progressive construction, allowing families to invest in housing solutions at their own pace, as their needs, aspirations and available resources change. Second, it guarantees that families' investments in their homes reflect their priorities and financial possibilities at every stage. Third, it facilitates the integration of informal companies in post-occupancy interventions. Fourth, by offering a wide range of products with different finishes, construction features, spatial conditions, stages of consolidation and prices, it increases household mobility. Fifth, it provides an appropriate balance between individual agency (giving households the capacity to finish, modify and enlarge their units according to individual desires) and collective agency (providing common infrastructure and shared patterns of urban design). Finally, it must be noted that buying a fully finished, complete house is a practice foreign to many traditional rural residents and new urbanities with a rural background. For many of them, housing is not a market transaction, but a process that engages family members in incremental, adaptive construction that may last for several generations. In the course of this process, the home becomes a valuable symbolic and economic investment, carrying family history and experiences, which can be transferred to children and other family members, Households often take pride in this collective effort. Core-housing provides (at least partially) a familiar mechanism for creating this collective narrative and family asset.

Innovative forms of core-housing, in which a basic two- or three-story structure is provided, leaving beneficiaries significant freedom to upgrade and enlarge their units, have been successfully developed by the Chilean firm *ELEMENTAL* in cities such as Constitución, Iquique, Rancagua and Santiago (all in Chile). In the Quinta Monroy project in Iquique (see Figures 10.12 to 10.14) and the Villa Verde project in Constitución (see Figures 10.15 to 10.18), the architects provided appropriate urban densities and a three-dimensional structure and infrastructure that can be completed and upgraded by individual households. They have created an inspiring architectural design and a development process that responds to both collective and individual needs and expectations (see www.elementalchile.cl). Identifying itself as a "Do Tank," *ELEMENTAL* is an organization deeply engaged in understanding and producing viable settlements for low-income families. Its work has demonstrated that lower-standard housing can be upgraded by individual households in post-construction interventions without compromising urban and architectural quality, thus preserving collective value.

FIGURE 10.12 Quinta Monroy, Iquique, Chile—Designed by *ELEMENTAL*. Image of the core-unit project before post-occupancy interventions (Photo: Tadeuz Jalocha, 2003–2004, design-construction period).

FIGURE 10.13 Quinta Monroy, Iquique, Chile—Designed by *ELEMENTAL*. Image of the core-unit project after post-occupancy interventions (Photo: Cristobal Palma).

FIGURE 10.14 Quinta Monroy, Iquique, Chile—Designed by *ELEMENTAL*. Image of the core-unit project after post-occupancy interventions (Photo: Takuto Sando).

FIGURE 10.15 Villa Verde, Constitución, Chile—Designed by *ELEMENTAL*. Image of the core-unit project before post-occupancy interventions (Photo: Cristian Martinez/ *ELEMENTAL*, 2010–2013, design-construction period).

FIGURE 10.16 Villa Verde, Constitución, Chile—Designed by *ELEMENTAL*. Image of the core-unit project after post-occupancy interventions (Photo: Cristian Martinez/ *ELEMENTAL*, 2010–2013, design-construction period).

Financing Incremental Construction

Previous chapters have shown that incremental construction is the principal homeownership strategy of the poor. Peer Smets found that incremental housing financing in the informal sector includes individual and group savings, windfalls, building materials production, sweat equity, credit from informal moneylenders, barter

FIGURE 10.17 Villa Verde, Constitución, Chile—Designed by *ELEMENTAL*. Image of the core-unit project before post-occupancy interventions (Photo: Cristian Martinez/ *ELEMENTAL*, 2010–2013, design-construction period).

FIGURE 10.18 Villa Verde, Constitución, Chile—Designed by *ELEMENTAL*. Image of the core-unit project after post-occupancy interventions (Photo: Cristian Martinez/ *ELEMENTAL*, 2010–2013, design-construction period).

arrangements, community self-help and remittances from friends and family members living abroad.[8] However, these resources are often insufficient or too expensive for a steady completion and upgrading process. In such cases, financial tools (including mortgages, subsidies, loans, cash-for-work and micro-financing) are needed.[9] However, incremental construction financing (in informal settlements or core-housing developments) is still one of the most under-developed areas of housing policy. What is needed are innovative solutions for credit and subsidies that give end-users sufficient decision-making power regarding their own individual projects and the means to accelerate the reinforcing and upgrading process.

Savings Mechanisms

In most developing countries, family savings are critically important for access to housing. Tran Thi Hanh, a UN-Habitat consultant, found that the Vietnamese need to save up to 80% of their incomes to purchase a house (the average rate worldwide is 33%).[10] However, with limited access to the financial system, the poor cannot rely on formal savings mechanisms. Economists have recently found that most banking services, including savings and checking accounts, are unaffordable for the poor in many countries. Minimum administrative fees are often disproportionately high, given the small amounts the poor can save. Besides, in most cases, the costs of travelling to the nearest financial institution branch can be higher than the amount for deposit. Partly because of these factors, savings that could be used to improve living conditions end up being spent on domestic emergencies, ostentatious parties, grandiose funerals and, all too often, alcohol.[11] Individual agency could improve by providing the poor with inexpensive saving mechanisms that allow them to set aside even very small amounts on a frequent (probably daily) basis. Innovative saving solutions that are affordable, safe and easy to access and manage must be developed to improve housing conditions in the Global South.

Home-Based Enterprises

Chapter 2 described the close relationship between domestic and income-generation activities in low-income housing. Analysing the results of detailed studies in four countries (South Africa, Bolivia, Indonesia and India), Peter Kellett found that families operating home-based businesses have significantly higher revenues than families that do not (in India and Indonesia, the differences are 27% and 34%, respectively). Other advantages include women's capacity to work while caring for children and elderly parents, the fungibility of space and investment, and reduced time and resources for commuting to work. Finally, home-based enterprises create (and are viable because of) dynamic, busy, vibrant streets and open spaces.[12] Park and sidewalk activity and proximity between interior and exterior spaces typically create safer and more enjoyable public spaces.

Urban policies in developing countries should encourage the development of income-generation activities within housing units, rather than suppress them. This requires changes to zoning laws, municipal codes and, sometimes, construction codes. It is a strategy that can both improve individual household capabilities and help create collective value in neighbourhoods.

Rental Housing

Rental housing plays a crucial role in informal settlements in developing countries. Alan Gilbert's research shows that only 11% of houses in selected formal settlements in

Bogotá are occupied by tenants, whereas two-thirds of self-help units in more informal settlements have rental space.[13] However, attempts to "fix" residential markets have almost inevitably promoted home-ownership as the only real solution to housing for the poor. In a brilliant article, that could well have inspired the title of this book, researchers Kavita Datta and Gareth A. Jones deplore the constant "invisibility of rental housing" in many countries. They argue that the emphasis on homeownership has come to be accepted, but it "fails to note that the attractions of ownership are—to some extent—'constructed' by government support through subsidies on services and building materials, 'right to buy' policies and pronouncements that ownership is a sound investment" (p. 340).[14] They contend that "urban policy often explicitly and implicitly represents the tenure trajectory of low-income households as a one-way process from renting/sharing to owning with the latter seen as the 'normal' goal of households" (p. 339).[15]

Governments in many developing countries support the goal of homeownership through subsidized programs that provide support to homeowners, but not to tenants.[16] An almost exclusive focus on homeownership (shared by most NGO-backed projects) has led to a general marginalization of the rental sector. Organizations have failed to recognize that rental housing provides three significant advantages. First, it provides income for landlords, allowing them to complete and upgrade their units more rapidly, which accelerates the process of consolidating neighbourhoods. Second, it provides a solution to those who cannot afford, or are not interested in, ownership (such as migrant workers, who prefer temporary accommodations). Third, an increased number of landlords investing in rental units helps support the construction industry, thus creating jobs.[17]

Financial support (in the form of credit and subsidies) and technical assistance is required to design and construct rental units.[18] Gilbert explains:

> In a Third World context, encouraging private landlords to build for rent is highly desirable, whether in the formal or the informal housing market. Loans to landlords in consolidating self-help settlements will allow them to enlarge their property to create more space for tenants.
>
> (p. 166)[19]

Rental housing can potentially increase landlords' and tenants' capabilities, and provide collective value by consolidating neighbourhoods that offer people mobility and attract inhabitants of varying financial means.

Engagement

We live in a world of profound inequalities between the rich and the poor. However, in the last 30 years there has been a significant institutional disengagement from low-cost housing in developing countries. Neoliberal thought, widely implemented through policies in the 1980s and 1990s, discouraged governments from direct participation in housing development. Public agencies, ministries and departments, formerly responsible for housing issues, were downsized, dismantled or assigned different priorities and agendas. As such, responsibilities were transferred from one stakeholder to another, and neither of them committed to reducing the growing qualitative and quantitative housing deficit. International agencies reduced credit and financial support to housing initiatives and in the 1990s, most international NGOs focused on other development objectives. Banks and financial institutions have no serious sustained engagement to provide housing credit to the poor. Universities in North America, the UK and Europe have downsized academic programs focused on housing in developing countries, turning instead to more general urban and development issues (authors cited in this book are some of the remaining, inspiring, leaders in the field).

As fewer academics conduct research on low-cost housing, many architects believe that there is little stimulating design possible in the field. When involved, they tend to simplify issues and focus on specific challenges. In many cases, much like mainstream engineers, they focus on solving technical challenges while ignoring financial, logistic, organizational and other important dimensions of urban development. Other professionals and institutions see urban housing today as a commodity that is (or should be) developed and negotiated in private markets—after policy-makers define minimum-standard levels. This approach typically ignores the roles that housing plays in individual lives, as a symbol of the occupying space, the environment and in the collective memory. NGOs still working on low-cost housing in developing countries rarely deploy sufficient resources or hire architects and urban planners with sufficient experience to study local living patterns and develop innovative, appropriate designs. Rather, they typically resort to short-term interventions, imported solutions or low-density single-story developments that they can design easily to be built using beneficiaries' sweat equity.

In grey literature studies on housing and social justice, the principle of individual freedom has been hijacked to further legitimize institutional disengagement. Meanwhile, the community participation paradigm has not led to much exploration of the effective responsibility of *individuals* and *all stakeholders* in a complex, widely interconnected urban system. In many cases, stereotypes of the poor have served to either further marginalize or romanticize communities, leading to abusive or patronizing approaches. The role of the informal construction sector remains largely ignored by most organizations and in academic literature.

In this book, however, we have seen that low-cost housing policy, program and project interventions today, more than ever, require the committed engagement of multiple stakeholders, including formal and informal institutions and individual and collective agents. This engagement requires that architects, urban planners, economists and other decision and policy-makers commit themselves to significant sustained efforts in research, organizational design, infrastructure, architectural and urban design, education, information, training and follow-up.

Engaged Research

Learning from the Poor

A social justice-based approach demands that architects and other professionals study and decode local, informal and vernacular forms of space appropriation (domestic,

FIGURE 10.19 Urban newcomers bring rural forms of space appropriation and occupation with them. A rural house, found in El Valle, Colombia, (top) is replicated in an informal urban settlement in Yumbo, about 60km away (bottom).

transitional and public), the city and the surrounding territory, and that they analyse local forms of incremental housing development. These forms of construction and space appropriation must be reflected in urban and architectural designs that allow residents to replicate culturally valued practices. Ideas must constantly be informed by

FIGURE 10.20 Careful observation and understanding of human settlements allows us to see the aesthetic value of informal constructions such as this one in Barrio Las Cruces in Bogotá, Colombia.

solutions (in construction and space use) created by the informal sector. Professionals must recognize that, in most cases, these solutions reflect the trade-offs, needs and aspirations of vulnerable, marginalized households. They also reflect their outstanding strengths and, as such, are significant representations of adaptive capacities and mechanisms of resilience. Since many informal settlements are inhabited by first- and second-generation rural migrants, these solutions are also information sources on how rural lifestyles slowly adapt to urban contexts (see Figure 10.19). Interpreting and understanding the use of space also reveals the aesthetic, functional and symbolic value of informal solutions (see Figures 10.20 and 10.21).

Academic Research

Academic research is enriched by including housing in development and urban studies. However, specific characteristics of housing, particularly its connection to a symbolic, culturally-based appropriation of space, the importance of land management, and the role of the construction industry and informal means of production, should not be minimized in favour of more general approaches. More research is needed to add to our understanding of the informal construction sector, to develop solutions for reinforcing informally constructed structures, and to design solutions that effectively reduce the vulnerabilities associated with floods, landslides, earthquakes and other hazards. Additional studies are also needed on adaptation mechanisms in the informal sector and informal settlements.

How do poor households, informal companies and informal workers save, learn, sell, socialize and obtain services, credit, construction materials, information, education and permits? What factors effectively increase mobility and accelerate housing

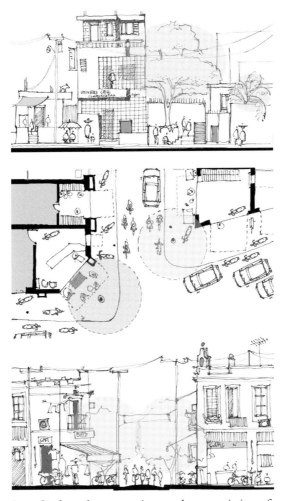

FIGURE 10.21   Sketches of informal constructions and appropriation of open space in Haiti (top) and Hanoi (bottom). Understanding and interpreting the use of space is the first step in understanding the value of informal solutions.

consolidation? How and why do the poor make decisions that involve significant trade-offs in their living conditions? Empirically-based answers to these and other questions could play an important role in informing policy and interventions and help reduce decision-making based on *ideology*, *ignorance* or *self-interest*. Such studies could also refine or possibly refute the arguments raised in this book. Finally, more empirical and theoretical work in the field could also serve to refurbish a lexicon so widely abused that original meanings have given way to superficial interpretations (notions such as community empowerment, participation, capacities, social capital and sustainable housing are a few).

Institutional Engagement

Integration and Differentiation

Institutional engagement does not mean that public or private organizations should concentrate decision-making power. In fact, it means quite the opposite—they must recognize that current challenges require multiple stakeholders to play fundamental, interconnected roles. Decentralization of housing responsibility in the 1980s and 1990s led to a transfer of responsibilities to the private sector and to insolvent, ill-prepared and understaffed municipalities. As we saw in Chapter 7, the results were, in some cases, catastrophic. This is not the type of decentralization required by the framework proposed in this book. Let's consider why.

The complexity of the built environment in developing countries is exacerbated by five important factors. First, threats to living environments (climate change, deforestation, violence, earthquakes, floods and others) do not respect community or urban boundaries. Their effects storm through regions and affect those who may or may not be held responsible for the unsafe conditions leading to death and destruction. Responses that concentrate exclusively on small geographical sectors or social groups tend to be woefully inadequate.

Second, most urban problems (including unemployment, waste disposal and increasing traffic, pollution and land prices) also exceed community and neighbourhood boundaries. Therefore, local solutions (greatly valued by most social scientists) rarely have a significant impact if they are not sufficiently integrated into larger systems. Third, the responses required to mitigate these common challenges and threats are beyond the competencies, and outside the mandates, of individual organizations; so changes that rely on a single sector (construction, health, transport, etc.) or on a single institution are bound to fail. Fourth, the physical boundaries and socially-constructed limits of communities, settlements, cities and metropolitan areas today rarely correspond to administrative districts and political constituencies. This challenges the representativeness of the elected and non-elected. It also puts the legitimacy of their decisions into question and renders negotiations more complex. Finally, policy documents defining resilience, sustainability and other popular agendas continue to multiply, making it more difficult to stay abreast of their contents and comply with them (especially as they sometimes promote diverging, or even conflicting objectives).

This increasing complexity means that two attributes are, more than ever, required of institutional interventions. The first, integration, involves creating conditions that permit institutions to work toward common goals. The second, differentiation, requires a clear definition of the mandate, responsibility and scope of each organization. Although these attributes seem contradictory at first glance, both are required to attain common objectives without redundancy. Institutional networks based on organizational integration and differentiation at the international, national, regional and municipal levels are required to deal with situations that are increasingly complex.

Decentralized Decision-Making

Previous chapters have demonstrated that decentralized decision-making is necessary for dealing with the dynamic and incomplete information characteristic of low-cost housing projects. To facilitate individual and collective agency, it is also crucial that power be fairly distributed among stakeholders. This means not only that more stakeholders become engaged in transparent open discussions on collective value, but also that individuals and groups are offered multiple choices. Residents should have several design alternatives, financial options and choices of construction methods, technologies and contractors. When companies compete with each other and end-users pass judgement on their solutions (by adopting them or not), companies have an incentive to improve quality and reduce costs.

To be legitimate, governance mechanisms in policy, programs and projects in the Global South must first identify, recognize and involve informal groups. Decentralization requires that formal institutions (ministries, government departments, municipalities, control agencies, financial institutions, NGOs, religious organizations, donors, private companies, etc.) work with informal entities such as local community-based organizations, informal enterprises and neighbourhood associations. Formal recognition of *Juntas de Acción Comunal* in Bogotá (and their ability to negotiate with authorities on behalf of social groups) has led, for instance, to the development of successful urban upgrading projects. This is an example that can, and should be, replicated in other contexts.

Freedom and Accountability in Resource Use

One of the most powerful tools for decentralizing decision-making power is transferring resources (such as cash, subsidies and credit) directly to end-users, and allowing them to manage them as they see fit for their needs and expectations. This implies trusting them and believing that they are capable of making choices that will provide value to their families and communities. It also means recognizing that they can (and should) be responsible for making choices to enable them to live lives that they value. Rather than providing finished solutions (a house, a plot or an apartment unit), direct resource provision gives households the freedom to respond to their own needs and aspirations, and adds incentives for finding inexpensive solutions in the market.

We have seen, however, that this freedom in resource use implies accountability. Programs and projects that transfer resources directly to individual households need efficient control mechanisms. Progressive instalments, subject to adherence to collectively decided core principles, are an effective tool for finding the right balance between household agency, collective value and individual responsibility. More innovative management tools are needed to promote individual capabilities while still developing coherent, efficient and properly integrated settlements.

Follow-Up Engagement

Public and private organizations must recognize that their responsibility does not end with the delivery of a house, subsidy, loan, public service, infrastructure or plot. Housing development is not about delivering a financial or shelter solution that ends with a ribbon-cutting ceremony. Policy, programs and projects have to anticipate and include effective governance mechanisms and structures to assess the short-, medium- and long-term impacts of interventions, the evolution of products and services, the appropriation of public and private space, and the use of infrastructure and open areas. Evaluation and follow-up programs must be aimed, not at congratulating elected officials or pursuing partisan political agendas, but at identifying both the difficulties and opportunities that arise in the post-occupation or appropriation process.

Trust between stakeholders cannot be achieved within the typically short time frame of a project or program. The trust that informal institutions and poor households may develop for governmental and other formal organizations is dependent on sustained support and continuous interaction over longer time periods. A sustained engagement with social groups and vulnerable households on the part of institutions can build this trust. Follow-up on interventions is also necessary so that policies, programs, services and products can be adapted to unintended effects, new market conditions and unexpected changes in the political, economic and social environments. It is important to identify the ideas and strategies that work best along with those that should be discarded or modified.

Examples

Although it is impossible to summarize here all the successful strategies of engaged institutions in the low-cost housing field, let's consider four relevant examples.

Community Architects

This Cuban institution, whose role in resilience development was explored in Chapter 7, has shown that directly engaging in local architectural practices and accounting for individual needs and household expectations can produce significant results. The *Arquitecto de la Comunidad* is a stakeholder that responds to Cuba's specific political and economic environment. Although it is probable that the Community Architect model cannot be entirely replicated in other contexts, its capacity for direct interaction with households in designing and planning construction work provides an inspiring example of institutional engagement.

Arturo Valladares, a researcher at McGill University, has highlighted some key aspects of this engagement.[20] First, consistent work in the same district allows Community Architects to accrue significant local knowledge and become familiar with local households. Second, the constant review of design work and ideas by several professionals provides scenarios for collective, committed debate and discussion among architects and other design professionals. Third, systematic learning about the local framework, regulations and strategies provides best practice continuity and successful strategies. Fourth, consistent use of a proven design method that involves designing several alternatives so families can choose the option that best suits their needs and aspirations. Fifth, implementing a standard system of progressive fees means end-users pay only for the services they receive and can space their investment over time. Finally, rigorous compliance with certain regulations and policies has led to housing development and upgrades that reduce vulnerabilities and enhance resilience. These principles and mission statements are not specific to the Cuban situation. They can be adapted to other contexts and other types of bottom-up institutions committed to developing individual capabilities and collective value.

Cajas de Compensación

Different types of organizations operate in Colombia under the name *"Cajas de Compensación Familiar"* (or Social Security Institutions). Although they are private (non-profit) corporations, their funds are supervised by the *Superintendencia del Subsidio Familiar* (part of the Ministry of Labour). They fulfil several social tasks, including redistributing the resources from a compulsory financial contribution by all affiliated employees.[21] Their socially-oriented activities include providing education, recreation, culture, tourism opportunities, health care and childhood programs. The *Cajas de Compensación* are also responsible for creating a link between government housing-subsidy programs and their beneficiaries. In this role, they collect valuable information about potential beneficiaries, organize selection processes (this often includes organizing a savings plan), provide soft loans to beneficiaries, help households obtain alternative forms of credit and subsidies, and manage housing programs bringing together housing developers, government agencies and households.

Their engagement in developing housing solutions for low-income families has become a crucial element of Colombia's welfare system. The *Cajas de Compensación* are information hubs facilitating access to housing services and promoting core values that improve the quality of housing solutions. Their commitment to these values (including "the wellbeing of all family members"), as well as the competition between them (there are more than 60 institutions), provide constant incentives for improving the services offered. By providing comprehensive services in different areas, the major *Cajas de Compensación* have gained the trust and respect of Colombian employees. This has made them effective intermediaries in subsidy programs.

There are, however, many operational aspects of the *Cajas de Compensación* that could be improved. Not all offer the same services or the same quality, the majority have failed to reach the poorest sectors of society and several of their housing projects have failed to respond to anything other than market forces. Nonetheless, they are an important example of sustained institutional commitment to accompanying households through the process of improving their living conditions.

Government of Gujarat

For more than 13 years, the Government of Gujarat (in western India) has maintained a steady engagement to reduce qualitative and quantitative housing deficits. When the 2001 earthquake hit the region, destroying millions of structures, the government adopted an ambitious owner-driven approach to providing affected rural and urban residents with housing solutions. Since then, the government has been committed to evaluating the program's effects, having a constant open dialogue with researchers and academics, holding public debates involving citizens, experts, elected officers and officers of other Indian states, publishing data on housing programs and explaining their benefits. Currently adapting the owner-driven program to "regular" housing development, the government is also committed to improving the approach by making it more efficient and inclusive. The Government of Gujarat exemplifies how a public institution can contribute to open, transparent dialogue on housing practices, bring together different stakeholders and collect valuable data for scientific research and policy improvement.

Cooperative Housing

It has become clear that other forms of housing production must be considered as alternatives to the neoliberal model. In South Africa and many other countries, housing cooperatives have become a powerful means of efficiently providing housing *for* and, especially, *with* the poor. Cooperative housing can overcome some of the drawbacks of centralized government investment and procurement. Through cooperatives, a group of families with common interests can gain increased control of the design, procurement and construction of their own project, with the possibility of developing multi-family housing and/or collective income-generating activities (farming, agriculture, commerce, etc.). Cooperative housing thus integrates individual and collective agency, and provides additional scenarios to the debate on notions of the "good life" and sustainable human settlements.

However, specialized institutions are often required to contribute to the establishment of cooperatives. These institutions must accompany and support families through the processes of registering the organization, obtaining credit, subsidies and permits and hiring design, construction and other services. Housing cooperatives are an inspiring form of bottom-up engagement in which low-income families collectively agree on living conditions.

Infrastructure and Services Engagement

In previous chapters, we have seen that all units must be serviced if living conditions for the poor are to be improved. Progressive forms of infrastructure that allow residents to improve their access to public services should be adopted, when necessary. A clear differentiation must be made between forms of infrastructure development that require skilled labour, centralized management and specialized technology (which must be provided by institutions) and the type of infrastructure that can be carried out, hired out and/or managed by households. Therefore, numerous decision-making institutions (with various levels of formality or informality) must be recognized and included in the process. A clear differentiation also has to be made between maintenance and upgrading activities that can be carried out through individual agency (at the household level) and those performed through collective, consensual decision-making within social groups and institutions.

Engaged Design

Architectural and urban designers have a significant role to play in low-cost housing. In many cases, their role is not to design finished housing units, but rather plots and three-dimensional spaces that can evolve, be progressively adapted and then occupied through individual and/or collective agency. Time (over extended periods), therefore, becomes a significant design tool in low-cost housing. Designs must anticipate that residents can, and will, expand and upgrade structures in the future. They have to facilitate and, in many cases, enhance these possibilities. This means that layouts, materials, structural joints, pipes, sections and foundations have to be designed so that later modifications will be structurally sound and inexpensive to carry out. It also requires that designs accommodate structurally sound horizontal and/or vertical additions. The anticipation of future modifications must not affect the light and ventilation in the initial spaces and designing to different (sometimes lower) standards should not, of course, compromise environmental or health and safety standards. Designers must propose a variety of alternatives so that individuals and social groups can select the solution they judge most appropriate. Finally, end-users and other stakeholders must be included at all stages of the design process.

Education, Training and Information

Education, training and information distribution must target informal companies, unskilled labourers, households and other stakeholders. For example, information and education on upgrades and extensions must be provided to end-users, informal construction companies and informal workers. Institutions must facilitate South–South knowledge transfer so lessons and strategies that have proven successful in other locations can be shared. Policy, program and project evaluations must produce reliable, accessible data to be used for later improvements.

Planning and Designing in a Complex Context

Many people recognize that the qualitative and quantitative deficits in low-cost housing are both a cause and a consequence of underdevelopment in most poor countries. However, fewer are aware that informal housing (the most tangible expression of this deficit) is created using efficient and sophisticated strategies that are invisible to most policy and decision-makers. Unfortunately, a lack of knowledge, institutional disengagement from housing problems, centralized decision-making power and focus on a limited number of variables have led to housing policy, programs and projects that fail to respond to the real needs and aspirations of the poor.

As our journey in this book has made clear, "the housing problem" is not, in fact, a problem of non-existent dwellings and its solution requires more than the provision of shelters. We have explored a framework for thinking about the meaning of sustainable, resilient human settlements, the uniqueness of contextual conditions and the tensions and long-term effects that can result from interventions. It suggests that the real challenge is not building houses but creating conditions in which individuals and social groups can live lives they have reason to value. This is an arduous task that must include social justice considerations, decentralizing decision-making power, integrating heterogeneous institutions and including the informal construction sector—doubtless the most powerful housing industry force. More importantly, it is a process that requires the demanding engagement of public and private organizations, NGOs, international agencies, social groups, end-users and many other stakeholders. Individual agency and intensive stakeholder interaction are prerequisites for a sustainable adaptive process which, evolving over time, allows the needs and desires of inhabitants to take shape. We can improve the living conditions of millions of people in the Global South if we accept this engagement, stop trying to simplify housing issues and embrace the challenge of planning and designing within a complex context.

Notes

1 Ceballos Ramos, O.L. "Rehabilitación de Vivienda y Recuperación del Patrimonio Construido: El Caso de Bogotá." *Scripta Nova—Revista electrónica de geografía y ciencias sociales* 10 (2007); Álvarez, M. "El inquilinato: Una alternativa de vivienda en el Barrio Las Cruces." *Revista Apuntes* 16, no. 23 (2003): 46–72.

2 Perelman, L.J. "Infrastructure Risk and Renewal: The Clash of Blue and Green." Paper presented at the Public Entity Risk Institute Symposium, 2008 (Fairfax, VA: Public Entity Risk Institute).

3 Lizarralde, G., C. Davidson and C. Johnson, eds. *Rebuilding after Disasters: From Emergency to Sustainability*. London: Taylor & Francis, 2009.

4 Smets, P. "Small is Beautiful, but Big is Often the Practice: Housing Microfinance in Discussion." *Habitat International* 30, no. 3 (2006): 595–613.

5 Datta, K. and G.A. Jones. "Housing and Finance in Developing Countries: Invisible Issues on Research and Policy Agendas." *Habitat International* 25, no. 3 (2001): 333–57.

6 Buckley, R.M. and J. Kalarickal. "Housing Policy in Developing Countries: Conjectures and Refutations." *The World Bank Research Observer* 20, no. 2 (2005): 233–57.

7 Bhatt, V. and W. Rybczynski. "How the Other Half Builds." In *Time-Saver Standards for Urban Design*, edited by Watson, D., A. Plattus and R. Shibley, 1.3.1–1.3.11. New York: McGraw-Hill, 2003.

8 Smets, "Small Is Beautiful, but Big is Often the Practice: Housing Microfinance in Discussion."

9 Keivani, R. and E. Werna. "Modes of Housing Provision in Developing Countries." *Progress in Planning* 55, no. 2 (2001): 65–118.

10 Institut des métiers de la ville. *Policies sought to manage housing industry*, 2011. Retrieved from www.imv-hanoi.com.

11 Banerjee, A.V. and E. Duflo. *Poor Economics: A Radical Rethinking of the Way to Fight Global Poverty*. New York: PublicAffairs, 2011; Karlan, D.S. and J. Appel. *More Than Good Intentions*. Dutton New York, 2011.

12 Kellett, P. and J. Hernández-García. *Researching the Contemporary City: Identity, Environment and Social Inclusion in Developing Urban Areas*. Bogotá: Editorial Pontificia Universidad Javeriana, 2013.

13 Gilbert, A. "A Home is for Ever? Residential Mobility and Homeownership in Self-Help Settlements." *Environment and Planning A* 31 (1999): 1073–92.

14 Datta and Jones, "Housing and Finance in Developing Countries: Invisible Issues on Research and Policy Agendas."

15 Datta, K. and G.A. Jones, eds. *Housing and Finance in Developing Countries*. London: Taylor & Francis, 1998.

16 Gilbert, "A Home Is for Ever? Residential Mobility and Homeownership in Self-Help Settlements."

17 Werna, E. "Shelter, Employment and the Informal City in the Context of the Present Economic Scene: Implications for Participatory Governance." *Habitat International* 25, no. 2 (2001): 209–27.

18 Ibid.

19 Gilbert, A. "Financing Self-Help Housing: Evidence from Bogotá, Colombia." *International Planning Studies* 5, no. 2 (2000): 165–90.

20 Valladares, A. "The Community Architect Program: Implementing participation-in-design to improve housing conditions in Cuba." *Habitat International* 38 (2013), 18–24.

21 Alm, J. and H. López-Castaño. "Payroll Taxes in Colombia." In *Reforming the Colombia Tax System*, edited by Richard Bird, James Poterba and Joel Slemrod. Boston: MIT Press, 2004.

BIBLIOGRAPHY

ACDI Agence Canadienne de Développement International. "Results-Based Management Tools at CIDA: A How-to Guide." ACDI, http://www.acdi-cida.gc.ca/acdi-cida/ACDI-CIDA.nsf/eng/NAT-92213444-N2H.

Aguilar, A. G. and E. P. Campuzano. "Informal Sector." In *International Encyclopedia of Human Geography*, edited by Rob Kitchin and Nigel Thrift, 446–53. Oxford: Elsevier, 2009.

Alexander, D. E. "Resilience and Disaster Risk Reduction: An Etymological Journey." *Natural Hazards and Earth System Sciences Discussions* 1 (2013): 1257–84.

Alkire, S. "Why the Capability Approach?" *Journal of Human Development* 6, no. 1 (2005): 115–35.

Alm, James and Hugo López-Castaño. "Payroll Taxes in Colombia." In *Reforming the Colombia Tax System*, edited by Richard Bird, James Poterba and Joel Slemrod. Boston: MIT Press, 2004.

Alter Chen, Martha. *Rethinking the Informal Economy: Linkages with the Formal Economy and the Formal Regulatory Environment, Research Paper No. 2005/10*. Helsinki: UNU-WIDER, United Nations University (UNU), 2005.

Álvarez, Mónica. "El inquilinato: Una alternativa de vivienda en el barrio Las Cruces." *Revista Apuntes* 16, no. 23 (2003): 46–72.

Anand, Paul. "New Directions in the Economics of Welfare: Special Issue Celebrating Nobel Laureate Amartya Sen's 75th Birthday." *Journal of Public Economics* 95, no. 3–4 (2011): 191–92.

Anvuur, A. and M. Kumaraswamy. "Better Collaboration through Cooperation." In *Collaborative Relationships in Construction: Developing Frameworks and Networks*, edited by H. Smyth and S. Pryke, 107–28. Oxford: Wiley-Blackwell, 2008.

Aristizabal, Nora C. and Andrés Ortíz Gómez. "Improving Security without Titles in Bogotá." *Habitat International* 28, no. 2 (2004): 245–58.

Arnstein, S. R. "A Ladder of Citizen Participation." *Journal of the American Planning Association* 35, no. 4 (1969): 216–24.

Barenstein, Jennifer Duyne. *Housing Reconstruction in Post-Earthquake Gujarat: A Comparative Analysis*. Humanitarian Practice Network Paper. London: Overseas Development Institute, 2006.

Barenstein, Jennifer Duyne, P. M. Phelps, D. Pittet and S. Sena. *Safer Homes, Stronger Communities: A Handbook for Reconstruction after Natural Disasters*. Washington: World Bank, 2010.

Baron, C. "La gouvernance: Débats autour d'un concept polysémique." *Droit et société*, no. 2 (2003): 329–49.

Bekker, M. C. and H. Steyn. "Defining 'Project Governance' for Large Capital Projects." *South African Journal of Industrial Engineering* November 20, no. 2 (2009): 81–92.

Bhatt, Vikram and W. Rybczynski. "How the Other Half Builds." In *Time-Saver Standards for Urban Design*, edited by D. Watson, Plattus, A. and Shibley, R., 1.3.1–1.3.11. New York: McGraw-Hill, 2003.

Blaikie, P. M., T. Cannoon, I. Davis and B. Wisner. *At Risk: Natural Hazards, People's Vulnerability, and Disasters*. New York: Routledge, 1994.

Boaden, B. and A. Karam. "The Informal Housing Market in Four of Cape Town's Low-Income Settlements". Working Paper. Cape Town: University of Cape Town, 2000.

Bouraoui, Dhouha and Gonzalo Lizarralde. "Centralized Decision Making, Users' Participation and Satisfaction in Post-Disaster Reconstruction: The Case of Tunisia." *International Journal of Disaster Resilience in the Built Environment* 4, no. 2 (2013): 145–67.

Bowbrick, Peter. "The Causes of Famine: A Refutation of Professor Sen's Theory." *Food Policy* 11, no. 2 (1986): 105–24.

Brighouse, H. and I. Robeyns. *Measuring Justice: Primary Goods and Capabilities*. Cambridge: Cambridge University Press, 2010.

Buckley, Robert M. and Jerry Kalarickal. "Housing Policy in Developing Countries: Conjectures and Refutations." *The World Bank Research Observer* 20, no. 2 (2005): 233–57.

Burgess, Rod. "Self-Help Housing: A New Imperialist Strategy? A Critique of the Turner School." *Antipode* 9, no. 2 (1977): 50–59.

Campbell, S. "Green Cities, Growing Cities, Just Cities? Urban Planning and the Contradictions of Sustainable Development." *Journal of the American Planning Association* 62, no. 3 (1996): 296–312.

Canada Mortgage and Housing Corporation. "Filtering in Housing." *Publications and Reports* (2013), http://www.cmhc-schl.gc.ca/odpub/pdf/63795.pdf.

Ceballos Ramos, Olga Lucía. "Rehabilitación de vivienda y recuperación del patrimonio construido: El caso de Bogotá." *Scripta Nova—Revista electrónica de geografía y ciencias sociales* 10 (2007).

CECI. *Projet De Reconstruction de maisons au profit des sinistrés de L'Ouragan Mitch: Rapport narratif final*. Montreal: CECI, 2001.

CEPRODE. *Caracterización de los desastres en El Salvador: Tipología y vulnerabilidad socioeconómica*. San Salvador: CEPRODE, 1994.

Chan, Paul and Christine Raisanen. "Informality and Emergence in Construction." *Construction Management and Economics* 27, no. 10 (2009): 907–12.

Cherns, A.B. and D.T. Bryant. "Studying the Client's Role in Construction Management." *Construction Management and Economics* 2, no. 2 (1984): 177–84.

Choguill, Charles L. "The Search for Policies to Support Sustainable Housing." *Habitat International* 31, no. 1 (2007): 143–49;

Comim, Flavio. "Operationalizing Sen's Capability Approach." Paper presented at the Conference Justice and Poverty: Examining Sen's Capability Approach. Cambridge, 2001.

Comim, Flavio, Mozaffar Qizilbash and Sabina Alkire. *The Capability Approach: Concepts, Measures and Applications*. Cambridge: Cambridge University Press, 2008.

Construction Industry Development Board (CIDB). *Annual Report 2004 2005*. Pretoria: CIDB, 2005.

Datta, Kavita and Gareth A. Jones. "Housing and Finance in Developing Countries: Invisible Issues on Research and Policy Agendas." *Habitat International* 25, no. 3 (2001): 333–57.

Datta, Kavita and Gareth A. Jones, eds. *Housing and Finance in Developing Countries*. London: Taylor & Francis, 1998.

Dávila, J., A. Gilbert, N. Rueda and P. Brand. "Suelo urbano y vivienda para la población de ingresos bajos. Estudios de caso: Bogotá-Soacha-Mosquera; Medellín y área metropolitana." Development Planning Unit, University College of London (2006).

Davis, Mike. *Planet of Slums*. London: Verso, 2006.

Department of Housing South Africa. "Design and Construction of Houses, Republic of South Africa." http://www.nhbrc.org, 2006.

Department of Housing South Africa. *Housing Programs and Subsidies*. Pretoria: Department of Housing, Communication Services, 2006.

Desai, V., Rob Kitchin and Nigel Thrift. "Aid." In *International Encyclopedia of Human Geography*, edited by Ron Kitchin and Nigel Thrift, 84–90. Oxford: Elsevier, 2009.

De Soto, Hernando. *The Mystery of Capital*. New York: Basic Books, 2000.

Doherty, Gareth and Moises Lino Silva. "Formally Informal: Daily Life and the Shock of Order in a Brazilian Favela." *Built Environment* 37, no. 1 (2011): 30–41.

The Economist. "City Limits." August 13, 2011.

The Economist. "Hot Spots: Plagues and Livestock." February 10, 2011.

The Economist. "Let Them Shoot Hoops." July 30, 2011.

The Economist. "Lighting Rural India: Out of the Gloom." July 23, 2013.

The Economist. "Slumdog Millions." March 24, 2010.

Feiler, Gil. "The New Towns in Egypt." In *Housing Policy in Developing Countries*, edited by Gil Shidlo, 121–39. London: Routledge, 1990.

Fellows, R. and A. M. M. Liu. "Managing Organizational Interfaces in Engineering Construction Projects: Addressing Fragmentation and Boundary Issues across Multiple Interfaces." *Construction Management and Economics* 30, no. 8 (2012): 653–71.

Ferguson, B. and J. Navarrete. "A Financial Framework for Reducing Slums: Lessons from Experience in Latin America." *Environment and Urbanization* 15, no. 2 (2003): 201.

Ferguson, B. and J. Navarrete. "A Financial Framework for Reducing Slums." In *Contemporary Readings in Globalization*, edited by Scott Sernau, 183–96. London: Sage, 2008.

Ferguson, B. and J. Navarrete. "New Approaches to Progressive Housing in Latin America: A Key to Habitat Programs and Policy." *Habitat International* 27, no. 2 (2003): 309–23.

Ferguson, B. and P. Smets. "Finance for Incremental Housing; Current Status and Prospects for Expansion." *Habitat International*, 34, no. 3 (2010): 288–298.

F.M.O. Finance for Development. "F.M.O Low Income Housing Roundtable Hanoi, Vietnam." The Hague: F.M.O. 2012.

Forester, J. *The Deliberative Practitioner: Encouraging Participatory Planning Processes*. Boston: The MIT Press, 1999.

Frediani, Alexandre Apsan. "Amartya Sen, the World Bank, and the Redress of Urban Poverty: A Brazilian Case Study." *Journal of Human Development* 8, no. 1 (2007): 133–52.

Frediani, Alexandre Apsan. "Planning for Freedoms: The Contribution of Sen's Capability Approach to Development Practice." *UCL Discovery* (2008): http://www.discovery.ucl.ac.uk.

Frediani, Alexandre Apsan. "The World Bank, Turner and Sen—Freedom in the Urban Arena." DPU Working Papers, no. 136 (2009): Development Planning Unit, University College London.

Frediani, Alexandre Apsan and Camillo Boano. "Processes for Just Products: The Capability Space of Participatory Design." In *The Capability Approach, Technology and Design*, 203–22. New York: Springer, 2012.

Freeman, R.E. *Strategic Management: A Stakeholder Approach*. Boston, MA: Pitman, 1984.

Friedman, Joseph, Emmanuel Jimenez and Stephen K. Mayo. "The Demand for Tenure Security in Developing Countries." *Journal of Development Economics* 29, no. 2 (1988): 185–98.

FUNDEMUN-USAID. "Estudio socio-económico y censo de población y vivienda, Ciudad Nueva, Choluteca." Unpublished, 2001.

Gaeta-Carrillo, Nubia. "La incursión de la comunicación en la prevención de desastres: El caso cubano." I Congreso de Salud y Desastres. La Habana, Cuba, 2011.

Gasper, Des. "What Is the Capability Approach? Its Core, Rationale, Partners and Dangers." *Journal of Socio-Economics* 36, no. 3 (2007): 335–59.

Gilbert, Alan. "A Home Is for Ever? Residential Mobility and Homeownership in Self-Help Settlements." *Environment and Planning A* 31 no. 6 (1999): 1073–92.

Gilbert, Alan. "Financing Self-Help Housing: Evidence from Bogotá, Colombia." *International Planning Studies* 5, no. 2 (2000): 165–90.

Gilbert, Alan and Ann Varley. *Landlord and Tenant: Housing the Poor in Urban Mexico*. London: Taylor & Francis, 1991.

Goebel, A. "Sustainable Urban Development? Low-Cost Housing Challenges in South Africa." *Habitat International* 31, no. 3–4 (2007): 291–302.

Gore, C. "Irreducibly Social Goods and the Informational Basis of Amartya Sen's Capability Approach." *Journal of International Development* 9, no. 2 (1997): 235–50.

Gough, Katherine V. and Peter Kellett. "Housing Consolidation and Home-Based Income Generation: Evidence from Self-Help Settlements in Two Colombian Cities." *Cities* 18, no. 4 (2001): 235–47.

Guaraldo Choguill, Marisa B. "A Ladder of Community Participation for Underdeveloped Countries." *Habitat International* 20, no. 3 (1996): 431–44.

Hansen, K. T. "Informal Sector." In *International Encyclopedia of the Social and Behavioral Sciences*, edited by J. Smelser Neil and B. Baltes Paul, 7450–53. Oxford: Pergamon, 2001.

Hawker, D. "Riding Wave of Shack Business Boom." *Cape Argus News*, 2006, May 29, 3.

Hernández-Bonilla, Mauricio. "People Shaping Public Space: Popular Urban Design Processes in Mexico." In *Researching the Contemporary City: Identity, Environment and Social Inclusion in Developing Urban Areas*, edited by Jaime Hernandez-Garcia and Peter Kellett, 137–50. Bogotá: Editorial Pontificia Universidad Javeriana, 2013.

Hernández-García, Jaime. "The Production of Informal Urban Space: The Barrios of Bogotá." In *Researching the Contemporary City: Identity, Environment and Social Inclusion in Developing Urban Areas,* edited by Jaime Hernandez-Garcia and Peter Kellett, 141–68. Bogotá: Editorial Pontificia Universidad Javeriana, 2013.

Hewitt, K. *Regions of Risk: A Geographical Introduction to Disasters*. Harlow: Longman, 1997.

Hoek-Smit, Marja C. and Douglas B. Diamond. "Subsidies for Housing Finance." *Housing Finance International* 17, no. 3 (2003): 3–13.

Huchzermeyer, Marie. "From 'Contravention of Laws' to 'Lack of Rights': Redefining the Problem of Informal Settlements in South Africa." *Habitat International* 28, no. 3 (2004): 333–47.

Hussmanns, Ralf. "Measuring the Informal Economy: From Employment in the Informal Sector to Informal Employment." Integration Working Paper, no 53. (2004) Geneva: ILO.

IFRC. *World Disasters Report 2004*. New York: International Federation of Red Cross and Red Crescent Societies, 2004.

Institut des métiers de la ville. "Policies Sough to Manage Housing Industry." (2011), http://www.imv-hanoi.com.

Institute for Security Studies. *Crime and Justice Hub*. Pretoria: Institute for Security Studies, 2013.

Jha, A. K., Jennifer Duyne Barenstein, P. M. Phelps, D. Pittet and S. Sena. *Handbook for Post-Disaster Housing and Community Reconstruction*. Washington: The World Bank, 2009.

Johnson, Cassidy. "Impacts of Prefabricated Temporary Housing after Disasters: 1999 Earthquakes in Turkey." *Habitat International* 31, no. 1 (2007): 36–52.

Johnson, Cassidy and Gonzalo Lizarralde. "Post-Disaster Housing and Reconstruction." *The International Encyclopedia of Housing and Home* (2012): 340–6.

Karlan, Dean S. and Jacob Appel. *More Than Good Intentions*. New York: Dutton, 2011.

Keivani, Ramin and Edmundo Werna. "Modes of Housing Provision in Developing Countries." *Progress in Planning* 55, no. 2 (2001): 65–118.

Keivani, Ramin and Edmundo Werna. "Refocusing the Housing Debate in Developing Countries from a Pluralist Perspective." *Habitat International* 25, no. 2 (2001): 191–208.

Kellett, Peter and Jaime Hernandez-Garcia. *Researching the Contemporary City: Identity, Environment and Social Inclusion in Developing Urban Areas*. Bogotá: Editorial Pontificia Universidad Javeriana, 2013.

Kellett, Peter and Graham Tipple. "The Home as Workplace: A Study of Income-Generating Activities within the Domestic Setting." *Environment and Urbanization* 12, no. 1 (2000): 203–14.

Khavul, Susanna, Garry D. Bruton and Eric Wood. "Informal Family Business in Africa." *Entrepreneurship Theory and Practice* 33, no. 6 (2009): 1219–38.

Kvan, Thomas. "Collaborative Design: What Is It?" *Automation in Construction* 9, no. 4 (2000): 409–15.

Lall, Somik V., Mila Freire, Belinda Yuen, Robin Rajack and Jean-Jacques Helluin. *Urban Land Markets: Improving Land Management for Successful Urbanization*. Washington: Springer, 2009.

Lewis, James. "The Worm in the Bud: Corruption, Construction and Catastrophe." In *Hazards and the Built Environment*, edited by Lee Bosher, 238–63. New York: Routledge, 2008.

Lizarralde, Gonzalo. "Organisational System and Performance of Post-Disaster Reconstruction Projects." Ph.D. Thesis, Université de Montréal, 2004.

Lizarralde, Gonzalo. "The Challenge of Low-Cost Housing for Disaster Prevention in Small Municipalities." In *4th International i-Rec Conference 2008. Building resilience: achieving effective post-disaster reconstruction*, edited by i-Rec, Electronic publication. Christchurch, New Zealand: i-Rec, 2008.

Lizarralde, Gonzalo. "Mythes et réalités de la reconstruction à la suite de désastres." *Revue ARQ* no. 144, 2008, 8–11.

Lizarralde, Gonzalo. "Project Management and Democracy: Owner Driven Reconstruction in Rural Colombia." Paper presented at the Owner Driven Reconstruction Conference, London, 2009.

Lizarralde, Gonzalo. "Stakeholder Participation and Incremental Housing in Subsidized Housing Projects in Colombia and South Africa." *Habitat International* 35, no. 2 (2010): 175–87.

Lizarralde, Gonzalo. "Decentralizing (Re)Construcion: Agriculture Cooperatives as a Vehicle for Reconstruction in Colombia." In *Building Back Better: Delivering People-Centered Housing Reconstruction at Scale*, edited by Michal Lyons and Theo Schilderman, 191–214. London: Practical Action, 2010.

Lizarralde, Gonzalo and Marie-France Boucher. "Learning from Post-Disaster Reconstruction for Pre-Disaster Planning." In *2nd International i-Rec Conference 2004. Planning for Reconstruction*, pp. 8-14–8-24. Coventry: Coventry University, Coventry Centre for Disaster Management, 2004.

Lizarralde, Gonzalo and Colin Davidson. "Learning from the Poor." In *3rd International i-Rec Conference 2006. Meeting Stakeholder Interests*, edited by David Alexander, Colin Davidson;,Andrew Fox, Cassidy Johnson, and Gonzalo Lizarralde. Florence, Italy: Firenze University Press, 2006.

Lizarralde, Gonzalo and Mark Massyn. "Unexpected Negative Outcomes of Community Participation in Low-Cost Housing Projects in South Africa." *Habitat International* 32, no. 1 (2008): 1–14.

Lizarralde, Gonzalo and Michel-Max Raynaud. "The Capability Approach in Housing Development and Reconstruction." In *Post-Earthquake Reconstruction: Lessons Learnt and Way Forward*. Ahmedabad, India: Government of Gujarat, 2011.

Lizarralde, Gonzalo and David Root. "Ready-Made Shacks: Learning from the Informal Sector to Meet Housing Needs in South Africa." Paper presented at the CIB World Building Congress Construction for Development, Cape Town, South Africa, 2007.

Lizarralde, Gonzalo and David Root. "The Informal Construction Sector and the Inefficiency of Low Cost Housing Markets." *Construction Management and Economics* 26, no. 2 (2008): 103–13.

Lizarralde, Gonzalo, Cassidy Johnson and Colin Davidson. "Houses of Candied Sugar: Comparative Research on Controversial Temporary Housing after Earthquake Disasters in Colombia and Turkey." Paper presented at the the International Association for Housing Science 31st World Congress on Housing Process and Product, Montréal, Canada, June 23–27, 2003.

Lizarralde, Gonzalo, Colin Davidson and Cassidy Johnson, eds. *Rebuilding after Disasters: From Emergency to Sustainability*. London: Taylor & Francis, 2009.

Lizarralde, Gonzalo, Stella Tomiyoshi, Mario Bourgault, Juan Malo and Georgia Cardosi. "Understanding Differences in Construction Project Governance between Developed and Developing Countries." *Construction Management and Economics* 31, no. 7 (2013): 711–30.

Lizarralde, Gonzalo, Arturo Valladares, Andrés Olivera, Lisa Bornstein, Kevin Gould and Jennifer Duyne Barenstein. "Towards Strategic Resilience: The Cuban Model to Vulnerability Reduction and Reconstruction." *Disasters* In press (2014).

Louis, Mosake Njomo. "The Effects of Conflict on the Youth of Mfuleni." Saarbrucken: LAP Lambert Academic Publishing, 2006.

Lozano, Juan. "Juan Lozano, Senador." http://www.juanlozano.com.co/noticias/2006/noviembre/20061126_01.html.

Luce, Edward. *In Spite of the Gods: The Strange Rise of Modern India*. London: Abacus, 2006.

Lungo, Mario and Sonia Baires. "Socio-Spatial Segregation and Urban Land Regulation in Latin American Cities." Paper presented at the International Seminar on Segregation in the City. Cambridge, MA, USA, 2001.

Lungo, Mario and Roxana Martel. "Ciudadanía social y violencia en las ciudades centroamericanas." *Realidad: Revista de Ciencias Sociales y Humanidades*, no. 94 (2003): 485–510.

Lyons, Michal. "Building Back Better: The Large-Scale Impact of Small-Scale Approaches to Reconstruction." *World Development* 37, no. 2 (2009): 385–98.

Macours, Karen and Johan F. M. Swinnen. "Rural-Urban Poverty Differences in Transition Countries." *World Development* 36, no. 11 (2008): 2170–87.

Manyena, S.B. "The Concept of Resilience Revisited." *Disasters* 30, no. 4 (2006): 434–50.

Martin-Breen, P. and J. M. Anderies. *Resilience: A Literature Review*. New York: Rockefeller Foundation, 2011.

Marx, Benjamin, Thomas Stoker and Tavneet Suri. "The Economics of Slums in the Developing World." *Journal of Economic Perspectives* 27, no. 4 (2013): 187–210.

Medicc. *In the Eye of the Storm: Lesson in Disaster Management from Cuba*. Decatour, GA: Medicc, 2005.

Mehta, Barjor and Arish Dastur, eds. *Approaches to Urban Slums: A Multimedia Sourcebook on Adaptive and Proactive Approaches*. Washington: The World Bank, 2008.

Mesa, G. "The Cuban Health Sector and Disaster Mitigation." *MEDICC Review* 10, no. 3 (2008): 5–8.

Mesa V. I. S. – Diego Echeverry Campos. "Reflexión sobre la propuesta del gobierno nacional en el tema de vivienda 2010–2014." Presentaciones, 2011. https://mesavis.uniandes.edu.co/Presentacion%202011/24%20de%20marzo%202011.pdf

Mlinga, R. S. and Jill Wells. "Collaboration between Formal and Informal Enterprises in the Construction Sector in Tanzania." *Habitat International* 26, no. 2 (2002): 269–80.

Mohsini, R. A. and Colin H. Davidson. "Determinants of Performance in the Traditional Building Process." *Construction Management and Economics* 10, no. 4 (1992): 343–59.

Morado Nascimento, Denise. "Auto Production Housing Process in Brazil: The Informational Practice Approach." In *Sustainable Slum Upgrading in Urban Area*, edited by Happy Santosa, Winny Astuti and Dyah Widi Astuti, 51–62. Surakarta: CIB, 2009.

Mukhija, Vinit. "An Analytical Framework for Urban Upgrading: Property Rights, Property Values and Physical Attributes." *Habitat International* 26, no. 4 (2002): 553–70.

Murray, Mike and Mohamed Rafik Meghji. "Corruption within International Engineering-Construction Projects." In *Corporate Social Responsibility in the Construction Industry*, edited by Mike Murray and Andrew Dainty, 141–64. New York: Taylor & Francis, 2009.

Naoum, Shamil. *People and Organizational Management in Construction*. London: Thomas Telford Books, 2001.

Newman, Oscar. *Creating Defensible Space*. Washington: Diane Publishing, 1966.

Newman, Oscar. *Defensible Space*. New York: Macmillan, 1972.

NHBRC. "Registration of Home Builders." http://www.nhbrc.org/Registrations/Registrationofhomebuilder.htm.

Norris, F. H., S. P. Stevens, B. Pfefferbaum, K. F. Wyche and R. L. Pfefferbaum. "Community Resilience as a Metaphor, Theory, Set of Capacities, and Strategy for Disaster Readiness." *American Journal of Community Psychology* 41, no. 1 (2008): 127–50.

Nussbaum, M. "Human Rights and Human Capabilities." *Harvard Human Rights Journal* 20 (2007): 21–22.

Office of the United Nations High Commissioner for Human Rights. "International Covenant on Economic, Social and Cultural Rights." Office of the United Nations High Commissioner for Human Rights, http://www2.ohchr.org/english/law/cescr.htm—art11.

Olivera, Andrés, Gonzalo Gonzalez and Adanay Rodriguez. "Cuba. Por una buena gestión pública municipal en la reducción del riesgo y la recuperación post-desastre." In *Prevención y respuesta a desastres: Estudios de caso*, edited by Foro Iberoamericano y del caribe sobre mejores prácticas. Rio de Janeiro: ONU Habitat, 2012.

Oliver-Smith, A. "Successes and Failures in Post-Disaster Resettlement." *Disasters* 15, no. 1 (1991): 12–23.

Payne, Geoffrey. "Land Tenure and Property Rights: An Introduction." *Habitat International* 28, no. 2 (2004): 167–79.

Perelman, L. J. "Infrastructure Risk and Renewal: The Clash of Blue and Green." Paper presented at the Public Entity Risk Institute Symposium. 2008.

Perlman, Janice. *The Myth of Marginality: Urban Poverty and Politics in Rio De Janeiro*. Los Angeles: University of California Press, 1980.

Perlman, Janice. *Favela: Four Decades of Living on the Edge of Rio De Janeiro*. Oxford: Oxford University Press, 2010.

PHP Policy Working Group. *Report on Progress in the P.H.P. Policy Working Group*. Pretoria: CSIR, 2006.

Pietroforte, Roberto. "Communication and Governance in the Building Process." *Construction Management and Economics* 15 (1997): 71–82.

Porio, Emma and Christine Crisol. "Property Rights, Security of Tenure and the Urban Poor in Metro Manila." *Habitat International* 28, no. 2 (2004): 203–19.

Rahman, Mohammed Mahbubur. "Problems of the NGOs in Housing the Urban Poor in Bangladesh." *Habitat International* 26, no. 3 (2002): 433–51.

Rakowski, Cathy A. "Convergence and Divergence in the Informal Sector Debate: A Focus on Latin America, 1984–92." *World Development* 22, no. 4 (1994): 501–16.

Ravallion, Martin. "On the Urbanization of Poverty." *Journal of Development Economics* 68, no. 2 (2002): 435–42.

Robeyns, I. "The Capability Approach in Practice." *Journal of Political Philosophy* 14, no. 3 (2006): 351–76.

Rodriguez, Adrian G. and Stephen M. Smith. "A Comparison of Determinants of Urban, Rural and Farm Poverty in Costa Rica." *World Development* 22, no. 3 (1994): 381–97.

Rodriguez, Carlos Manuel and Ada Luisa Perez. "Componentes de la gestión del riesgo en la prevención de desastres naturales: Caso Cuba." In *Jornadas Iberoamericanas sobre el hábitat, vulnerabilidad y desastres*. Bolivia: Centro de formación de la cooperación Española, 2004.

Rusen, Keles. "Housing Policy in Turkey." In *Housing Policy in Developing Countries*, edited by Gil Shidlo, 140–72. London: Routledge, 1990.

Rust, Kecia and FinMark Trust. "Analysis of South Africa's Housing Sector Performance." (2006), http://www.hic-net.org.

Sandel, Michael J. *Justice: What's the Right Thing to Do?* London: Penguin, 2010.

Sanyal, Bishwapriya and Vinit Mukhija. "Institutional Pluralism and Housing Delivery: A Case of Unforeseen Conflicts in Mumbai, India." *World Development* 29, no. 12 (2001): 2043–57.

Sen, Amartya. *Development as Freedom*. New York: Anchor Books, 1999.

Sen, Amartya. *The Idea of Justice*. Cambridge, MA: Belknap Press, 2009.

Sims, H. and K. Vogelmann. "Popular Mobilization and Disaster Management in Cuba." *Public Administration and Development* 22, no. 1 (2002): 398–400.

Sliwinsky, Alicia. "The Politics of Participation: Involving Communities in Post-Disaster Reconstruction." In *Rebuilding after Disasters: From Emergency to Sustainability*, edited by Gonzalo Lizarralde, Colin Davidson and Cassidy Johnson, 188–207. London: Taylor & Francis, 2010.

Smets, Peer. "Small Is Beautiful, but Big Is Often the Practice: Housing Microfinance in Discussion." *Habitat International* 30, no. 3 (2006): 595–613.

Smith, Neil. "Disastrous Accumulation." *South Atlantic Quarterly* 106, no. 4 (2007): 769–87.

Smyth, H. "Measuring, Developing and Managing Trust in Relationships." In *The Management of Complex Projects: A Relationship Approach*, edited by S. Pryke and H. Smyth, 97–120. Oxford: Blackwell Publishing, 2006.

Strassmann, P. "The Timing of Urban Infrastructure and Housing Improvements by Owner Occupants." *World Development* 12, no. 7 (1984): 743–53.

Strassmann, Paul. "Home-Based Enterprises in Cities of Developing Countries." *Economic Development and Cultural Change* 36, no. 1 (1987): 121–44.

Strassmann, Paul. "Oversimplification in Housing Analysis, with Reference to Land Markets and Mobility." *Cities* 11, no. 6 (1994): 377–83.

The White House. "The Vice President Visits Favela Santa Marta." (2013), http://www.whitehouse.gov/photos-and-video/video/2013/06/11/vice-president-visits-favela-santa-marta.

The World Bank. *Housing: Enabling Markets to Work. A World Bank Policy Paper.* Washington, DC: The World Bank, 1993.

Thompson, M. and I. Gaviria. *Weathering the Storm: Lessons in Risk Reduction from Cuba.* Boston: Oxfam, 2004.

Tickamyer, A. R. "Poverty, Rural." In *International Encyclopedia of Human Geography*, edited by Ron Kitchin and Nigel Thrift, 416–20. Oxford: Elsevier, 2009.

Tipple, Graham and Suzanne Speak. *Hidden Millions: Homelessness in Developing Countries.* New York: Taylor & Francis, 2009.

Tomlinson, Mary R. "The Development of a Low-Income Housing Finance Sector in South Africa: Have We Finally Found a Way Forward?" *Habitat International* 31, no. 1 (2007): 77–86.

Turner, J. R. "Towards a Theory of Project Management: The Nature of the Project Governance and Project Management." *International Journal of Project Management* 24, no. 2 (2006): 93–95.

Turner, John F. C. *Housing by People: Towards Autonomy in Building Environments.* New York: Pantheon Books, 1977.

UN-Habitat. *The Challenge of Slums: Global Report on Human Settlements 2003.* London: Earthscan, 2003.

UN-Habitat. "Measuring the Size of the Informal Economy." *Habitat Debate* 13, no. 2 (2007): 19.

UN-Habitat. *Enhancing Urban Safety and Security: Global Report on Human Settlements 2007.* London: Earthscan, 2007.

UN-Habitat. *State of the World's Cities 2010/2011.* London: Earthscan, 2008.

UN-Habitat. *Planning Sustainable Cities: Global Report on Human Settlements 2009.* London: Earthscan, 2009.

UNISDR. "Preventionweb." UNISDR, http://www.preventionweb.net.

Vakil, A. "Confronting the Classification Problem: Toward a Taxonomy of NGOs." *World Development* 25, no. 12 (1997): 2057–70.

Valladares, Arturo. "The Community Architect Program: Implementing Participation-in-Design to Improve Housing Conditions in Cuba." *Habitat International* 38 (2013): 18–24.

Viel, Laurent , Isabelle Thomas-Maret, Fella Amina Maherzi and Gonzalo Lizarralde. "L'influence des parties prenantes dans les grands projets urbains: Les cas du quartier des spectacles de Montréal et de Lyon Confluence." *Cybergéo: European Journal of Geography* 604 (2012): http://cybergeo.revues.org/25310.

Webb, Justin W., Garry D. Bruton, Laszlo Tihanyi and R. Duane Ireland. "Research on Entrepreneurship in the Informal Economy: Framing a Research Agenda." *Journal of Business Venturing* 28, no. 5: 598–614.

Wells, Jill. "Construction and Capital Formation in Less Developed Economies: Unravelling the Informal Sector in an African City." *Construction Management and Economics* 19, no. 3 (2001): 267–74.

Werna, Edmundo. "Shelter, Employment and the Informal City in the Context of the Present Economic Scene: Implications for Participatory Governance." *Habitat International* 25, no. 2 (2001): 209–27.

Winch, Graham M. "Governing the Project Process: A Conceptual Framework." *Construction Management and Economics* 19, no. 8 (2001): 799–808.

Wisner, B. "Risk and the Neoliberal State: Why Post-Mitch Lessons Didn't Reduce El Salvador's Earthquake Losses." *Disasters* 25, no. 3 (2001): 251–68.

Zanetta, C. "The Evolution of the World Bank's Urban Lending in Latin America: From Sites and Services to Municipal Reform and Beyond." *Habitat International* 25, no. 4 (2001): 513–33.

INDEX